D1488627

ALABAMA'S
CIVIL RIGHTS TRAIL

Alabama

THE FORGE OF HISTORY

A Series of Illustrated Books

ALABAMA'S
CIVIL RIGHTS TRAIL

An Illustrated Guide to the Cradle of Freedom

Frye Gaillard

With Jennifer Lindsay and Jane DeNeefe

Foreword by Juan Williams

The University of Alabama Press • Tuscaloosa

Designer: Michele Myatt Quinn
Typeface: Minion Pro, Corbel

∞

The paper on which this book is printed meets the minimum
requirements of American National Standard for Information
Sciences—Permanence of Paper for Printed Library Materials,
ANSI Z39.48-1984.

Library of Congress Cataloging-in-Publication Data

Gaillard, Frye, 1946–
    Alabama's civil rights trail : an illustrated guide to the
cradle of freedom / Frye Gaillard; with Jennifer Lindsay and
Jane DeNeefe; foreword by Juan Williams.
        p.   cm.—(Alabama : the forge of history)
    Includes bibliographical references and index.
    ISBN 978-0-8173-5581-4 (pbk.: alk. paper) 1. African
Americans—Civil rights—Alabama—History—20th century.
2. Civil rights movements—Alabama—History—20th century.
3. Alabama—Race relations. 4. Historic sites—Alabama—
Guidebooks. 5. Alabama—Guidebooks. I. Lindsay, Jennifer,
1972– II. DeNeefe, Jane. III. Title.
E185.93.A3G34 2009
323.1196'0730761—dc22   2009020073

The University of Alabama Press wishes to gratefully acknowledge
Ed Rogers and the Office of the Provost of The University of
Alabama for their generous support of this book.

Contents

8

Mobile: City of Progress, City of Backlash 257

9

Other Places of Interest 293

Alabama's Civil Rights Timeline

The Foundation

August 1864 Wallace Turnage, a runaway slave in Mobile, escapes
to the Union garrison on Dauphin Island. His flight to freedom,
which would be chronicled 140 years later in the best-selling book
A Slave No More, represents the aspirations of millions of African
Americans.

November 1865 A group of fifty-six former slaves meet in Mobile and
resolve that education should be their number one priority.

1867 Two former slaves, William Savery and Thomas Tarrant, open a
school that will become Talladega College, the first black college in
Alabama.

1867 Lincoln Normal School is established in Marion. Part of its
program is later moved to Montgomery and becomes Alabama
State University.

1870 Benjamin Sterling Turner, a former slave, becomes Alabama's first
African American member of Congress.

1875 Alabama A&M is established in Huntsville by revered educator
William Hooper Councill.

1881 Booker T. Washington opens what will soon be known as
Tuskegee Institute.

1901 Alabama adopts a new constitution, stripping most African
Americans of the vote. Black leaders debate the best path to
equality.

March 1931 Nine young black men who soon become known as the
Scottsboro Boys are accused of raping two white women on a

freight train. Their death sentences prompt an international outcry.

1944 Mobile civil rights leader John LeFlore files a lawsuit challenging Alabama's all-white Democratic primary. He finds white allies in his struggle.

The Beginning

December 1955 Rosa Parks is arrested in Montgomery for refusing to relinquish her seat on a bus to a white man. The Montgomery bus boycott begins with Dr. Martin Luther King Jr. as its leader.

February 1956 Autherine Lucy becomes the first black student to attend classes at the University of Alabama. She is driven out by a mob.

May 1956 At Spring Hill College in Mobile, Fannie Ernestine Motley becomes the first African American graduate of a formerly all-white college in Alabama.

December 1956 The U.S. Supreme Court issues its final order requiring desegregation of the Montgomery buses.

December 1956 Birmingham civil rights leader Fred Shuttlesworth announces he will test the Montgomery Supreme Court ruling in Birmingham. On Christmas night, his house is bombed and he narrowly escapes injury, but the next day he leads a group of black riders to desegregate the buses.

September 1957 Shuttlesworth is attacked by a mob as he attempts to enroll his children in a previously all-white Birmingham school.

May 1958 Arch-segregationist John Patterson wins Alabama governor's race against racial moderate George Wallace. Wallace vows never to be "outniggered" again.

December 1958 Selma native and Howard University law student
Bruce Boynton is arrested in Virginia for desegregating an all-white
bus terminal. He files a federal lawsuit.

Direct Action

February 1960 Students at Alabama State College sit in at the all-white
cafeteria at the state capitol. Leaders of the protest are expelled
from school.

December 1960 U.S. Supreme Court rules in favor of Bruce Boynton,
ordering desegregation of interstate bus terminals and providing
the legal basis for the freedom rides.

May 1961 Freedom riders are attacked in Anniston, Birmingham, and
Montgomery.

Spring 1962 Students at Birmingham's all-black Miles College
lead demonstrations and a boycott aimed at segregated public
accommodations.

January 1963 Newly elected Alabama governor George Wallace
delivers his inaugural address pledging "segregation forever."

April 1963 Dr. Martin Luther King Jr. joins local Birmingham leaders in
massive demonstrations opposing segregation.

May 1963 Birmingham police commissioner Eugene "Bull"
Connor orders fire hoses and police dogs used against peaceful
demonstrators.

June 1963 Alabama governor George Wallace stands in the
schoolhouse door, attempting unsuccessfully to block the
enrollment of African American students Vivian Malone and James
Hood at the University of Alabama.

August 1963 Alabama public safety commissioner Al Lingo and his state troopers use cattle prods on demonstrators in Gadsden.

September 1963 Birmingham's Sixteenth Baptist Church, a staging ground for the civil rights movement, is bombed, killing four little girls.

July 1964 President Lyndon Johnson signs the Civil Rights Act of 1964, ending segregation in public accommodations. Events in Birmingham are a major factor in the bill's passage.

May 1965 Vivian Malone becomes the first black graduate of the University of Alabama.

The Right to Vote

January 1965 Dr. Martin Luther King Jr. comes to Selma to lead voting rights protests, building on the work of the Student Nonviolent Coordinating Committee (SNCC) and local Selma leaders.

February 1965 Jimmie Lee Jackson, a black U.S. Army veteran, is killed by police during a voting rights protest in Marion.

March 7, 1965 Peaceful marchers are attacked on Bloody Sunday at Selma's Edmund Pettus Bridge.

March 9, 1965 Unitarian minister James Reeb, who has come to Selma to support voting rights demonstrations, is attacked and fatally injured.

March 25, 1965 More than 20,000 marchers led by Dr. Martin Luther King Jr. complete a five-day trek to Montgomery.

March 25, 1965 Movement volunteer Viola Liuzzo is murdered by members of the Ku Klux Klan after helping drive marchers back to Selma.

May 7, 1965 An all-white jury is unable to reach a verdict in the trial of Collie Leroy Wilkins, identified by an FBI informant as the murderer of Mrs. Liuzzo.

August 6, 1965 President Lyndon Johnson signs the Voting Rights Act of 1965, perhaps the greatest single achievement of the civil rights era. Events in Alabama play a major role in passage of the bill.

The Struggle Continues

May 1966 More than 900 African American voters in Lowndes County cast ballots in the Black Panther primary, establishing an all-black political organization using the black panther as its symbol.

May 1966 Lucius Amerson, a thirty-two-year-old Korean War veteran from Macon County, becomes Alabama's first black sheriff.

December 1967 African American dentist John Cashin in Huntsville unveils plans for the National Democratic Party of Alabama, a racially integrated organization.

March 1968 Dr. Martin Luther King Jr. tours rural Alabama seeking to build support for a Poor People's march on Washington.

March 1968 Presidential candidate Robert Kennedy, once a pariah in Alabama, visits the University of Alabama and is cheered by 9,000 people as he makes a strong plea for equal rights.

1970 After years of intensive voter registration, blacks win control of county governments in parts of rural Alabama where they are in a majority. Alabama leads the nation in the number of black elected officials.

This is not a complete list of the sites and events described in this book. It is intended simply as a summary to help set the larger stories into context.

Abbreviations

Listed below are abbreviations for various organizations referred to in this book.

AMA American Missionary Association

CORE Congress of Racial Equality

FAME Florence Alabama Music Enterprises

FQB Freedom Quilting Bee

ILD International Labor Defense (legal arm of the Communist Party)

NAACP National Association for the Advancement of Colored People

NDPA National Democratic Party of Alabama

NOW Neighborhood Organized Workers

SCLC Southern Christian Leadership Conference

SCOPE Summer Community Organization and Political Education

SNCC Student Nonviolent Coordinating Committee

TCA Tuskegee Civic Association

UKA United Klans of America

Foreword

A white friend from Alabama tells this story:

As he is walking through the lobby of a Birmingham hotel, he sees a young white mother, holding her children by the hand. They stop at the registration desk, and the mom asks the lady behind the counter for directions to the sites of several historic civil rights events.

The hotel clerk pulls out a pad of stapled mimeographed sheets, complete with maps and directions. She explains that the hotel gets so many questions about historic civil rights events that they finally printed up the information to hand to their many guests.

In that moment my friend, Ed Rogers, who was born in Alabama some fifty years ago, said he realized that a generational shift had taken place and civil rights history had become a plus for Alabama.

As a black person who has written extensively about civil rights history, I listened to Ed's story about watching the mom and children in that hotel lobby and thought how incredibly fast change comes to people and places. The children and their mother in his story could be black or white and still share a common experience—today they are not nursing bruises from Alabama's past racial battles. It is all history to them.

They feel little weight, if any, from the heavy burdens of guilt, bitterness, blame, and redemption of Alabama's past. What happened fifty years ago is history to them. It might even be an amazing story told by your mom while she holds your hand and points to a statue or an old building. But it is just history.

The white mother and her children know a black president. They know black mayors and police chiefs, and see black and white people laughing together on TV. They know about racial tensions and arguments, but the history of the racial clashes in Alabama from the 1950s and 1960s seems so distant and so unbelievable to Ed's children, to my children, to any child of the twenty-first century.

So much time has passed that the people who love Alabama, be they black or white, have arrived at a new appreciation of Alabama's controversial history. They now understand that by any fair and objective look at their state Alabama is the setting for compelling chapters of American history. That is a cold, honest fact.

Alabama is known around the world for its natural beauty, the Crimson Tide football team, and its southern traditions. And Alabama is also known to the world as the scene, the intriguing and mythic place, for so many vital lessons of American history—specifically civil rights history.

The state has the same powerful pull that attracts people to Independence Hall in Philadelphia where the U.S. Constitution was written, or to Ground Zero in New York City where terrorists attacked skyscrapers in the heart of the big city's financial district. People come to these places to get a better understanding of history, feel the power of the past, and gain a personal, up-close experience.

The same can be said of Anniston, Birmingham, Selma, and Tuscaloosa.

That is why Alabama's relationship to its treasure trove of history is so very intense—it is personal. And for many in Alabama there is a sense of protecting family secrets and family pain, not wanting to air dirty laundry. After all, there are heroes and villains, racists and agitators, activists and traditionalists in the story. There are murderers and liars, too, on every side of the tale. They all have their stories to tell, and every story has a power to it, insight and inspiration that comes with each soul's version of his or her Alabama history.

It was in Alabama that the Montgomery Bus Boycott took place. It was in Alabama that Martin Luther King Jr. and Rosa Parks came to be nationally known. Alabama was the site of Autherine Lucy's entrance to The University of Alabama in 1956 and the site of Governor George Wallace's 1963 stand in the schoolhouse door to block the entry of black students.

It was in Alabama in 1961 that Freedom Riders had their buses bombed for riding in interracial groups. And it was in Alabama in 1965 that the small town of Selma became the center of the nation's struggle over guaranteeing voting rights for blacks.

There is so much history in Alabama.

To walk into Alabama's buildings, courthouses, schools, storefronts, and churches, it is easy to go about your business and get on with daily life without thinking about or remembering all the history. That is especially true when family names are tied to the past for better or worse. Some might say it is better to forget than to stir up all those potentially upsetting feelings.

But so many places in Alabama are bridges from the past to modern America. Those simple courthouses and churches have the power to evoke tremendous memories back to the era of Civil War as well as the time of the civil rights movement. These are places that harbor the spirits of human struggle with right and wrong, triumphs and despair, courage and cowardice. They are the sites of historic struggles for justice under law and human rights, central to the ideals of America's Founding Fathers.

Much as Alabama is the heart of the American South, it is at the heart of the story of how generations of Americans turned a blind eye to the concept of "Justice for All" because of race.

What makes the experience of traveling to Alabama so powerfully evocative is also comparing the past to the present. Alabama has made so much progress in race relations—to an extent beyond imagination just a generation ago—and yet Alabama and America is not finished fulfilling its promise.

I remember the first time I visited the Birmingham Civil Rights Institute. I had been invited to give a lecture on civil rights history. Before my trip I read about the museum and its programs and found them fascinating—absolutely first rate.

But when I arrived at the Institute, I was stunned to see that it was across the street from Kelly Ingram Park, the place renown in history books as the gathering site for so many civil rights protests and clashes between police and demonstrators.

The main door to the institute was practically across the street from the Sixteenth Street Baptist Church, a living shrine to four black Sunday school girls killed there by a segregationist's bomb. And a short ride from the museum will take you to what remains of the jail where Dr. King wrote an American classic known to every high school student—"Letter from Birmingham Jail."

It is mind boggling that there is so much American history concentrated in any one place, but it is in Alabama.

To walk around Alabama's towns and cities is to come face-to-face with not so distant ghosts that Dr. King spoke about in his "I Have a Dream" speech. King described Alabama as a place with some "vicious racists," but also predicted it will one day be a place where "little black boys and little black girls will be able to join hands with little white boys and little white girls as sisters and brothers. . . . I have a dream today."

To visit Alabama today is to see and feel Dr. King's vision come to life. The fight for racial equality has made so many strides. The state today is a testament to the many people—black and white, young and old— who took heroic stands at these schools, courthouses, and churches, who fought and shed blood for equal rights.

Alabama's Civil Rights Trail: A Traveler's Guide to the Cradle of Freedom highlights many of these momentous places and events in the ways that they should be viewed and remembered, and never forgotten. Far more than just places and buildings though, Alabama's unique civil rights history is the story of people, and Frye Gaillard artfully narrates the lives of those who took the first steps toward freedom, those who risked everything to carry the fight forward, those who fought every step of the way, and those who paid the ultimate sacrifice for their convictions.

Alabama's role in the history of civil rights in America is truly exceptional, as this guide to the "Cradle of Freedom" makes abundantly evident. As Gaillard suggests in the very title of this book, one may see Alabama for its history of hatred and oppression, but just as valid is the opposite view—that Alabama is a forge of freedom, a place where the promises made so long ago by our nation's founders finally began to be fulfilled.

Some bridges that we never imagined we would cross, we now cross freely. Let us cross those bridges and view these sites in the extraordinary spirit that this book makes possible, inspiring us to dream again about crossing over to new victories and making the most of the potential in all of us in the great American experiment.

—Juan Williams

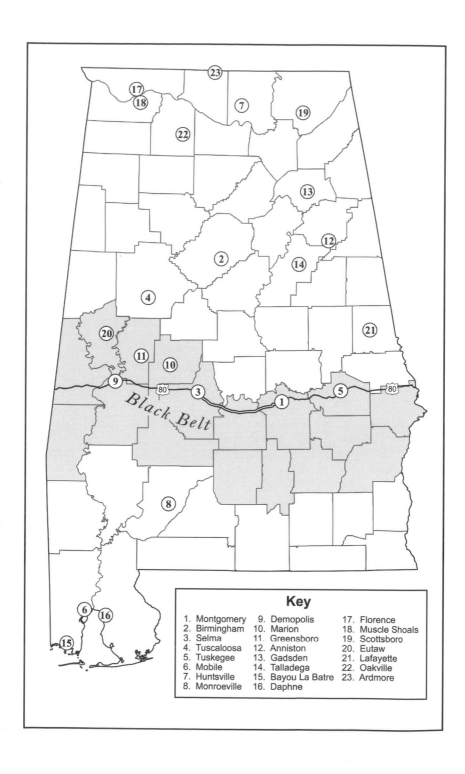

Key

1. Montgomery	9. Demopolis	17. Florence
2. Birmingham	10. Marion	18. Muscle Shoals
3. Selma	11. Greensboro	19. Scottsboro
4. Tuscaloosa	12. Anniston	20. Eutaw
5. Tuskegee	13. Gadsden	21. Lafayette
6. Mobile	14. Talladega	22. Oakville
7. Huntsville	15. Bayou La Batre	23. Ardmore
8. Monroeville	16. Daphne	

Introduction

No state has done a better job of preserving its civil rights history than Alabama, and no state has a more important history to preserve. In Montgomery, Birmingham, and Selma—scenes of some of the most turbulent civil rights struggles—there are museums and markers that chart the course of those years.

But Alabama's racial story is much bigger than that, and the reminders of it are scattered quite literally from Mobile in the south to the Tennessee border. In Mobile, for example, just a few miles west of downtown, the oak-shaded campus of Spring Hill College, Alabama's oldest, has long borne witness to the moral imperative of integration. And far to the north in the town of Scottsboro, a civil rights struggle in the 1930s centered on the fate of nine black men, accused of raping two white women.

Even earlier on the long upward climb, there were slaves who ran away, and former slaves who built colleges and schools, and ran for public office, and established an economic base for the future. And all of this, too, is a part of the story.

But Alabama is best known for events that occurred in more recent years. Arguably the most famous of those came in December 1955, on a cool winter evening when Rosa Parks, a Montgomery seamstress, refused to relinquish her seat on a bus. Her act of courage, spontaneous and calculated all at once, triggered the Montgomery bus boycott, one of the most important protests in the civil rights struggle.

Among other things, it was the event that introduced the nation to Dr. Martin Luther King Jr., a Montgomery minister who would soon emerge as the most eloquent civil rights leader of his time. But the bus boycott was a movement of the masses—a dramatic demonstration of a community's ability to take a stand for its freedom. And most critically of all, the boycott ended in a moment of victory for a movement still in its embryonic stages.

Five years later, in 1961, the freedom riders came to Alabama, enduring attacks of the most vicious kind in Anniston, Birmingham, and Montgomery. But the riders served an unmistakable notice that the civil rights movement would not be cowed. In 1963, the Birmingham demonstrations—and the televised images of fire hoses and dogs—reaffirmed that message and touched the conscience of the country as nothing else had. The following summer Congress passed the Civil Rights Act of 1964, ending legal segregation in the South.

And then came Selma. In 1965 this small river town, home of Alabama's first black congressman in the days of Reconstruction, became a new battleground in the struggle for the vote. On March 7, 1965, peaceful marchers were attacked at the Edmund Pettus Bridge, and the horrifying footage shocked the country and won even greater support for the movement. Two weeks later, more than twenty-five thousand demonstrators completed a five-day march to Montgomery, where they cheered the words of Dr. Martin Luther King Jr. as he promised that the day of justice was at hand.

These were bloody times in Alabama. In the spring and summer of 1965, Jimmie Lee Jackson, James Reeb, Viola Liuzzo, and Jonathan Daniels became the latest in a line of civil rights martyrs. The violence, however, only stiffened the resolve of people in the movement—and of President Lyndon B. Johnson, who pushed for the passage of a voting rights bill that would soon bring democracy to the South.

On August 6, 1965, Johnson signed the bill into law, and the struggle in much of rural Alabama became more local but no less dramatic. In Lowndes County, where there were no black voters at the time of the Selma to Montgomery march, African Americans by the thousands turned out to register, and established their own political party, with a black panther as its symbol.

In the months that followed, young militant leaders from California would borrow that symbol as they formed the Black Panther Party for Self-Defense. But in Lowndes County and the others around it, African Americans simply wanted to be part of the system—to help govern the communities in which they lived. In retribution, many of the new black voters were evicted from their rented farmhouses, and tent cities sprang up across the rural countryside, a reminder that freedom didn't come without a price.

Throughout these years, adding their own layers to the story, people from nearly every walk of life—educators, musicians, lawyers, and athletes—took their places in a changing racial landscape. And most remarkably for our purposes here, they left a physical trail that we can follow. The Edmund Pettus Bridge, the dynamite scar on Dr. King's porch, the Birmingham park where Bull Conner unleashed his hoses and dogs are only the most dramatic stops on the trail.

This book is intended in part as a guide. But its larger purpose is to help tell the story for anyone interested in those times. It is a book, we hope, that a reader can open to any page and find pieces of a story that needs to be preserved—one, in fact, that *has* been preserved in the physical reminders that abound in the state. Many readers, no doubt, will want to visit those sites and soak up the history that all of them contain. But the journey can also be made within these pages. Either way, we hope this book will help the story come alive.

ALABAMA'S
CIVIL RIGHTS TRAIL

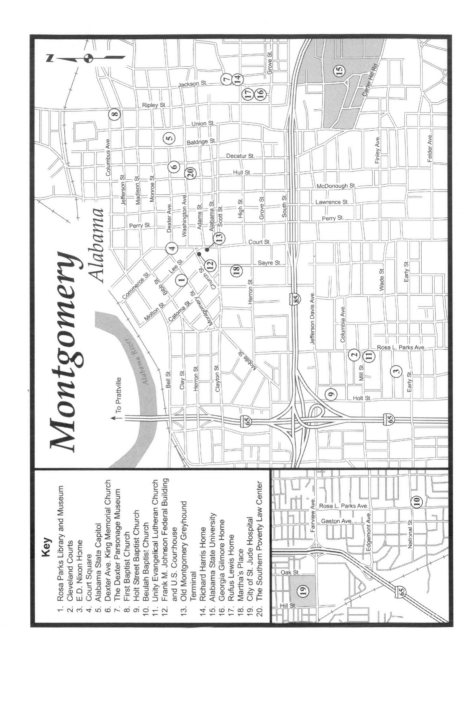

Montgomery
Alabama

Key

1. Rosa Parks Library and Museum
2. Cleveland Courts
3. E.D. Nixon Home
4. Court Square
5. Alabama State Capitol
6. Dexter Ave. King Memorial Church
7. The Dexter Parsonage Museum
8. First Baptist Church
9. Holt Street Baptist Church
10. Beulah Baptist Church
11. Unity Evangelical Lutheran Church
12. Frank M. Johnson Federal Building and U.S. Courthouse
13. Old Montgomery Greyhound Terminal
14. Richard Harris Home
15. Alabama State University
16. Georgia Gilmore Home
17. Rufus Lewis Home
18. Martha's Place
19. City of St. Jude Hospital
20. The Southern Poverty Law Center

THE MONTGOMERY STORY
Hallowed Ground

The city of Montgomery, always central to the history of Alabama, was the birthplace of the civil rights movement in the state—and a critical part of the struggle nationwide. The Montgomery bus boycott, which gave the movement such iconic figures as Rosa Parks and Dr. Martin Luther King Jr., was also a massive grassroots effort that ended in unequivocal success. Pursuing their goals on parallel fronts, the black leaders of Montgomery not only maintained their yearlong boycott but also secured a U.S. Supreme Court ruling that segregation of buses was unconstitutional.

The victory did not come easily. In the winter of 1956, the homes and churches of many leaders were bombed as tension in the city reached a fever pitch. But both in the courts and as a model for action on a grassroots level, the boycott gave hope to African Americans all over the country. Nor was it the only role Montgomery played. In May 1961, a group of freedom riders were beaten at the Montgomery Greyhound station, but they vowed to continue their ride to Mississippi, serving notice to the nation that violence would not intimidate nonviolence.

And in March 1965, Montgomery made national headlines again when thousands of marchers made the trek from Selma, demonstrating powerfully for the right to vote. In the simultaneous battles against legal segregation and in the pursuit of genuine democracy in the South, no other community played a more important role, and no group of citizens demonstrated greater courage.

Here, tied to the sites at which they occurred, are some of the stories of the Montgomery movement.

E. D. Nixon and Rosa Parks: Drawing the Line

The Site

The Rosa Parks Museum in Montgomery stands at the place where history was made, where Mrs. Parks, in December 1955, refused to relinquish her seat on a bus. That act of defiance would soon become one of the most celebrated moments of the civil rights era. More specifically, it would launch the Montgomery bus boycott, a movement of the masses in which Mrs. Parks became the dignified symbol of resistance. But she was only one player in the drama. Indeed her act of personal courage might have passed unnoticed if not for the toughness of E. D. Nixon, an African American labor leader who believed, as strongly as anyone in Montgomery, that it was time for his community to take a stand.

Rosa Parks. Photograph courtesy of Carl Clifford.

The Story

Rosa Parks didn't know that this would be the day. On December 1, 1955, she boarded the bus as she had many times when it stopped at Court Square in the heart of downtown. Almost certainly, she didn't give a lot of thought to the history of that corner—how it had once been the site of the old slave market, or how in 1866, in a triumphant moment just after the Civil War, the emancipation parade had passed nearby, the first such celebration in the city.

To be sure, those things mattered to Mrs. Parks. She knew the history of racial oppression in the South and was becoming more active in the struggle against it. But on the afternoon of December 1, she was

Rosa Parks being fingerprinted by Deputy Sheriff D. H. Lackey in Montgomery, Alabama, 1956. Photograph courtesy of the Library of Congress, Prints and Photographs Division [LC-USZ62-109643].

simply tired. She had put in another long day at the Montgomery Fair department store, and with her bursitis acting up, she settled gratefully into the first vacant seat. At the next stop, in front of what was then the Empire Theater, a white man boarded the bus and found no empty seats in the front. Mrs. Parks was sitting just behind the dividing line between black and white, and the driver, James Blake, ordered her to move.

Like many other black citizens, Mrs. Parks had had previous run-ins with Blake. At a time when discourtesy was too often the rule, the driver had developed a nasty reputation, and once again he was living up to it. "You better make it light on yourselves and let me have those seats," he told several blacks who were sitting near the front.

Three other passengers got up to move, but Mrs. Parks did not. When Blake threatened angrily to have her arrested, she looked up calmly from where she was sitting and replied, "You may do that."

The police came quickly and took her to jail, and it was then that she felt her first rush of fear. She noticed that her throat felt scratchy and dry, but there was only one water fountain at the jail, and the policemen told her it was only for whites. They did allow her to make a phone call, and by the time she was able to reach her family, word of her arrest was beginning to spread. One of the first to hear was E. D. Nixon, which was

E. D. Nixon. Photograph courtesy of the Alabama Department of Archives and History, Montgomery, Alabama.

no surprise, for if you were black and in trouble in Montgomery, Nixon was usually the person you called.

He was a handsome man, ramrod straight at the age of fifty-six, with neatly cropped hair that was starting to gray. He was already a veteran civil rights leader, having led a voting rights march in 1940 and having served as president of the NAACP. He lived a quarter of a mile from Mrs. Parks in a sturdy brick house on Clinton Avenue, and after posting her bond on December 1, accompanied by a white attorney, Clifford Durr, he asked her to serve as a symbol for the movement.

He knew she was not the first to be arrested or to refuse to relinquish her seat on a bus. But he also knew that in the African American community of Montgomery, there was nobody more universally respected. Like Nixon, Mrs. Parks was a leader in the NAACP, where her passion was working with children, teaching them their rights, but also their responsibilities, as citizens.

Nixon also knew that, earlier in the year, she had experienced a moment of personal revelation, a watershed interlude in her life, when she visited the Highlander Folk School in Tennessee. It was a beautiful place nestled back in the hills, where a native southerner by the name of Myles Horton had set out to train a generation of activists. Beginning in 1932, when the Depression's grip grew deeper in the South, Horton, a white man, was determined to create a sanctuary—a place where disaffected people could gather and talk about ways to build a better world.

In the beginning, most of his constituency was white—miners, mill workers, and pulpwood cutters who made a living from the forests. But twenty years into Myles Horton's experiment, the prevailing issue was racial understanding. During Rosa Parks's two-week visit, she found herself part of an integrated group, and the experience was like nothing she had known. Never, she said, in her forty-two years had she been around white people who were willing to accept a black person as an equal. It was an encounter that left her with a new understanding, for if she had always known that segregation was wrong, now at Highlander she could see the alternative.

The following December, in the wake of her arrest, she felt herself driven by a heightened sense of purpose. As Nixon made the case for massive protest, she told him quietly she would do what she could.

"I'll go along with you, Mr. Nixon," she said.

Nixon immediately set the grapevine humming. He left a message for Fred Gray, an African American attorney in Montgomery, who, as soon as he received it, put in a call to Jo Ann Robinson. Mrs. Robinson, at the time, was an English professor at Alabama State College and president of the Women's Political Council. She was a woman of influence who was ready to move, and who thought it was time to boycott the buses.

Around midnight on December 1, she and her closest friends on the council gathered at Alabama State, and began to draft a letter of protest. "Another Negro woman has been arrested and thrown into jail because she refused to get up out of her seat on the bus for a white person to sit down," they wrote. "Negroes have rights too. . . . We are, therefore, asking every Negro to stay off the buses Monday in protest."

As the women were running off flyers at the college, Mrs. Robinson telephoned Nixon, letting him know of their idea for a boycott. Nixon immediately endorsed the plan, saying he had been thinking of the same thing himself. At the very least, it could buttress the battle he was seeking in the courts. But it was already 3:00 A.M. on Friday, and if the boycott was really to start on Monday, that left them three days to organize the most far-reaching protest in the history of Montgomery. Nixon knew that they would need more help.

At 5:00 A.M., he called Ralph Abernathy, a twenty-nine-year-old Baptist minister, and told him of the boycott. Nixon knew that Montgomery's strong community of black ministers would be essential in spreading the word, and he was pleased to get Abernathy's promise of support. A short time later, Nixon called another of Montgomery's ministers, a relative newcomer named Martin Luther King Jr. Now twenty-six, King had come to the city in 1954 and taken over the pulpit at Dexter Avenue Baptist, one of Montgomery's most prestigious black churches.

In a pair of conversations on Friday morning, Nixon asked King to make his church available for a strategy session that afternoon. King cautiously agreed, and late in the day, about fifty black leaders gathered in the basement. Their meeting lasted until nearly midnight, as they ran off more flyers to help spread the word and debated details of their massive undertaking. By Saturday, December 3, more than thirty-five thousand flyers were circulating in the African American community, and the following morning the message went out again from the pulpits.

And there was one other thing. Already on Friday, Nixon had telephoned Joe Azbell, a white reporter for the *Montgomery Advertiser,* offering him a major news tip. He told Azbell about the boycott, knowing that the slant of the story wouldn't matter. As long as the reporter wrote about their plans, even a hostile account would spread the word. But in fact when the article appeared on Sunday, Nixon found it evenhanded enough, its headline cutting to the heart of the news: Negro Groups Ready Boycott of City Lines.

All in all, he thought, the preparations could not have gone better. He was eager to see the results on Monday.

When the morning came, he rose at dawn, and the results exceeded anything he had hoped for. Buses that were normally filled with black workers were now rumbling empty through the streets of Montgomery. It didn't take much of a leap to understand that the community was poised on the brink of major change.

What to See

Montgomery is rich in historical markers, many of which tell the story of the boycott. At the Cleveland Courts public housing project on what is now Rosa Parks Avenue, a marker on a hill at the horseshoe entrance takes note of the fact that this is where Mrs. Parks once lived, and where she and Nixon first met to talk about her arrest. Her apartment itself, unit 634, is now on the National Register of Historic Places.

At 647 Clinton Avenue, less than a quarter of a mile to the south, another marker stands at E. D. Nixon's former home, a brick house in a modest residential neighborhood.

The Rosa Parks Library and Museum at 232 Montgomery Street now dominates the site of her famous arrest, and the displays inside, including a replica of the bus, carry a visitor powerfully back in time.

A long city block to the south is Court Square, where Mrs. Parks first boarded the bus, and where other markers note the long and complicated history of the area. This crossroads corner in the heart of downtown was once the site of the old slave market. But another, more hopeful marker celebrates the passing of the first Emancipation Parade on January 2, 1866.

And finally, outside the museum, another gold-lettered sign points precisely to the site of the arrest, which occurred in front of the old Empire Theater.

The Rosa Parks Library and Museum, 232 Montgomery Street.
Photograph courtesy of Ann Webb.

FLIP SIDE OF THE MARKER

On the other side of the historical marker denoting the watershed arrest of Rosa Parks, there's an account of an unrelated event—the first public concert by Hank Williams, a soon-to-be country star, who appeared at the Empire Theater in 1938. The marker points out that Williams, an Alabama native, went on to greater fame at the Grand Ole Opry. But it says very little about the forces that shaped him, specifically the black musicians he knew in his boyhood.

Williams grew up in Georgiana and Greenville, a pair of small towns in Butler County, where his closest friend and musical mentor was a black street singer by the name of Rufus Payne. Payne, who also worked part-time as a janitor, was a consummate musical performer, a man in his fifties who sang the blues, played the slide guitar, and taught young Hank how to sing from his heart.

In a harshly segregated South, Payne, whose nickname was Tee-Tot, worried occasionally about what people would think, particularly when the young white boy, not yet in his teens, brought along his own Silvertone guitar and began playing with Payne on the sidewalks of town. More than a decade later, when Williams emerged as a country music star, he carried with him the memories of Tee-Tot, as well as the black and white hymns of the South's rural churches, and all of it came together in his songs.

Some scholars have argued that long before the legal cracks in the walls of segregation, with performers such as Hank Williams the cultural lines began to blur in the music of the South (see chapter 9).

Hank Williams historical marker, on the flip side of the Rosa Parks historical marker, at the site of the Empire Theater, now the Rosa Parks Library and Museum. Photograph courtesy of Frye Gaillard.

Vernon Johns and Dr. Martin Luther King Jr.: Men of God

The Site

The Dexter Avenue Baptist Church, home pulpit of Dr. Martin Luther King Jr., stands almost literally in the shadow of the capitol on a corner where history has passed in review. Jefferson Davis was inaugurated nearby as the first president of the Confederacy; Governor George Wallace gave his inaugural address just one block away; and the Selma to Montgomery march passed by the church on the final leg of that history-making journey.

Dexter Avenue King Memorial Baptist Church, 454 Dexter Avenue, at the corner of Decatur and Dexter Avenues. Photograph courtesy of Kenny Shackleford.

But more than anything else, this unimposing brick church on Dexter Avenue—a staging ground for the Montgomery bus boycott—provided a home in the 1950s for King and his predecessor Vernon Johns, two of the most powerful voices that the black community of Montgomery had ever heard.

The Story

Dr. Martin Luther King Jr. was not the first to cry freedom from the pulpit of Dexter Avenue Baptist Church. Before King came to Montgomery in 1954, the Reverend Vernon Johns had emerged as one of the venerated preachers in the country. Even before his arrival at Dexter, one of Johns's sermons, "Transfigured Moments," had been included in an anthology of America's greatest sermons. "It is a heart strangely un-Christian," he had written, "that cannot thrill with joy when the least of men begin to pull in the direction of the stars."

The Reverend Vernon Johns, lecturing at Morehouse College.

Photograph courtesy of the family of Vernon Johns.

At Dexter Avenue, where Johns served from 1947 to 1952, the congregation loved the sound of such words, but found Johns somewhat frightening as well. He was a fiery, barrel-chested man, who wore disheveled suits and wire-rimmed glasses and was fluent in Hebrew, Latin, and Greek. He loved the poetry of Byron and Keats, and the Negro spirituals written by slaves. He hated the indignities that went with segregation, and was not afraid to say so.

Once in Montgomery, after police beat an African American man with a tire iron, Johns announced that he would preach the next Sunday on the following topic: "It's Safe to Murder Negroes in Montgomery." The Klan burned a cross at his church that Saturday, but Johns was undeterred. Before an overflow crowd the following morning, he compared police brutality, and the ugly history of lynchings in the South, with the "lynching" of Jesus Christ himself. Many church members were uneasy with the message. They feared that Johns would only stir people's anger—white as well as black—in a part of the country where nothing ever changed.

They responded differently to Dr. Martin Luther King Jr., who came to Dexter after Johns's departure in 1952. King was only twenty-five years old. He was a smallish, mostly soft-spoken man, with large, dark eyes and an affability that was somehow tinged with reserve. But he was a powerful force in the Dexter Avenue pulpit, a preacher with the eloquence of Vernon Johns and an equally strong concern for social justice. After the arrest of Rosa Parks, King was chosen to lead the bus boycott in part because he was new to Montgomery and was not yet entrenched, or identified with any one faction, in the various turf wars of the black community.

As King already understood clearly, there were a number of other strong leaders in town—ministers, including Ralph Abernathy, who had developed major followings of their own; and the labor leader E. D. Nixon, who was fearless and wise and willing to lay his life on the line; and the African American attorney Fred Gray; and brilliant educators

Dr. Martin Luther King Jr., March 26, 1964. Photograph by Marion S. Trikosko, courtesy of the Library of Congress, Prints and Photographs Division [LC-U9-11695-5].

at Alabama State College. But if talented leaders in Montgomery were abundant, King quickly took his place at the center of the group.

One of his fellow ministers, John Porter, who was then an assistant at Dexter Avenue, thought King had a curious gift of humility, a steady ego that seldom drew him into pointless conflict and that helped him treat his fellow leaders with respect. As Porter noted with deep admiration, King could allow debates over strategy to swirl, and then state his own case in a way that usually pulled people together. But more than anything, he offered inspiration. On December 5, 1955, after the first successful day of the boycott, King addressed a rally at Holt Street Baptist Church—a massive gathering of more than four thousand people, who spilled from the pews to the streets outside.

"We are not wrong," he told the crowd that night. "If we are wrong, the Supreme Court of this nation is wrong. If we are wrong, the Constitution of the United States is wrong. If we are wrong, God Almighty is wrong. If we are wrong, justice is a lie."

As historians have noted, the black people of Montgomery found a leader that night, but King's appeal soon spread nationwide. Almost from the moment of that first speech, he managed to frame the issues of injustice in a way that most people couldn't ignore. He could buoy the resolve of African Americans, and touch the conscience of ordinary whites, in a way that few other leaders ever could.

And yet he had his frailties as well. More than once during the months of the boycott, as the controversy dragged on for more than a year, he wondered if he was the man for the job. Perhaps, he would often say to himself, if he had only demonstrated more skill, progress might have come more quickly. And there was always the matter of the mind-numbing fear. Later, he would write about the January night in 1956 when he came home late from a strategy session and the telephone rang with another death threat. He hung up on the caller and went to the kitchen to fix a pot of coffee.

He said he thought about the danger to his family, and the feeling that he hadn't accomplished much at all, and he could feel a prayer taking shape in his mind: "Lord, I must confess that I'm weak now. I'm faltering. I'm losing my courage. And I can't let the people see me like this."

He knew that as a leader he had to be strong, allowing the people to feed off his courage, but he soon discovered that the roles could be reversed. Three nights later, at a meeting at Ralph Abernathy's First Baptist Church, an old woman came up and put her arms around him, and told him he looked tired that night. King recognized Mother Pollard right away. She was a community elder widely known for her wisdom, having once declared in support of the boycott, "My feets is tired but my soul is

Audience at the First Baptist Church during a standing ovation for leaders of the Montgomery bus boycott, February 1956. Photograph courtesy of the Library of Congress, Prints and Photographs Division, NYWT&S Collection [LC-USZ62-135428].

rested." And now on the night of January 30, she told King simply that everything would be fine. "God's gonna take care of you," she said.

A few minutes later, word reached the church that King's house had been bombed. His wife, Coretta, and new baby, Yolanda, had both been at home, and nobody knew whether or not they were hurt. King remembered later that he felt strangely calm, encouraged by Mrs. Pollard's simple words. When he reached the parsonage he discovered remarkably that his family was fine. They were shaken, of course, by the dynamite that had exploded on the porch, blowing out windows and leaving a gash near the concrete steps. But Coretta told him that as soon as she heard somebody outside, she had taken the baby to the back of the house, where they escaped the major force of the blast.

King was relieved and his concern quickly shifted to the angry crowd that had gathered near the house. He lived in the Centennial Hill neighborhood, an area of African American professionals, who were shocked at the ugly act of terrorism. As word of the bombing spread across town, many of the people in the crowd came armed, ready to fight to protect Dr. King. But he urged them instead to stay calm.

"We are not advocating violence," he said, in a voice that was authoritative and strong. "I want you to love our enemies. Be good to them. . . . I did not start this boycott. I was asked by you to serve as your spokesman. I want it known the length and breadth of this land that if I am stopped, this movement will not stop. If I am stopped, our work will not stop. For what we are doing is right. What we are doing is just. And God is with us."

That multilayered message became King's gift, the fundamental legacy of his brief public life. On the one hand, he was resolutely committed to nonviolence, even in moments of personal peril. But he also promised that the movement would continue, pushing an agenda that was radical for its times, and he held out the hope that the movement would win. It was, he said, nothing more or less than a matter of justice.

What to See

In Montgomery, there are many reminders of King's message and life, and to a lesser extent, the prophetic legacy of Vernon Johns. The Dexter Avenue Memorial Baptist Church at the corner of Decatur Street and Dexter Avenue is a place of historic dignity and beauty.

The small brick structure might seem overwhelmed by the capitol building only one block away if not for the powerful history it produced. Markers on the corner record that history, while another marker a few feet away makes note of the fact that in another time, Jefferson Davis took the oath of office just up the street. On that same day, February 18, 1861, "Dixie" was first played as the fight song of the Confederacy.

The parsonage where King lived, and where his wife and daughter survived the bombing on January 30, 1956, is located at 309 South Jackson Street. A marker out front tells its story, and a plaque imbedded on the cement floor of the porch marks the spot where the bomb exploded. Inside, the parsonage is preserved as it was when the Kings' lived there, including much of the furniture that was there at the time.

The Dexter Parsonage Museum, 309 South Jackson Street.
Photograph courtesy of Ann Webb.

You can see the study where King worked and the kitchen where he sometimes brooded late at night about the slow pace of progress. An interpretive center stands next to the parsonage, where volunteers will provide background on the history of the site and take visitors on a guided tour of the home. Admission to the interpretive center is five dollars.

At the King-Johns Garden for Reflection behind the parsonage, visitors are encouraged to contemplate the principles of the movement: equality, forgiveness, hope, unity, peace, and understanding.

First Baptist Church, where King was speaking when he learned of the bombing of his home and where Mother Pollard offered her words of reassurance, stands at 347 North Ripley Street, less than a mile from the parsonage.

The church, which is still in use, is one of Montgomery's oldest. At the time of the boycott, it was pastored by the Reverend Ralph Abernathy, who became King's friend and closest adviser.

Holt Street Baptist Church, site of the first mass meeting that helped launch the boycott, is located at 903 South Holt Street, just off I-65 on the corner of Jefferson Davis Avenue. At this writing, the church, though one of the most important sites of the civil rights era, is in a state of disrepair. King's now famous "We are not wrong" speech, delivered on the night of December 5, 1955, ranks as one of the most inspiring that he ever gave. More than four thousand people gathered to hear it, and some historians have argued that the Montgomery movement sprang to life that night.

Another important church in the Montgomery movement, Beulah Baptist Church at 3703 Rosa Parks Avenue was organized at a different location in 1880. A marker erected by the Alabama Historical Association at the current location explains that in its earlier days the church provided classroom space for Alabama Colored People's University, which became Alabama State College. In the twentieth century it was the home church for the family of Nat King Cole, a Montgomery native who went on to international fame as an entertainer. And on January 23,

1956, the church was the site of an important mass meeting in support of the Montgomery bus boycott.

Robert Graetz: A White Preacher's Courage

The Site

Trinity Evangelical Lutheran Church, now renamed Unity Evangelical Lutheran, is located on the corner of Rosa Parks Avenue and Mill Street, where a historical marker on the neatly manicured lawn tells its story. In the 1950s, the church offered its building to Rosa Parks for her civil rights workshops for neighborhood children. On two occasions in 1956 and 1957, the church parsonage was bombed in retribution for the minister's support of civil rights. There were other bombings in Montgomery at the time. What made these unusual was that Robert Graetz, the minister at Trinity Lutheran, was white.

Unity Evangelical Lutheran Church, formerly Trinity Evangelical Lutheran Church, corner of Rosa Parks Avenue and Mill Street, where Robert Graetz was minister. Photograph courtesy of Frye Gaillard.

The Story

Robert Graetz, a native West Virginian, came to Montgomery with his young wife, Jeannie, arriving just before the bus boycott, to take over the pulpit at an all-black church. He was happy enough with that assignment, and he had promised his superiors in the Lutheran church that he would do his best to stay out of trouble.

But then came the arrest of Rosa Parks, a neighbor and friend who lived in Cleveland Courts immediately across the street from his church. Bob and Jeannie, as many people called them, knew there were dangers in getting involved. Indeed, their race, which could provide a certain immunity in more normal times, might turn them into targets as the situation became more tense. They also had their own family to consider—two small children whose lives, like their own, could suddenly be in danger.

But the more they talked about it and prayed, the more certain they became that this was a moment in which they had to play a part. It was, said Graetz, a time so fraught with possibility and hope that they could only understand it as the handiwork of God.

The dangers, however, proved to be very real. Graetz was arrested for driving black people to work, and on two different occasions the Ku Klux Klan threw bombs at his home. The second of those attacks proved to be the most serious. On January 10, 1957, as the family was sleeping, a dynamite blast shattered windows on the house and blew in the door and left the roof sitting tilted on the frame. Graetz rushed first to his children's room, and finding them unhurt, he hurried outside. In the darkness, he stumbled over something in the driveway—a second bomb that had not gone off. It consisted of eleven sticks of dynamite and some TNT. The police, who quickly arrived on the scene, informed him gravely that if that bomb had worked, it could easily have leveled the whole neighborhood.

"They were obviously trying to kill us," Graetz said.

But terrifying as it was, the episode, for Bob and Jeannie Graetz, was somehow less memorable than the first bomb attack. They were out of town on that particular night, having traveled to Tennessee with their friend Rosa Parks. It was August 1956, and the bus boycott had dragged on for eight months without any visible signs of progress. Mrs. Parks, to renew her spirits, wanted to return to the Highlander Folk School. It was the place where, the previous summer, she had attended an integrated workshop and drawn inspiration for the struggle just ahead.

When she returned in August with Bob and Jeannie Graetz, they spent a week in the company of Benjamin Mays, the great black educator from Atlanta, and Septima Clark, a member of the teaching staff at Highlander. But after seven inspirational days, Graetz received a telephone call from Alabama, telling him his parsonage had been bombed. With Mrs. Parks and Jeannie, he returned as quickly as he could to Montgomery, and found a deep crater in the middle of his yard and some broken dishes and windows in the house. He surveyed the damage and wandered in a daze through an area now roped off by police. Suddenly, he noticed that Mrs. Parks had disappeared.

Worried momentarily, he soon found her in the kitchen cleaning up dishes that had shattered in the blast. She had called no attention to herself in the process, but was simply acting as a neighbor and a friend, doing what she could to be of help. Graetz was deeply touched by the gesture, but he also knew it was typical of Mrs. Parks—an unpretentious woman of decency and grace who had always wanted to do her part.

What to See

The handsome brick sanctuary of Trinity Lutheran, now known as Unity Evangelical Lutheran, faces Rosa Parks Avenue on the corner of Mill Street. Directly across Mill Street is Unit 634 of Cleveland Courts, where Rosa Parks lived—a proximity that at least partially explained her close friendship with Bob and Jeannie Graetz. In front of the small brick and shingle-sided parsonage adjacent to the church, a hackberry tree in the

Hackberry tree planted at Robert Graetz's parsonage, in a crater left by a bombing. Photograph courtesy of Frye Gaillard.

front yard now towers more than forty feet high. As a marker at the base of the tree explains, it was planted by neighbors and members of the church in one of the craters created by a bomb.

The Frank M. Johnson Jr. Federal Building and U. S. Courthouse: Victory in the Courts

The Site

The Frank M. Johnson Jr. Federal Building and U. S. Courthouse in

Frank M. Johnson Jr. Federal Building and U.S. Courthouse, 15 Lee Street.
Photograph courtesy of Ann Webb.

downtown Montgomery has been the scene of major civil rights litigation, none more important than the Montgomery bus boycott case, filed on February 1, 1956. The case, which led to a U.S. Supreme Court ruling overturning segregation of the Montgomery buses, made judicial icons of the judges who heard it, particularly U.S. district judge Frank Johnson. But there were other, lesser-known heroes from the trial, especially the black women who were called to offer historic testimony.

The Story

Two days after the bombing of the parsonage of Dr. Martin Luther King Jr., attorney Fred Gray filed a motion in federal court, seeking total desegregation of the buses. As historian Taylor Branch later noted, the motion was regarded by white Montgomery as "the social equivalent of atomic warfare."

Until that time, Dr. King and the other boycott leaders had not been demanding complete integration but rather an arrangement like the one in Mobile. That city's white leaders had agreed to a simple, two-part plan, designed to preserve the dignity of both races within the basic laws of segregation: Whites would fill bus seats from the front, and blacks from the rear. But when they met in the middle, it was first-come, first-served, and no one would have to give up a seat.

As reasonable as that plan sounds, Montgomery's white leaders refused to consider it. And when their rejection was compounded by bombings and other violence, the black community escalated its demands. As King said later, the boycott leaders had made a mistake by being too moderate. The time had come for the courts to overturn segregation entirely.

The case landed on the desk of U.S. district judge Frank Johnson, who was still a relative newcomer to the bench. Johnson was a Republican, a rarity in Alabama in those days, appointed to his post in 1955 by President Dwight D. Eisenhower. Before that time, he had been a U.S. attorney who vigorously prosecuted racial crimes. In 1954, he secured a conviction from an all-white jury against several members of a prominent white family who had beaten a black farm worker to death.

Johnson was a formidable man in the courtroom, with his hawklike features and piercing eyes, and whenever the occasion seemed to call for it, a cool and efficient sense of outrage. As a judge, he proved to be fearless and firm, but he decided not to tackle the bus case alone. He arranged for a three-judge federal panel consisting of himself and two of his most distinguished colleagues, Judges Richard Rives and Seybourn Lynne, both of them regarded as fair-minded men.

On May 11, 1956, the panel convened at the federal courthouse that now bears Johnson's name. The first witness that day was Aurelia Browder, a young woman who carried herself with great poise. She was already a widow at the age of thirty-four, a nurse's aide and mother of four who was also a student at Alabama State College. When attorney Fred Gray

Judge Frank M. Johnson. *Birmingham News.*

asked her why, as an African American, she supported the boycott, she said it was simple: "I wanted better treatment."

There was similar testimony from Susie McDonald, a black woman seventy-seven years old, and from Mary Louise Smith, who was only nineteen. But the most powerful testimony of the day came from Claudette Colvin. Like Smith, she had refused to give up her seat on a bus—had done it, in fact, before Rosa Parks—but she was only sixteen at the time of her arrest, and her case had largely passed unnoticed. But now she was playing a historic role, summoning what seemed to be a different kind of courage—not the spontaneous anger she had shown on the bus, but a resolve that had to be far more deliberate, requiring an ongoing level of calm.

During cross-examination, the white attorney for the city of Montgomery accused her of simply being part of a plot, "a scheme" by Martin Luther King and other black leaders, to disobey the law and bring pressure on the city. Colvin said no, she was speaking for herself. But the attorney persisted. There had to be somebody in charge, some organizer behind a movement so elaborate. The whole community, after all, had abandoned the buses on the same Monday morning. "Why," said the lawyer, his voice more intense, "did you stop riding on December 5?"

Colvin didn't hesitate. "Because," she said, to scattered murmurs of approval from the crowd, "we were treated wrong, dirty and nasty."

The hearing lasted five hours that day, and when the judges withdrew to consider the evidence, it took them only a few minutes to decide. Judge Johnson spoke first, addressing Richard Rives, the senior member of the group. "Judge," he said, "as far as I'm concerned, state-imposed segregation on public facilities violates the Constitution. I'm going to rule with the plaintiffs here."

"You know," replied Rives, "I feel the same way as you."

Judge Lynne dissented. Though he would later become sympathetic to civil rights, he was uneasy with the idea of judicial activism, with the courts essentially making new law. But he was outvoted, and on June 5, 1956, the three-judge panel issued its opinion: "There is no rational basis upon which the 'separate but equal' doctrine can validly be applied to public transportation in the city of Montgomery."

The city appealed, but on December 20, 1956, the U.S. Supreme Court upheld the ruling. The following morning, a small group of bus riders gathered at dawn—Martin Luther King Jr., Rosa Parks, Ralph Abernathy, and a white man by the name of Glenn Smiley, who had been a supporter of the civil rights movement. At 6:00 A.M., they boarded a bus and sat near the front.

"I believe," said the driver, "that you are Reverend King."

"Yes, I am."

"We are glad to have you this morning."

Rosa Parks took a symbolic ride in the formerly whites-only section of a city bus in Montgomery on December 21, 1956, the day after the U.S. Supreme Court banned segregation of the city's public transit vehicles. Photograph courtesy of the Library of Congress, Prints and Photographs Division [LC-USZ62-111235].

For the embryonic civil rights movement, it was a critically important moment of triumph. At a time in the South when whites held every instrument of power, a grassroots movement of ordinary people had refused for a year to ride segregated buses and eventually had won a victory in the courts. It was true that many of them took heart in the fairness of Judge Johnson and his colleagues. But the triumph belonged to the rank and file—to the people like Colvin, Smith, McDonald, and Browder, who had managed in the halls of the federal courthouse to summon the courage to do what they must.

What to See

The Frank M. Johnson Jr. Federal Building and U.S. Courthouse is now on the National Register of Historic Places. Built in 1933 and designed by Montgomery architect Frank Lockwood Sr., the five-story granite and limestone structure sits on a parcel of downtown land bounded by Lee, Court, Clayton, Catoma, and Church Streets. Its address is 15 Lee Street, but the primary entrance faces Church Street. Immediately behind it is the former Greyhound bus terminal, site of a bloody attack on a group of freedom riders in May 1961.

Inside the federal building, Frank Johnson's courtroom is on the second floor. He presided there for nearly three decades, ruling on a number of civil rights issues, including voting rights, school desegregation, and a case allowing the Selma to Montgomery march to occur. For much of his career, he was vilified by many of Alabama's white citizens. But in 1992, his judicial legacy was enshrined when the federal court building was named in his honor.

There is no equivalent tribute to the black women who testified in the bus case. But at least one of them, Aurelia Browder, became a part of judicial history when her name, alphabetically, came first in the case of *Browder v. Gayle,* the Supreme Court's landmark ruling on the buses.

The Freedom Riders

The Site

The Reverend Ralph Abernathy's First Baptist Church, bombed at the time of the Montgomery bus boycott, became the site of another tense drama in 1961 when the freedom riders came to Montgomery. In May of that year, an integrated group boarded Greyhound and Trailways buses in Washington, D.C., and headed south to test recent rulings on interstate transportation. One group of riders was attacked in Anniston and their bus set aflame, while a second group was beaten in Birmingham. On May 20, 1961, another group continued the ride to Montgomery, where, once again at the Greyhound station, an angry mob was waiting

THE LEGACY OF ALABAMA STATE UNIVERSITY

Aurelia Browder, a student at Alabama State College when she testified in the Montgomery bus case, was one of many people at that institution to play an important role in the civil rights movement.

Many historians give credit to Jo Ann Robinson, an English professor, for first conceiving the idea of the bus boycott. On the night after Rosa Parks's arrest, Ms. Robinson and several of her colleagues came to the campus and ran off more than thirty-five thousand flyers urging black citizens to stay off the buses. There are differing accounts about whether this act of defiance took place in Councill Hall or Patterson Hall, both of which still stand on the Alabama State campus. Wherever it occurred, if it had been reported at the time, it could easily have cost the women their jobs.

Once the boycott was under way, one of the most important organizers was former Alabama State football coach Rufus Lewis, who lived close to campus at 801 Bolivar Street (on the corner of what is now Dericote Street and Rufus Lewis Lane). Not only did Lewis, who had a long history of civil rights activism, first nominate Dr. Martin Luther King Jr. to be the spokesman for the boycott, he also organized the elaborate carpool system that enabled black citizens, throughout the course of the yearlong protests, to make it to their jobs.

In February 1960, some three years after the boycott was over, the sit-in movement swept through the South, and Alabama State students were caught up in its fervor. On February 25, thirty-five students sat in at the basement cafeteria at the state capitol, prompting Governor John Patterson to demand their expulsion from the state-supported college. In protest the following week, more than half the student body gathered in front of Councill Hall, the administration building, and marched downtown.

In the end, nine student sit-in leaders were expelled, including their spokesman, Bernard Lee, who soon became an aide to Dr. King.

to attack them. The following day, a Sunday, civil rights leaders from all over the country assembled at Abernathy's Montgomery church to rally in support of the riders, only to confront still another white mob.

The Story

John Lewis remembered the eerie moment of calm as the bus pulled slowly into the station. There seemed to be nobody there. But then a crowd of angry whites, many of them backers of the Ku Klux Klan, suddenly appeared and attacked the freedom riders as they stepped off the bus.

Lewis was the leader of this group of riders, a young Alabamian who had left his family farm near the community of Troy to become a ministerial student in Nashville. While at American Baptist Theological Seminary, he became involved with the sit-in movement, as he and other young students in Nashville refused to compromise with segregation. Day after day in the winter and spring of 1960, they took their seats at the city's lunch counters, risking both arrest and physical assault.

Now in Montgomery, the risk included the possibility of being killed. Already in May 1960, two groups of riders had been seriously injured during attacks in Anniston and Birmingham, and Lewis was expecting more of the same. He knew, in fact, that many of the young riders who shared the bus with him had written their wills before leaving Birmingham.

As the Greyhound approached the outskirts of Montgomery, some of the passengers may have been reassured that things had gone smoothly between the two cities. Floyd Mann, Alabama's director of public safety and a consummate law enforcement professional, had arranged an impenetrable police escort—highway patrol cars traveling with the bus, and surveillance planes flying overhead, searching for snipers, reporting regularly by radio to Mann.

Montgomery police had agreed to take over protection as soon as the bus crossed into the city. But at the Greyhound station, there were no police anywhere to be found. Lewis knew that it didn't feel right, and he said as much to another freedom rider as they stepped off the bus.

"And then, out of nowhere," he wrote years later in his autobiography,

> from every direction, came people. White people. Men, women and children. Dozens of them. Hundreds of them. Out of alleys, out of side streets, around the corners of office buildings, they emerged from everywhere, from all directions, all at once, as if they'd been let out of a gate. To this day I don't know where all those people came from.
>
> They carried every makeshift weapon imaginable. Baseball bats, wooden boards, bricks, chains, tire irons, pipes, even garden tools—hoes and rakes. One group had women in front, their faces twisted in anger, screaming, "Git them niggers, GIT them niggers."

Lewis himself was one of the first to be attacked, knocked to the ground by a Ku Klux Klansman swinging a crate. Jim Zwerg, a young white man who was standing next to him, knelt down to pray and another of the Klansmen delivered a kick to his back that was hard enough to break it. But the most horrifying moment came a few seconds later when the mob attacked William Barbee, a black freedom rider. They threw him to the ground, and as he lay there stunned, a white man stood with his shoe at Barbee's throat, and jammed a lead pipe into his ear.

Not far away, a Justice Department official named John Seigenthaler was left bleeding on the pavement with a fractured skull, and many observers and historians agree that people would have died at the station that day if not for the intervention of Floyd Mann. The director of public safety never quite trusted the Montgomery police, and despite the repeated assurances they had offered, he decided to drive to the Greyhound station just to assess the situation for himself.

Horrified by the scene when he arrived, he waded into the fray and fired two warning shots with his pistol. "There'll be no killing here to-

John Lewis talks with fellow freedom rider James Zwerg who was brutally beaten in Montgomery after riding into town on a Greyhound bus, May 1961. Photograph courtesy of the Library of Congress, Prints and Photographs Division, NYWT&S Collection [LC-USZ62-117558].

day," he declared. But a few feet away, a Klansman with a baseball bat kept swinging, and Mann walked over and put his gun to the white man's temple. "One more swing and you're dead," he said. He called in a contingent of seventy-five state troopers and within a few minutes the riot at the Greyhound station was over.

The most seriously injured victims that day, including Seigenthaler, Barbee, and Zwerg, had to be hospitalized in Montgomery. The remaining freedom riders, shell-shocked and battered, spent the night at the home of Richard Harris, an African American pharmacist who had long been a backer of the civil rights movement. During the bus boycott, Harris lived three houses down from Dr. Martin Luther King Jr. and was always around to offer his support. And now despite the dangers to himself and his family, he offered his home as a kind of sanctuary.

The following day, the community gathered in support of the riders. They chose Ralph Abernathy's First Baptist Church, the oldest African American church in the city, built at the end of the Civil War by an eager congregation of former slaves. The church had played a major role in the bus boycott, with mass meetings held in the sanctuary, and on January 10, 1957, it was one of four churches bombed during a reign of Klan terror.

But at the time of the freedom rides, the damage from that explosion had long since been repaired, as the black citizens of Montgomery, proud of the movement they had helped to start, began to assemble once again in the pews. On May 21, 1961, they trickled in throughout the afternoon, and by early in the evening the church was nearly full. They had heard of the attack at the Greyhound station, and they knew the roster of speakers that night would be a veritable who's who of the civil rights movement. Martin Luther King was coming over from Atlanta, where he had moved in 1960 to become copastor of his father's church. James Farmer, director of the Congress of Racial Equality, initial sponsor of the freedom rides, was flying in from Washington D. C., and Fred Shuttlesworth, the brave and dynamic leader in Birmingham, was coming in as well.

As it happened, Shuttlesworth and Farmer drove in together from the Montgomery airport, and when they arrived, they found the church surrounded by a mob. Unable to drive directly to the door, they parked their car on the other side of a cemetery and made their way through the scattered gravestones. When they emerged from a cluster of cedars near the church, Shuttlesworth boldly walked toward the mob.

"Coming through, gentlemen!" he announced. "Give us some room."

Remarkably, the crowd of white people parted like the sea, but their mood grew worse with the coming of night. They began throwing rocks and periodically surging toward the doors of the church, while a thin and haggard line of federal marshals tried to keep them at bay. Inside, the civil rights leaders urged the people in the pews to stay calm, even

National Guardsmen remain on alert as freedom riders board a bus in Montgomery, Alabama, for the next leg of their trip, to Mississippi. May 24, 1961. Photograph courtesy of the Library of Congress, Prints and Photographs Division, NYWT&S Collection [LC-USZ62-117558].

as the mob began smashing windows and turning over cars that were parked outside.

Dr. King and the other leaders were worried. In addition to the threat that was posed by the whites, they knew there were blacks that night who were armed, and they feared a bloodbath in which people would die. But they prayed and sang old hymns, and when they came to one of the standards—"Love lifted me when nothing else could help"—Solomon Seay Jr., one of the Montgomery stalwarts, urged the people to mean every word.

Finally, some time after midnight, Alabama governor John Patterson declared martial law and sent in a contingent of National Guardsmen. For the first time in many days, the freedom riders and their supporters were safe.

Three days later, twenty-seven riders on two separate buses left Montgomery and continued their journey into Mississippi. They knew already that they had sent a message. There was no place too dangerous for the movement to go.

What to See

The First Baptist Church stands at 347 North Ripley Street. A marker out front recounts the history, not only of the church's role in the civil rights struggle but also of its founding in 1866. After a fire destroyed the original church, a new one designed by architect W. T. Bailey of Tuskegee Institute was built between 1910 and 1915, using bricks donated by the congregation. In black communities in Montgomery and beyond, First Baptist became known as the Brick-a-Day Church.

First Baptist Church, 347 North Ripley Street. Photograph courtesy of Ann Webb.

The Oakwood Cemetery from which Fred Shuttlesworth and James Farmer emerged to make their way through the mob is diagonally across from the church on the corner of North Ripley and Columbus Streets. The Richard Harris house, where the battered freedom riders spent a night of safety, is at 333 South Jackson Street, half a block from Martin Luther King's former parsonage. A historical marker out front tells the story of the house and the role of the Harris family in the movement.

But perhaps the most dramatic reminder of the freedom rides is the former Greyhound station itself.

Located at 210 South Court Street immediately behind the Frank M. Johnson Federal Building, its exterior is now lined with plaques and photographs recounting the historic events that occurred there.

Old Montgomery Greyhound bus terminal, 210 South Court Street.
Photograph courtesy of Ann Webb.

Georgia Gilmore: Food for the Body and Soul

The Site

On a side street in one of Montgomery's residential neighborhoods, a historical marker stands in front of Georgia Gilmore's house, recording her unique contributions to the movement. She was a full-time foot soldier who offered her home as a place for meetings that often took place over heaping platters of soul food. Her cooking became a legend in the movement, and even today, a few blocks away, her spirit lives on. One of her protégées, Martha Hawkins, has opened a restaurant featuring the same kind of food, served up, many of the old-timers say, with the same feelings of community and common ground.

The Story

Those who knew Martin Luther King Jr. have spoken with affection about his love of good food. R. D. Nesbitt, a deacon at Dexter Avenue Baptist Church, remembered the first time he met Dr. King. It was a Friday afternoon in 1953, and Nesbitt had made the short trip to Atlanta to try to persuade King to become pastor of the Dexter Avenue church. They met at the home of Martin Luther King Sr., and, as Nesbitt remembered it many years later, the younger King was busily at work on a plate of pork chops.

After King made the move to Montgomery and assumed leadership of the bus boycott, one of the people he came to know well was Georgia Gilmore. Like many others in the black community, he loved her cooking and loved her personality as well. He and other leaders in the movement would gather around the table in her den, which could accommodate up to sixteen people, and they would settle in with her stuffed bell peppers, her cakes and pies, and very often a steady dose of her sass.

"She was a lady of great physical stature," remembered Thomas E. Jordan, a Montgomery minister. "She didn't take any junk from anybody. It

Georgia Gilmore House, 453 Dericote Street. Photograph courtesy of Frye Gaillard.

didn't matter who you were. Even the white police officers let her be. She wasn't a mean person, but like it was with many black people, there was a perception that she might be dangerous. The word was, 'Don't mess with Georgia Gilmore, she might cut you.' But Lord that woman could cook. I loved to sit down at her table for some good greasing."

Writing first for the *Oxford American* and later for National Public Radio, John T. Edge of the University of Mississippi described Gilmore as "a mountain of a woman, nearly 250 pounds of girth." And as Edge noted, she played a critical role in the movement. Among other things, as her sister Betty Gilmore told him, "she organized a group to start selling cakes and pies all over town, to beauty parlors and laundries and cab stands and doctor's offices. She called it the Club from Nowhere, so those people who were afraid of losing their jobs could still work for the movement. It was like, 'Where did this money come from?' 'It came from nowhere.'"

In addition to selling food to help fund the bus boycott, Gilmore also offered her home as a place for meetings—a place where delicate negotiations could occur beyond the prying eyes of the public. President Lyndon Johnson once met with Dr. King at her table, as did Attorney General Robert Kennedy, the two of them sharing a platter of collard greens.

"I just served 'em and let 'em talk," Mrs. Gilmore said.

One of the people inspired by Gilmore's example was a young woman by the name of Martha Hawkins. In 1965, during the Selma to Montgomery march, Hawkins made sandwiches for the marchers, having absorbed the lesson from Mrs. Gilmore that she was providing food for the body, but also for the soul.

"I idolized her," Hawkins said of Georgia Gilmore. "Just like her, I love people and I love to cook. My experience in the civil rights movement gave me a desire to have a place to bring people together."

Because of that desire, Hawkins is now the proprietor of Martha's Place, a Montgomery restaurant that features home cooking in the old southern style, and offers a place for people to meet much as they did at Georgia Gilmore's house.

Martha's Place, 458 Sayre Street. Photograph courtesy of Marcia Jones Media.

Randall Williams, a Montgomery historian, writer, and publisher, offers this assessment of Martha's Place: "Martha Hawkins is not simply cooking and running a café. She is trying to build a community."

What to See

Georgia Gilmore's house, where presidents and civil rights leaders came to eat, is located at 453 Dericote Street. The historical marker reads as follows:

> Georgia Gilmore, cited as a "solid, energetic boycott participant and supporter," lived in this house during the days of the Montgomery bus boycott. Once arrested on a bus, Gilmore was ardent in her efforts to raise funds for the Movement and organized the "Club from Nowhere" whose members baked pies and cakes for sale to both black and white customers. Opening her home to all, she tirelessly cooked meals for participants including such leaders as Dr. Martin Luther King Jr. and Dr. Ralph David Abernathy. Her culinary skills contributed to the cause of justice as she actively worked to encourage civil rights for the remainder of her life.

Martha's Place Restaurant, where Martha Hawkins seeks to keep that tradition alive, is located at 458 Sayre Street.

The Southern Poverty Law Center: Keeper of the Flame

The Site

The Civil Rights Memorial outside the Southern Poverty Law Center is one of the most striking monuments to the civil rights era. Designed by renowned artist and architect Maya Lin, whose credits also include the Vietnam Veterans Memorial in Washington D. C., the civil rights

CITY OF ST. JUDE

On March 24, 1965, the final night of the Selma to Montgomery march, more than two thousand demonstrators spent the night at the City of St. Jude Hospital just a few miles from the Alabama capitol. Many of the marchers slept on the grass at the hospital's thirty-six-acre campus and were treated that evening to a concert of freedom songs that featured some of the most popular entertainers in the country—Harry Belafonte, Odetta, Pete Seeger, Mahalia Jackson, Joan Baez, and Peter, Paul, and Mary, among many others. The following morning, another twenty thousand people gathered at the site and marched the final six miles to the capitol, where Dr. Martin Luther King Jr. gave one of his most famous speeches.

"The arc of the moral universe is long," he declared, "but it bends toward justice."

St. Jude's had opened in the 1930s to provide health care, education, and social services for African Americans. In 1951, it became the first racially integrated hospital in the South, and it played a notable role at the end of the Selma to Montgomery march. When civil rights supporter Viola Liuzzo was shot while driving marchers back to Selma, staff members at the hospital tried in vain to save her life.

Located at 2048 West Fairview Avenue in Montgomery, the hospital closed in 1985 but is now a well-marked historic site. In 1990, it was the site of the twenty-fifth anniversary celebration of the Selma to Montgomery march. Alabama's former governor George Wallace came to St. Jude's that day to greet the marchers and praise the changes that earlier demonstrators had helped to bring about.

City of St. Jude Hospital, 2048 West Fairview Avenue.

Photograph courtesy of Ann Webb.

Southern Poverty Law Center, 400 Washington Avenue. Photograph courtesy of the Southern Poverty Law Center.

remembrance combines the serenity of water flowing perpetually over the chiseled names of civil rights heroes with a stark reminder that these were people who died for the cause. There is also the unsettling fact that the memorial stands next to a heavily guarded and fortified building, where the Southern Poverty Law Center wages a sometimes dangerous crusade against the country's remaining hate groups.

The Story

For Morris Dees, director of the Southern Poverty Law Center, the idea for a memorial came at a deeply troubling time. He had just won a case against the Ku Klux Klan, a violent faction of the oldest hate group in Alabama. In March 1981, Michael Donald, a young black man in Mobile, was lynched by members of the United Klans of America (see chapter 8).

It was a shocking crime, considered by some to be the last lynching in the South, but to Dees and his colleagues it was one more piece of horrifying evidence that hate groups were still a danger to the country.

The center filed suit against the UKA on behalf of Beulah Mae Donald, Michael's mother, and in 1987 won a federal judgment on her behalf for the staggering amount of $7 million. Though most of the money was never collected, the case sent the UKA into bankruptcy, and soon afterward Mrs. Donald and Morris Dees were honored by the NAACP. Dees was struck by the fact that many young people attending the event didn't know the stories of the civil rights martyrs, and with that realization the idea for a memorial was born.

Dees turned to Maya Lin, who, at the age of twenty-one, when she was still an undergraduate at Yale University, had won a national design competition for the Vietnam Veterans Memorial. Lin said her concept for the Civil Rights Memorial, which was unveiled in 1989, came to her in a rush during her first visit to Montgomery. As she began to absorb the city's civil rights history, she came upon a quote from Martin Luther King, taken from his "I Have a Dream" speech in 1963.

"We are not satisfied," King had proclaimed, "and we will not be satisfied until justice rolls down like waters and righteousness like a mighty stream."

"Immediately I knew," said Maya Lin, "that the memorial would be about water and that the words would connect the past and the future. Sitting on the plane, I sketched the memorial on a napkin."

The result is a stark and handsome black granite structure with water flowing constantly across it and martyrs' names chiseled into the stone. In the building next to it, there is an interpretive center, or small museum, recalling the drama of the civil rights years and making the case that racial hatred is not yet dead. Security at the museum is tight, largely because it's immediately adjacent to the Southern Poverty Law Center itself, where dangerous legal work is an everyday occurrence.

Since its founding in 1971, the center has waged a continuing battle against racist groups nationwide. In 1979, for example, Dees and his attorneys filed suit against the Ku Klux Klan in Decatur, Alabama, after Klansmen attacked people attending a civil rights meeting there. In 1981, Dees set his sights on a Klan organization in Texas that was burning the boats and threatening the lives of Vietnamese fishermen near Galveston. And then in 1987 and 1988, the center secured judgments against two Klan groups and helped drive them into bankruptcy. Because of such activities, Dees and the center have been targeted for attack by members of white supremacist groups; more than thirty people have been jailed in connection with those plots.

In addition to its legal activities, the center is known for its educational programs, especially its *Teaching Tolerance* magazine, distributed free to more than four hundred thousand educators nationwide. Its other major publication is *Intelligence Report,* which monitors hate groups and extremist organizations in the United States.

What to See

The Southern Poverty Law Center is located at 400 Washington Avenue, just around the corner from Martin Luther King's former church, Dexter Avenue Baptist. The Civil Rights Memorial, which stands out front, is a mesmerizing structure made of granite with water flowing constantly over the names of martyrs.

But chiseled into the stone also are reminders of the movement's achievements, including the Civil Rights Act of 1964 and the Voting Rights Act of 1965. The powerful message of the memorial overall is that freedom hasn't come without a price, but neither have the martyrs perished in vain.

Southern Poverty Law Center. Photograph courtesy of the Southern Poverty Law Center.

The Civil Rights Memorial, designed by Maya Lin, was unveiled in 1989 at the Southern Poverty Law Center. Photograph courtesy of the Southern Poverty Law Center.

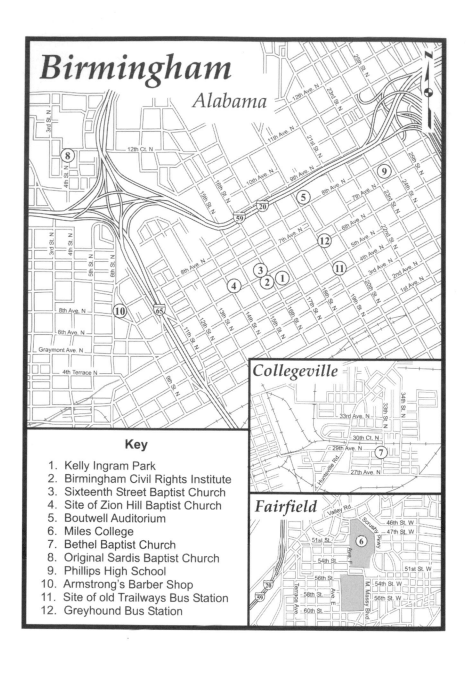

Birmingham
Alabama

Collegeville

Fairfield

Key

1. Kelly Ingram Park
2. Birmingham Civil Rights Institute
3. Sixteenth Street Baptist Church
4. Site of Zion Hill Baptist Church
5. Boutwell Auditorium
6. Miles College
7. Bethel Baptist Church
8. Original Sardis Baptist Church
9. Phillips High School
10. Armstrong's Barber Shop
11. Site of old Trailways Bus Station
12. Greyhound Bus Station

BIRMINGHAM AND THE AMERICAN CONSCIENCE

In the civil rights era, no other city in the South touched the national conscience more completely than Birmingham. During demonstrations in the spring of 1963, the city's racist police commissioner, Eugene "Bull" Connor, unleashed fire hoses and police dogs on civil rights protesters and African American bystanders. The televised images of those events left an indelible scar on Birmingham's reputation and reminded the country of the ugly brutality at the heart of segregation.

Dr. Martin Luther King Jr. came to the city to lead demonstrations, along with Birmingham minister Fred Shuttlesworth, one of the most fearless leaders in the movement. Following his arrest in April 1963,

Dr. King wrote his famous "Letter from Birmingham Jail," one of the most powerful documents of the civil rights era. "There comes a time," he wrote, "when the cup of endurance runs over, and men are no longer willing to be plunged into the abyss of despair."

Five months later, on September 15, 1963, a bomb exploded at Sixteenth Street Baptist Church, a primary staging ground for the movement, and four little girls died in the blast. For many in the movement, it was an emotional low point, a horrifying crime that tested their faith in the philosophy of nonviolence. For President John F. Kennedy, who would himself be murdered barely two months later, the bombing added urgency to the push for a civil rights bill that would overturn legal segregation in the South.

The turbulence in Birmingham did not begin in the 1960s. Thirty years earlier, during the depths of the Depression, protests rocked the city in some of the same areas—especially the now-famous Kelly Ingram Park—that shocked the nation in 1963. Here, beginning with events in the 1960s, is the Birmingham story.

Dr. King and the Children

The Site

Just a few blocks west of downtown, Kelly Ingram Park is shrouded in history, adorned today by statues and monuments telling the story of the civil rights years. Two other landmarks, the Birmingham Civil Rights Institute and the Sixteenth Street Baptist Church, stand just across the street, and for those who honor the history of civil rights, there is no more hallowed ground in the state.

The Story

Many years after his moment of truth, Freeman Hrabowski would re-

Statue in Kelly Ingram Park, Birmingham.

Photograph courtesy of Marcia Jones Media.

member the knot of fear in his stomach. He was leading a children's march in Birmingham and found himself, at the age of twelve, face to face with Eugene "Bull" Connor, the city's commissioner of police. Connor already had a fearsome reputation, a segregationist who ruled with an iron hand, parading through the streets in a custom-made tank, ordering his forces on multiple occasions to unleash the fury of fire hoses and dogs.

On this particular morning in May 1963, Hrabowski, with the reluctant blessing of his parents, started out at the head of a column of young people. They marched from Sixth Avenue Baptist Church all the way to city hall, where they were suddenly confronted by Connor himself. "I was so scared," Hrabowski remembered, but he did his best to stare back at Connor, who was gazing at him with a look of pure hate.

"What do you want, little nigger?" Connor demanded.

"We want our freedom, sir," Hrabowski responded, and with that Connor grabbed him and spat in his face.

In Birmingham in the spring of 1963, this was not an unusual occurrence. Martin Luther King Jr. and the staff of his Southern Christian Leadership Conference had arrived in the city, joining forces with Fred Shuttlesworth and other Birmingham leaders for something they were calling Operation C. "C" stood for confrontation, disruptive demonstrations that would begin with sit-ins, move from there to an economic boycott, and then to marches through the heart of downtown. And if at that point, the walls of segregation still stood, King would put out a national call for volunteers.

As the starting date for the protests approached, King had no illusions about the stakes. The previous year, 1962, had not been a good one for

Police block demonstrators in downtown Birmingham, 1963. Photograph courtesy of the Birmingham Civil Rights Institute.

him. For much of that time, he and his backers had found themselves bogged down in Albany, Georgia, a town in the southern part of the state where the sheriff, Laurie Pritchett, had proven to be a worthy adversary. Pritchett had discouraged violence on the part of his forces, choosing simply to arrest as many demonstrators as he could. The cost of paying bail had nearly exhausted the resources of the movement, without any visible signs of progress.

For the first time in King's career, national reporters had begun writing stories wondering whether he was losing his touch. He knew that he badly needed a victory, and he was hoping that Birmingham would provide it.

Part of that hope was tied to Bull Connor. King and others in the civil rights movement had long understood an ironic truth: Things went better when there was a villain, an opponent who embodied the qualities

Birmingham police commissioner Eugene "Bull" Connor, spring 1963.
Birmingham News. All rights reserved. Used with permission.

of meanness that added some melodrama to the struggle. Connor had long been that kind of man. Most recently, in 1962, when students at predominantly black Miles College had organized a boycott of downtown merchants, Connor had sought to cut off a government food program on the grounds that most of its recipients—the poorest of the poor in Birmingham—were black.

King and his coleader, Fred Shuttlesworth, were counting on Connor for more of the same, and it didn't take long for him to oblige. On April 7, 1963, during a Palm Sunday march, police dogs attacked a black teenager at Kelly Ingram Park, providing the kind of horrifying footage that inevitably generated sympathy for the cause. But the momentum this time was slower to develop. Despite the flashes of national publicity, the ranks of the demonstrators were thin. In these early days of the Birmingham protests, there were not enough people, or so it seemed, who were ready to go to jail for the cause.

King's first response was to go to jail himself. On April 12, 1963, which was, symbolically, Good Friday afternoon, he led a group of fifty demonstrators from Zion Hill Baptist Church toward Kelly Ingram Park. When they reached the corner at Seventeenth Street, where the dogs had attacked just a few days before, the marchers turned right along the edge of the park, then east again on Fifth Avenue. Three blocks later, Connor had them arrested, and a pair of burly policemen shoved King roughly toward a paddy wagon.

A few hours later, alone in his cell with its concrete walls and its cold, metal bed, King began to brood about the state of the movement and about the criticisms it had endured. He had read reports in the Birmingham papers about a group of white ministers who had urged greater patience and condemned the protests for being "ill-timed." As King considered what the ministers had said, he decided to try to formulate an answer.

The result was his "Letter from Birmingham Jail," which would soon

Left to right: Fred Shuttlesworth, Ralph Abernathy, and Martin Luther
King Jr. march on Good Friday, April 12, 1963, in Birmingham.
Photograph courtesy of the Birmingham Public Library Archives.

become one of the most famous documents of the civil rights era. The
actual text, written over a period of several days, was scrawled in the
margins of newspaper stories, on pieces of paper smuggled in by his visitors, and even on bits of toilet paper from his cell. His staff put the scraps
together like a puzzle, and then released the letter to the press.

"I guess it is easy," King had written,

for those who have never felt the stinging darts of segregation to say,
"Wait." But when you have seen vicious mobs lynch your mothers and fathers at will and drown your sisters and brothers at whim; when you have
seen hate-filled policemen curse, kick, brutalize and even kill your black
brothers and sisters with impunity; when you see the vast majority of your
twenty million Negro brothers and sisters smothering in an air-tight cage

of poverty in the midst of an affluent society; when you suddenly find your tongue twisted and your speech stammering as you seek to explain to your six-year-old daughter why she can't go to a public amusement park; . . . when you are harried by day and haunted by night by the fact that you are a Negro, living constantly at tip-toe stance . . . then you will understand why we find it difficult to wait.

Eight days later, King emerged from his cell only to discover that the movement, despite his eloquence and example, still suffered from a frustrating lack of volunteers. But then James Bevel, one of his most flamboyant staff members, had an idea. A sit-in veteran and former freedom rider, Bevel had been holding workshops for Birmingham students, talking about the gap between the promise of democracy and the actual conditions in which black people lived. He was sure that the students were ready to march, and he strongly urged King and other leaders to let them.

King was worried, unsure of the moral implications of the plan, for what if the children were hurt or even killed? But at noon on May 2, before he had even made up his mind, young people by the hundreds burst from the doors of Sixteenth Street Baptist Church and into Kelly Ingram Park across the street. As policemen began to make their arrests, the children kept pouring from the doors of the church, more than a thousand by the end of the day, filling jails in Birmingham and beyond.

The next day there were more, and Bull Connor called in the fire hoses and dogs, but the protest wouldn't die. On Tuesday, May 7, small groups of teenagers gathered unobtrusively in downtown Birmingham and began to picket the segregated stores. As police rushed down from Kelly Ingram Park to see what was happening, hundreds of young marchers burst from the church and made a "freedom dash" to downtown, adding to a mounting sense of chaos.

About the same time, a group of business leaders had assembled for

Police turn fire hoses on protestors in Kelly Ingram Park, 1963. Photograph courtesy of the Birmingham Civil Rights Institute.

a meeting of the Chamber of Commerce to talk about their city under siege. Suddenly, it seemed to be coming apart. Clearly it was time to negotiate, and the businessmen were led by Sidney Smyer, a Chamber official who had evolved through the years from a staunch defender of the racial status quo to a pragmatist who knew it was time to give ground. For the next several days, Smyer and a small delegation of whites—with the Kennedy administration running interference—hammered out a pact with Dr. King.

The agreement called for a phased integration of downtown business—a ninety-day window to remove the last of the "whites only" signs and the colored water fountains and to hire black clerks in the downtown stores. The agreement was announced on May 10, 1963, raising hopes for the possibility of peace. But that same night, a thousand members of the Ku Klux Klan gathered in a field outside of Birmingham. As a burning cross cast shadows on the crowd, their leader Robert Shelton called for "stiff-backed men . . . willing to go out and fight the battle for the Lord Jesus Christ."

A few hours later, bombs exploded at the home of A. D. King, Martin Luther King Jr.'s younger brother, who was also a stalwart leader in the movement. As blacks began to gather at the scene by the hundreds, many of them armed and calling for revenge, A. D. King worked hard to calm them down. He was making some progress, channeling their rage into a haunting chorus of "We Shall Overcome," when another bomb exploded not far away.

Word quickly spread that the second blast came from the Gaston Motel, where Martin Luther King Jr. himself had been staying. King was not there, but the attempt on his life was more than the black community could stand. Within a few minutes, a screaming mob gathered at Kelly Ingram Park and a full-scale riot erupted in the city. It lasted all night, and in the cold light of morning, it was clear that Birmingham still had a long way to go.

In the spring and summer of 1963, there was a legacy of violence to be overcome.

What to See

Kelly Ingram Park where so much of the drama unfolded covers a full city block, bounded by Sixteenth Street on the west and Seventeenth Street on the east, and by Fifth Avenue on the south and Sixth Avenue on the north. Sixteenth Street Baptist Church, the staging ground for many of the demonstrations, stands across from the northwest corner of the park.

Zion Hill Baptist Church, where King began the Good Friday march that led to his arrest—and thus to his "Letter from Birmingham Jail"—stood west of Kelly Ingram Park at 1414 Sixth Avenue North near the corner of Fourteenth Street, where the Deliverance Temple Interfaith Church stands today. Though the name of the church has changed, the building is the same. King's actual arrest occurred four and a half blocks east of the park on Fifth Avenue North, between Richard Arrington Boulevard and Twenty-second Street North. The Redmont Hotel stands near that spot. The actual bars from King's jail cell are now on display in the Birmingham Civil Rights Institute, which is located across from Kelly Ingram Park on Sixteenth Street North. In the same exhibit, there is a tape of King reading the famous letter he composed in that cell.

Boutwell Auditorium: Dark Days Ahead

The Site
Standing unobtrusively on Birmingham's Eighth Avenue North, Boutwell Auditorium seems an unlikely place for civil rights history. But it was here in 1956 that Alabama native Nat King Cole was attacked by a group of white supremacists as he sang for an all-white audience. It was not the first time that this municipal auditorium was the site of disturbing racial controversy.

The Story
Some in Nat King Cole's entourage had been expecting trouble from the start. But on April 10, 1956, Cole himself had simply said that it was good to be home. A native of Montgomery, he had returned to Alabama on a concert tour, appearing first in Mobile and then in Birmingham, and carrying himself on both of those occasions with the dignity and ease that had become his trademark.

His Mobile stop had gone smoothly enough, but in Birmingham there were hints of trouble before he had even made it to the stage. The White Citizens Councils in Alabama, a newly formed organization of white supremacists, had begun a campaign against black music. Leaders of the group were particularly enraged by the recent emergence of rock 'n' roll—a blend of black and white musical forms that they saw as a frightening form of integration.

Cole, of course, didn't play rock 'n' roll. He was a brilliant jazz pianist turned successful balladeer, but he was still an African American and that, apparently, was all it took. A few miles down the road in Anniston, the owner of a gas station and five other men planned to round up a mob of a hundred or more and storm the stage at Cole's Birmingham appearance. Their initial goal was to kidnap the singer and spirit him away, but when the mob of support troops failed to show, the original plotters were forced to scale back to a simple assault.

As Cole was starting to sing "Little Girl," his third song of the night, four white men bolted toward the stage. Before police could intervene, the attackers knocked Cole from his piano stool, injuring his back. The thugs were arrested along with two others waiting in the car with an arsenal that included two rifles, a blackjack, and brass knuckles. All six white men were sentenced to jail, and the two ringleaders, W. R. Vinson and Kenneth Adams, were convicted of assault with intent to commit murder.

Cole, meanwhile, returned to the stage for a standing ovation from the all-white crowd, and after doctors found nothing broken, he performed his second concert of the evening—this one reserved, under the laws of segregation, for an all-black audience. He told reporters before leaving the city that he was "not mad at anyone" in Alabama and believed he had "many friends in the state."

"I just hope I can get back to Alabama again soon," he said.

Ironically, for a time, his graciousness thrust him into controversy, as some blacks accused him of being too kind—a few even using the words "Uncle Tom." Cole was said to be hurt by the charge. It was true that he had never been political. But like many other African Americans, he hated the practice of racial segregation, had performed benefit shows for the NAACP, and had become a life member.

"There is only one opinion in this matter, and that is the right one," he wrote in a letter to *Down Beat* magazine. "Full equality for all people, regardless of race, creed or religion. . . . I had hoped through the medium of my music I had made many new friends and changed many opinions regarding racial equality."

The attack that repudiated such hopes was not the first disappointment that occurred within the walls of Boutwell Auditorium. Eighteen years earlier, in 1938, a group of black and white southerners from all walks of life—politicians, educators, community organizers, and others—gathered in Birmingham for the Southern Conference on Human Welfare. The conference came out of the work of Joseph Gelders, a Jewish intellectual from Birmingham who taught physics at the University of Alabama.

In the summer of 1936, Gelders had taken up the cause of Bart Logan, a Communist organizer during the Depression, who had been sentenced to an Alabama chain gang for the "seditious" literature in his possession. Included among the offending publications were recent issues of the *New Republic*. Gelders crusaded for Logan's release, and one night after a meeting about the case, he was kidnapped and beaten by a gang of white men.

But the experience only stiffened his resolve to put together a coalition of southern progressives who could chart a new course around the issue of race. On November 20, 1938, a remarkable cross section of southerners, black and white, heeded Gelders's call and assembled at the Birmingham auditorium. Alabama governor Bibb Graves was there, and Communist organizer Hosea Hudson, and Eleanor Roosevelt, the wife of the president. They gathered without regard for segregation, salt-and-peppered throughout the auditorium, as Frank Porter Graham, president of the University of North Carolina, delivered the keynote address.

"The black man," he declared, "is the primary test for American democracy and Christianity. The Southern Conference on Human Welfare takes its stand here tonight for the simple thing of human freedom. . . . We take our stand for the Sermon on the Mount, the American Bill of Rights, and American democracy."

Virginia Durr, one of Alabama's leading white liberals, would remember that speech and the opening night of the conference as "one of the happiest experiences of my life." But the next day, Birmingham's new police commissioner, Eugene "Bull" Connor, who would gain greater infamy in the 1960s, burst into the conference backed by a squadron of Birmingham police and demanded that the participants separate by race. Meekly, they complied, and almost immediately the soaring feelings of hope disappeared. Bull Connor left the auditorium flush with the power of his own success, and segregation became his holy crusade.

Meanwhile, the progressives left the meeting flustered and confused, and the conference was suddenly their symbol of failure. As historian John Egerton would later conclude, "It would be a long, cold winter in Dixie."

What to See

The Boutwell Auditorium, as the building is now known, is located on Eighth Avenue North between Fifteenth Street and Richard Arrington Boulevard.

Fred Shuttlesworth: Birmingham's Man of Steel

The Site

Standing sentinel in front of the Birmingham Civil Rights Institute is a statue of Fred Shuttlesworth. This work of art, created in 1992 by Birmingham sculptor John W. Rhoden, captures the intensity that made Shuttlesworth the most important civil rights leader in Birmingham, a man who grew up during the harsh segregation of the 1930s and became one of the bravest figures in the movement.

MILES COLLEGE: "WE SHALL OVERCOME"

Nestled in the hills of Fairfield, Alabama, six miles west of downtown Birmingham, Miles College has long been a beacon for the African American community, an "educational sanctuary" founded in 1905. In the 1960s its president, Lucius Pitts, was a cautious supporter of the civil rights movement. He was a tenant farmer's son from rural Georgia who understood the deprivations of segregation and poverty, and believed in the cause of racial equality.

Pitts was proud of the students at his school, including young men like U. W. Clemon, a future valedictorian who would later become the first African American federal judge in Alabama. In 1962, Clemon and other students helped spearhead a boycott of segregated stores, setting a tough-minded tone for the Birmingham movement. And then in 1963, as the civil rights protests gained momentum, Miles became a footnote to musical history.

Protest singer Joan Baez, already a committed supporter of civil rights, appeared at the college and recorded part of her concert there, including her version of "We Shall Overcome." The song by then was the preeminent anthem of the nonviolent movement, introduced to a whole generation of activists by a young folk singer named Guy Carawan. Carawan, a native of North Carolina, had studied the songs handed down in black churches and in the labor movement of the 1930s, and in 1960 he appeared at a demonstration in Nashville. He began strumming out the chords to one of his favorites, an old church standard called "I'll Overcome Someday," and he simply changed the pronoun to "we."

Joan Baez was one of many folk singers who was moved by the anthem, and her rendition of it at Miles, which appeared on her album *Joan Baez in Concert—Part 2*, was considered a classic in the folk music world. A few weeks after her recording at Miles, Baez was asked to sing the song at the 1963 March on Washington, shortly before Martin Luther King Jr.'s "I Have a Dream" speech.

In the years after that, she remained a committed supporter of the movement and participated in the 1965 Selma to Montgomery march. She performed both on the last night of the march—at Montgomery's City of St. Jude Hospital, where the marchers made camp—and the following day on the steps of the Alabama capitol.

Joan Baez leads singing of freedom songs at a postmarch rally on the steps of the Alabama State capitol in Montgomery, 1965. Photograph © 1978 Matt Herron/ Take Stock.

Statue of the Reverend Fred Shuttlesworth outside the Birmingham Civil Rights Institute. Photograph courtesy of the Birmingham Civil Rights Institute.

The Story

Nobody was surprised during the Birmingham demonstrations of 1963 that the Reverend Fred Shuttlesworth was in the thick of it. On May 7, peaceful marches near the heart of downtown were about to turn ugly. More than two thousand student protesters, most of them orderly, were suddenly confronted by firefighters and police, many of them armed with fire hoses and dogs. And on the fringes of the crowd at Kelly Ingram Park, there was yet another group of blacks—angry bystanders untrained in the nonviolent ways of the movement, who began throwing rocks and bottles at police.

Shuttlesworth quickly waded into the fray, trying to lead demonstrators away from the violence. A firefighter saw him and in a gesture of contempt for this militant warrior in the cause of nonviolence, he took aim with his hose. The force of the blast cracked Shuttlesworth's rib and knocked him back into the wall of a church. One of the demonstrators, a young activist by the name of James Orange, rushed immediately to Shuttlesworth's side and was startled when the minister, lying crumpled on the sidewalk, forced himself to whisper through the pain:

"Let's go! I'm ready to march."

Such was the character of Fred Shuttlesworth.

A Birmingham native, he had grown up poor just outside of town in a house with no electricity or plumbing. During World War II, he worked as a truck driver at an air force base in Mobile, then returned to Birmingham after the war and soon began his career as a preacher. As the newly called pastor at Bethel Baptist Church, he was drawn more and more to the civil rights movement. Many years later, he remembered being stirred in 1954 by the Supreme Court's ruling in *Brown v. Board of Education.* Here was the highest court in the land, ruling that racial segregation was wrong.

"That did something to me," he recalled. "That was God moving in the world."

Two years later, at the time of the Montgomery bus boycott, Shuttlesworth was determined to launch his personal crusade for civil rights. In December 1956, when the Supreme Court ruled that the buses of Montgomery had to be integrated, Shuttlesworth announced that on the day after Christmas he intended to test the ruling in Birmingham. On Christmas night, just a few hours before the protest, he was lying in his bed when a bomb exploded underneath his house, reducing it to rubble.

Remarkably enough, Shuttlesworth was unhurt, and the following morning, just as he promised, he led a large group of African Americans to conduct their own bus protest in Birmingham. Twenty-one people were arrested. No matter what the Supreme Court said, as far as the city fathers were concerned, segregation was still the law in Birmingham.

Shuttlesworth was undeterred. Already, he and four other ministers—

The Reverend Fred Shuttlesworth surveys the damage to Bethel
Baptist Church after his home, which sat next door, was bombed on
December 25, 1956. *Birmingham News.* All rights reserved. Used with permission.

R. L. Alford, T. L. Lane, G. E. Pruitt, and N. H. Smith—had established
the Alabama Christian Movement for Human Rights, and using that
organization as his platform, Shuttlesworth turned his attention to the
schools. In September 1957, he sought to enroll two of his children at
Phillips High School, which was still all white.

On September 9, he arrived at the school with his wife, Ruby; daughters, Ricky and Pat; and a fellow clergyman, J. S. Phifer, who was driving

The Reverend Fred Shuttlesworth preaching at a mass meeting in Bethel Baptist Church shortly after the bombing of the Sixteenth Street Baptist Church in September 1963. Photograph © 1978 Matt Herron/Take Stock.

the car. A mob was waiting, approaching from every possible direction, and to everyone's amazement Shuttlesworth got out of the car to confront them. A small contingent of policemen simply watched as the mob began to beat Shuttlesworth, many of its members using clubs and bicycle chains.

The lone exception was police lieutenant E. T. Rouse, one of those unheralded heroes, who, on this occasion, waded into the fray and began to pull the attackers away. With Rouse's help, Shuttlesworth and his family were able to escape, though Ruby Shuttlesworth had been stabbed in the hip as she attempted to go to the aid of her husband. Fred, meanwhile, had gotten the worst of it, but battered as he was, he addressed a civil rights rally that night.

"I don't want any violence," he said. "We have to control ourselves and keep on fighting."

Four years later, when the freedom riders came to Birmingham, it was Shuttlesworth who gave them sanctuary. And then came the demonstrations of 1963. Once again, he was at the center of it, sharing a leadership role with Dr. Martin Luther King Jr.

The two men had known each other for several years, and on one level, there was always a simmering rivalry between them. Too many people, in Shuttlesworth's opinion, were "goo-goo eyed" over King's credentials, including his PhD from Boston University, while Shuttlesworth was more of a self-made man. King, for his part, though indisputably brave, envied Shuttlesworth's physical courage and his charisma in moments of verbal confrontation.

"Fred," he once said, "you always have a ready answer. I wish I could do that."

"That's my gift," Shuttlesworth replied. "We all have our gifts."

But if they had their occasional moments of tension, the two leaders viewed each other with respect—a fact that was never more apparent than at the historic March on Washington, August 28, 1963. Initially, the march organizers had omitted Shuttlesworth when they drew up their list of speakers, and King had interceded on his behalf. But when the day was over and the speeches were done, Shuttlesworth understood that the hero was King.

He listened with amazement, and a little bit of awe, as King delivered the most famous speech of his career: "I have a dream today!" Many years later, when asked about the moment, Shuttlesworth simply smiled and said: "Every once in a while, God intervenes in such a way that you know that only God could do it. That was God preaching to America through King."

And yet if King, in his eloquence, became the preeminent spokesman for the movement, Shuttlesworth worked to give it an edge, to make it a nonviolent war for black freedom. He approached that task with a reckless courage that made some people wonder if he might be crazy. And he never actually denied it. "It takes a divine insanity," he said. "I didn't think it was bravery. I was just driven by divine impulse."

What to See

The memorial statue of Fred Shuttlesworth stands in front of the Birmingham Civil Rights Institute at 520 Sixteenth Street North, just across from Kelly Ingram Park, where many of the demonstrations were held. Shuttlesworth's home church, Bethel Baptist, where his parsonage was bombed on Christmas night 1956, is located at 3233 Twenty-ninth Avenue North.

The original Sardis Baptist Church, where Shuttlesworth launched the Alabama Christian Movement for Human Rights, is at 1240 Fourth Street North. On December 26, 1956, Shuttlesworth led a large group of African Americans in a challenge against segregated city buses. Their protest occurred between Second and Third Avenues North, near what is now the McWane Science Center. And Phillips High School, where Shuttlesworth was beaten by a mob of whites in 1957, is located at 2316 Seventh Avenue North.

Armstrong's Barber Shop and the "Ushers"

The Site

On Eighth Avenue North just west of downtown, there is an unmarked and little noticed civil rights site. Armstrong's Barber Shop, among other things, was the place where Martin Luther King Jr. got his haircuts whenever he needed one in Birmingham. But more importantly, the shop provided an independent living for its owner, James Armstrong, making him immune to economic pressure as he emerged in the 1950s and 1960s as one of the most important foot soldiers in the Birmingham movement.

On September 10, 1963, his two young sons, Dwight and Floyd, entered the previously all-white Graymont Elementary School, breaking the color barrier in Birmingham. Five days later, in apparent retaliation for that event, the Ku Klux Klan bombed the Sixteenth Street Baptist Church.

Armstrong Barber Shop, Eighth Avenue North and Sixth Street North.
Photograph courtesy of Frye Gaillard.

The Story

James Armstrong never forgot his first encounter with Fred Shuttlesworth. It was a Tuesday evening, June 5, 1956, and Armstrong was sitting in the balcony of Sardis Baptist Church, listening to Shuttlesworth in the pulpit. A few days earlier, an Alabama judge had essentially outlawed the NAACP, issuing an injunction forbidding it to operate in the state. Shuttlesworth had been a leader in the Birmingham chapter, and he was incensed.

"You can't stop people from trying to be free," he declared, and on the night of June 6, he announced the formation of a new organization, the Alabama Christian Movement for Human Rights, which would attack segregation in all of its forms. It would be a nonviolent war, he said. "Not one hair on the head of one white person will be harmed." But it would also be a battle to the end, and if there had to be any suffering for the cause, Shuttlesworth himself would be there to lead it.

"If anybody gets arrested," he proclaimed, "it'll be me; if anybody goes to jail, it'll be me; if anybody suffers, it'll be me; if anybody gets killed, it'll be me."

James Armstrong listened with deep admiration. He had rarely ever seen such fire, such passion for the cause, and he decided to cast his lot with Shuttlesworth and try to help him any way that he could. Armstrong was a veteran of World War II, who returned from the battlefields of Europe wanting a piece of the freedom he had fought for. But in Birmingham he found a segregated world—a place of "whites only" signs where blacks had to sit in the back of the bus and where his children were sentenced to inferior schools. Armstrong wanted to be a part of the resistance, and as his first assignment in support of Shuttlesworth he became a member of the "ushers."

These were the bodyguards, men who might believe in nonviolence but who were also willing to stand guard with their guns. Their name, the "ushers," was a reference to the fact that they often stood duty at the churches. With the movement drawing strength from these sacred sanctuaries, places of worship became a favored target of the Klan. In 1956, there was the Christmas night bombing at Shuttlesworth's parsonage, and two years later a pair of bodyguards found smoldering dynamite at his church. They were able to throw it in a ditch, just a few seconds before it exploded.

In 1957, Armstrong himself had rushed to the scene when Shuttlesworth was beaten at Phillips High School, trying to get his two daughters enrolled. Shortly afterward, Shuttlesworth announced he intended to file a desegregation lawsuit, and he asked for people to sign up as plaintiffs. James Armstrong was first in line, and first alphabetically when the case went to court. There were others who were forced to hold back, fearing violence or economic reprisals, but Armstrong knew he was in it until the end.

He waited patiently as the case made its torturous way through the courts. Finally in the summer of 1963, U.S. District Judge Seybourn Lynne issued a clear and unequivocal order: Birmingham schools would open their doors to black students in the fall. There were similar cases in Tuskegee and Huntsville, and Alabama governor George Wallace fought until the bitter end for segregation. He sent state troopers to close down the schools, and talked often about the possibility of violence.

Armstrong was nervous on September 10, when President Kennedy federalized the National Guard to assure safe passage of black children to the schools. Everybody in Birmingham knew that there was the likelihood of retribution. And indeed, over the next several days, Armstrong's two sons, Dwight and Floyd, endured epithets and petty assaults at the formerly all-white Graymont Elementary. But they handled the difficulties with good humor and grace, and as a father Armstrong couldn't help feeling proud.

Then came the morning of September 15, a warm summer Sunday with bright blue skies and the singing of birds, when a bomb went off at

Sixteenth Baptist Church. Four little girls were killed in the blast, and it was clear that headlines about civil rights progress, including the desegregation of the schools, had stirred the passions of the Ku Klux Klan.

For Armstrong and many others in the city, this was the low point—a time that would make nearly anyone wonder if the soul of the South could ever be redeemed. Such was the terrible history of the times.

But Armstrong discovered that there were the moments of hope, moments when everything seemed worth it, and one of them came less than two years later when he joined the Selma to Montgomery march—that epic journey in pursuit of the vote. On March 21, 1965, the first day of the march, he set out in the row behind Dr. King, selected to carry the American flag because of the bravery he had shown in Birmingham.

Armstrong knew that events in his city had touched the conscience of the country and helped ensure passage of the Civil Rights Act of 1964. Now in the spring of 1965, they were marching by the thousands for the right to vote, more certain every day that victory was at hand.

When they came at last to the Alabama capitol, it was easy to believe, as Dr. King put it, that "the God of History" was on their side.

What to See

Armstrong's Barber Shop, with its Coca-Cola sign hanging out front, is in an unimposing brick storefront on the corner of Eighth Avenue North and Sixth Street North.

The Sixteenth Street Baptist Church: Four Little Girls

The Site

Still the home of a vibrant congregation, the Sixteenth Street Baptist Church was a staging ground for the Birmingham civil rights movement,

Freedom riders Jim Zwerg (*right*) and Paul Brooks entering the Birmingham
Greyhound bus station in May 1961. The men were arrested for sitting
together in the front of the bus as they entered Birmingham city limits on
May 17, 1961. *Birmingham News.* All rights reserved. Used with permission.

and on September 15, 1963, it became the target of a bombing by the
Ku Klux Klan. Four little girls died in that Sunday morning blast, and
for many of Birmingham's black citizens—and many of the nation's civil
rights leaders—that terrible tragedy was nearly more than they could
bear. For me as a writer, I had always known the broad outlines, but the
story in all its nobility and pain never fully took on a face until some of
the people who were there that day bravely, generously sat down to share
their memories with me.

BIRMINGHAM AND THE FREEDOM RIDES

At the corner of Nineteenth Street and Fourth Avenue North, a marker offers a sketchy reminder of the horrific Mother's Day of 1961. That was the day, Sunday, May 14, when a Trailways bus carrying a group of freedom riders—some black, some white—pulled slowly into the Birmingham station. Earlier in the day, another group of riders had been attacked in Anniston, barely escaping with their lives as their bus was burned by the Ku Klux Klan (see chapter 7).

In Birmingham, the Trailways riders were greeted at first by an unnatural quiet. But as soon as they disembarked from the bus, a mob attacked with fists and clubs and bicycle chains. CBS reporter Howard K. Smith, who was there on assignment to cover their arrival, offered this account in his memoirs: "The riders were being dragged from the bus into the station. In a corridor I entered they were being beaten with bicycle chains and blackjacks and steel knucks. When they fell they were kicked mercilessly, the scrotum being the favored target, and pounded with baseball bats. One man made his way to the waiting room still vertical, but his head was a red mass of blood. Another was on all fours and could not get up."

One of the most seriously injured was Jim Peck, a white freedom rider and member of the Congress of Racial Equality, the organization that had sponsored the rides. Peck had been the first to step from the bus, followed closely by an African American rider, Charles Person. The two of them absorbed the first brunt of the attack. What the riders didn't know was that police officials in Birmingham had made a deal with the Ku Klux Klan, giving the hate group fifteen minutes to commit whatever mayhem they wanted.

When the police at last moved in to stop it, some of the demonstrators, including Peck, were injured too seriously to continue with the journey. Battered and bleeding, they gathered at Fred Shuttlesworth's house, the only safe haven they knew, and began to consider what to do next.

Up in Nashville at about the same time, a group of young leaders in SNCC decided that the freedom rides had to continue. It was simply not acceptable, they reasoned, for violent forces to intimidate the movement, for if such intimidation succeeded it was an invitation to more violence in the future. Three days later, on the morning of May 17, a new group of riders set out from Nashville and assembled in Birmingham, ready to continue the historic protest.

They were harassed at the Greyhound station and some were arrested, but they avoided any serious attacks until their bus arrived in Montgomery. There, the Klan was waiting once again (see chapter 1).

Note: The current Greyhound Station at 618 North Nineteenth Street stands at the same location from which the Freedom Riders departed in 1961. It is about three blocks from the former Trailways Station.

Freedom riders historical marker, Birmingham, Alabama. Photograph courtesy of Frye Gaillard.

Sixteenth Street Baptist Church, 1530 Sixth Avenue North. Photograph courtesy of Marcia Jones Media.

The Story

It was more than a decade after the event when the Reverend John Cross first agreed to do an interview with me. It was obviously wrenching for him even then. He remembered the sound the dynamite made, but somehow, he said, it was hard to believe it, hard to process what was going on. That late summer's morning had been so perfect, full of bright sunshine, with a trace of autumn in the September air.

Then came the explosion, and Cross thought at first it must be the hot water heater at the church. They had been having trouble with it, and in the initial blur of his own confusion he thought that maybe the pipes had finally blown. But then he heard the screaming, and as he rushed through

Firefighters and church members examine the debris left by the bombing of the Sixteenth Street Baptist Church, September 15, 1963. Photograph courtesy of the Alabama Department of Archives and History, Montgomery, Alabama.

the downstairs door of the church, the horrible scene came quickly into focus. There was a gaping hole in the side of the building, almost big enough to walk through, and as Cross prepared to search through the wreckage, there were people who begged him not to go in for fear that the rest of the wall would collapse. But with one of his church leaders, M. W. Pippin, Cross began to crawl through the rubble and came immediately to a patent leather shoe.

Pippin looked stunned. "That's Denise's shoe," he said, speaking of his granddaughter, Denise McNair, who had been at Sunday school that morning.

"Mr. Pippin," said Cross, "that could be anybody's shoe. A lot of little girls wear shoes like that."

But soon they came to the tangle of bodies—Addie Mae Collins, Cynthia Wesley, Carole Robertson, and Denise—young girls who had come from their Sunday school class to the women's rest room in order to primp for the main Sunday service. Their lesson that day had been "The Love That Forgives," a topic rendered hideously ironic by the bomb. In the immediate aftermath, Birmingham exploded. For the better part of fifteen years, dynamite had been a fact of life in the city, with the homes of local civil rights leaders becoming the favored target of the Klan. But now a line had been crossed with the Sunday morning bombing of a church, and blacks by the hundreds poured into the streets, many of them armed, breaking windows, throwing rocks at police. By the early morning of September 16, Birmingham teetered on the edge of racial war.

Martin Luther King Jr. was in Atlanta when he first received word that the church had been bombed, and at first he sank into deep depression, worried that somehow he was to blame. It was he, after all, who had asked John Cross to make his church available to the movement, and he had known in his heart that some kind of violence was likely to follow. And of course they had already seen a lot of it—the fire hoses, police dogs, the bombing of a motel where King had stayed. And now as violence took hold of the city, the death toll was rising. In addition to the four little girls, two more black children were shot and killed in the rioting that followed.

For King the crisis had a curious effect, pulling him out of his personal depression, forcing him to return to Birmingham and try to heal the city's bitter wounds. The first task he confronted was preaching the eulogy at the funeral for the girls, and he knew that for some of the people in the church his message would probably be a hard one to swallow. He intended to say that it was time to forgive.

"History," he declared, "has proven over and over again that unmerited suffering is redemptive. . . . So in spite of the darkness of this hour, we must not despair. We must not become bitter, nor must we harbor the desire to retaliate with violence. We must not lose faith in our white brothers. Somehow we must believe that even the most misguided among them can learn to respect the dignity and worth of all human personalities."

I had read that speech early in my years of covering the civil rights movement and always wondered how it was received. How could the families of the murdered girls, and the thousands of people who were grieving with them, possibly respond to such a noble call? I put that question to the Reverend John Porter, who had offered his church as the site for the funeral. Porter had been intimately connected to the movement. He had worked with Martin Luther King Jr. in Montgomery, and later in Birmingham he had become one of the stalwart figures in the city, leading marches, preaching strong sermons at his own Sixth Avenue Baptist Church.

He was also a close friend of John Cross, and on the morning of the bombing he had left his own service and, knowing there were casualties, had rushed to the hospital to offer his support. "I got there," he said, "as they were bringing the babies in."

Porter had vivid memories of the funeral, including King's eulogy, and he said if I wanted to understand the response I should visit Claude Wesley, whose daughter Cynthia had died in the bombing. I knew Mr. Wesley had been an educator, first a teacher and then a principal, in the Birmingham schools, a man who wanted his students to understand the power and the subtlety of black history. He believed, he said, that the current generations were connected to the past, to the taproots of freedom going back a hundred years.

When I went to his house, he explained that he saw the bombing that way, as a terrible, heartbreaking, personal loss that was nevertheless part of a much bigger story. As he talked he glanced at a portrait of Cynthia, hanging prominently on the living room wall, a radiant smile on her round, pretty face. "She was a very happy child," Wesley said. "She always liked to be in the forefront. Her teachers would say if they could get Cynthia on their side, they could get the whole class."

When I asked him directly about King's eulogy, how it felt to be called to forgiveness when bitterness and rage would have been more natural, he was emphatic. "We never felt bitter," he said. "That wouldn't have been fair to Cynthia. We try to deal with her memory the same way we dealt with her presence, and bitterness had no place in that. And there was something else we never did. We never asked, 'Why us?' because that would be the same thing as asking 'Why not somebody else?' But as far as the movement went, we continued to feel about it the way we always had. We supported it. We felt it was seeking necessary change."

And finally, of course, the changes did come, as Birmingham moved past the dark days of bombings and into a calmer, interracial future. But there were people who never forgot what it cost. Many years later, I met for a final time with John Cross, the minister who led with such dignity and grace, and we talked again about his days in the movement. His daughter, Barbara, was with us this time, and she remembered how, at the age of twelve, she was already a seasoned protester when the bomb exploded at her father's church. Just a few minutes earlier she had been with the four little girls who had died and would certainly have been in the rest room herself if her Sunday school teacher hadn't sent her on an errand.

As Barbara and her father talked about that day, and about his discovery of the bodies, it was clear that the passage of nearly forty years had not managed to drive away the pain. The Reverend Cross was now an old man, and as the shadow of the memory spread across his face, I knew that I had pushed him a little too far.

"This has to be the last time," he said, his voice now dropping nearly to a whisper. "I don't think I'll tell this story again."

What to See

The Sixteenth Street Baptist Church was Birmingham's first black church, organized in 1873. The current building, which was designed by the black architect Wallace Rayfield and completed in 1911, stands on the corner of Sixth Avenue and Sixteenth Street North, diagonally across from Kelly Ingram Park. A display in the basement recounts the church's civil rights history, and visitors can see the display and tour the sanctuary by making an appointment. The church's number is 205-251-9402. Visitors are also welcome at the Sunday morning services, where attendance sometimes approaches two thousand.

THE BIRMINGHAM CIVIL RIGHTS INSTITUTE

Located across the street from the Sixteenth Street Baptist Church, the Birmingham Civil Rights Institute is one of Alabama's most impressive museums. But from its inception it was also intended to be something more. The idea originated in 1978 with Birmingham mayor David Vann, a liberal lawyer in the civil rights years who had been a clerk at the U.S. Supreme Court when the landmark ruling *Brown v. Board of Education* was handed down in 1954. During the 1960s Vann supported civil rights, and as mayor he wanted to see the city embrace its past.

Birmingham Civil Rights Institute, 520 Sixteenth Street North. Photograph courtesy of the Birmingham Civil Rights Institute.

In 1979, Vann was succeeded as mayor by Richard Arrington Jr., the first African American to hold that position. Arrington, a Birmingham educator before he entered politics in the 1970s, embraced Vann's vision for a museum. As a city council member in the 1970s, he had pushed the community to confront such issues as police brutality. But during his twenty-year tenure as mayor, he also pushed for reconciliation, and he envisioned an institute for civil rights as a potential cornerstone of that goal.

In 1986, Arrington established a task force under the leadership of Birmingham educator Odessa Woolfolk, and the idea of a civil rights institute assumed a more definite shape. Since its opening in 1992, the institute has become what its executive director Lawrence Pijeaux calls "a beacon for research in civil and human rights." In addition to its state-of-the-art archives, the institute has served as a kind of conference center on human rights, and its bookstore offers such Birmingham classics as Diane McWhorter's *Carry Me Home*, Andrew Manis's *A Fire You Can't Put Out*, and Frank Sikora's *Until Justice Rolls Down*.

But visitors are drawn to the museum component of the institute as well, transported back in time by ten different galleries and exhibits covering the African American experience. Nearby, in addition to the Sixteenth Street Baptist Church, is Kelly Ingram Park, where many of the demonstrations took place, and only a couple of blocks away is the Fourth Avenue Historic District, which was the heart of black business life in Birmingham. Among the featured attractions in the business district is the Alabama Jazz Hall of Fame, located in the old Carver Performing Arts Theater. The Hall of Fame members whose work is celebrated inside include James Reese Europe, a Mobilian who conducted the first black orchestra to play Carnegie Hall, and Lionel Hampton, a Birmingham native, who joined the Benny Goodman Quartet in 1936 and became the first black player in an all-white band.

As this book goes to press, another Hall of Fame member, Frank Adams, whose brother Oscar Adams Jr. became the first black justice of the Alabama Supreme Court, still conducts tours of the Hall of Fame facility and will often play improvised clarinet solos for guests.

On Fourth Avenue, between Sixteenth and Seventeenth Streets, a marker notes the location of the Fraternal Hotel, whose soul food café was a favorite eating place for Martin Luther King, Jackie Robinson, and Jesse Jackson, among many others. On Fifth Avenue, just across from Kelly Ingram Park, a plaque honors the work of Birmingham civil rights attorney Arthur Shores.

Former Birmingham mayor Richard Arrington and family greet supporters, 1987. Photograph courtesy of the City of Birmingham Public Information Office.

SELMA AND THE RIGHT TO VOTE

In the winter and spring of 1965, Selma emerged as the decisive battle-ground in the struggle for black voting rights in the South. With the passage of the Civil Rights Act of 1964, legal segregation in public accommodations had been effectively dismantled. There were no more "whites only" signs, no more restrictions about where whites and blacks could sit on a bus. But in many heavily African American counties, especially in the Deep South, blacks still faced major obstacles at the polls.

In Freedom Summer of 1964, civil rights workers risked their lives in Mississippi promoting black voter registration, and then in 1965 the focus shifted to rural Alabama. In Selma and surrounding Dallas County,

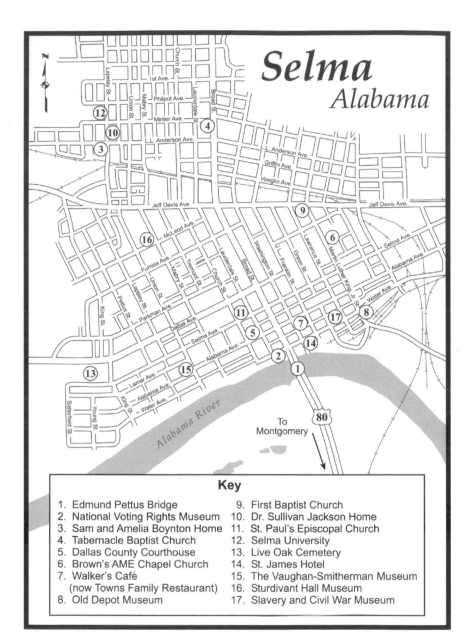

Key

1. Edmund Pettus Bridge
2. National Voting Rights Museum
3. Sam and Amelia Boynton Home
4. Tabernacle Baptist Church
5. Dallas County Courthouse
6. Brown's AME Chapel Church
7. Walker's Café
   (now Towns Family Restaurant)
8. Old Depot Museum
9. First Baptist Church
10. Dr. Sullivan Jackson Home
11. St. Paul's Episcopal Church
12. Selma University
13. Live Oak Cemetery
14. St. James Hotel
15. The Vaughan-Smitherman Museum
16. Sturdivant Hall Museum
17. Slavery and Civil War Museum

only a few hundred African Americans were registered to vote, out of a population of sixteen thousand. In neighboring Lowndes County, no African Americans were registered at all.

Civil rights leaders understood that the right to vote for sheriff or mayor or the local school board could represent a major stride toward freedom. By 1965, demanding that right had become the primary focus of the civil rights movement, but the effort had actually begun years before. Activists in Selma, Tuskegee, and Mobile, among other places, had worked on the issue of voter registration at least since the 1930s and 1940s.

But the 1960s were a turning point. The Student Nonviolent Coordinating Committee sent organizers to Selma in 1962, and Dr. Martin Luther King Jr. began leading demonstrations in 1965, culminating in the Selma to Montgomery march. In August 1965, passage of the Voting Rights Act, which grew directly out of the events in Selma, became perhaps the greatest triumph of the civil rights era. In the wake of its passage, democracy, at last, became a reality in the South.

The Quiet Beginning

The Site

In a residential neighborhood west of downtown, the struggle for the right to vote in Selma can be traced to a yellow wood-frame house, now in the process of being restored. The house once belonged to Sam and Amelia Boynton, indigenous leaders of the Selma movement, and among the guests who visited through the years were George Washington Carver, Ralph Bunche, and Dr. Martin Luther King Jr. The Boyntons were pillars of the civil rights aristocracy, who believed, quite simply, that every American should have the right to vote.

The Story

The struggle started quietly in the 1930s, much of it taking shape on Lapsley Street, where Sam and Amelia Boynton came naturally to their crusade for simple justice, as if it were a part of their DNA. On Amelia's side of their long family story, one of the ancestors was Robert Smalls, the first black congressman from South Carolina. During the Civil War, Smalls had been a hero for the Union. On May 12, 1862, he and a rebellious crew of black seamen who had been impressed into service by the Confederate Navy commandeered a steamer and turned it over to the Union, winning their own freedom in the process.

When the war ended and Reconstruction came, Smalls set out to take his rightful place as a citizen. He was elected first to the South Carolina legislature and then in 1875 to the first of five terms in the U.S. Congress. As white southerners reasserted their power and by the turn of the twentieth century managed to strip most African Americans of the vote, Smalls spoke out strongly against that trend. "We do not intend to go anywhere," he declared, "but will remain right here."

Growing up in Georgia, Amelia Boynton knew the story of Robert Smalls well and understood its meaning for her own generation. When she married Sam Boynton and moved to Selma, they talked often about how to make things better. Sam was an agricultural agent who traveled the back roads of Dallas County. He knew every farmer and sharecropper on the lands of white planters and knew the conditions under which they lived. Specifically, he knew that in a county split equally between black and white, almost all of the voters were white.

Starting in the 1930s, the two of them encouraged black people to register, regardless of their economic standing. It was a slow process, due in part to the fatalism of the times—a feeling among blacks that nothing would change—and due also to the hoops and impediments of the law. There were poll taxes that had to be paid, and hostile registrars, and the particularly galling requirement for a while that in order for an African American to register, a white person had to vouch for his or her character.

Despite all that, the Boyntons and their allies were making slow but steady progress until a backlash against the civil rights movement gained intensity in the 1950s and 1960s. At that point, the struggle became more bitter. With a few hundred Negroes already registered (out of a black population of sixteen thousand), white leaders decided that enough was enough. They intended to stop the movement in its tracks.

By the early 1960s, many blacks faced economic reprisals if they even attempted to get their names on the rolls. Annie Cooper, for example, was an African American who worked at a nursing home in Selma. She had lived in other parts of the country and had always voted—believing, in fact, that it was her patriotic obligation to do so. After returning to Selma in 1962, she joined a long line of people at the courthouse seeking to register, and while she was waiting, she noticed her employer writing down names. The following morning, he told her she was fired.

Such was the prevailing climate in Selma, but to the astonishment of white officials in the town, the intimidation failed. For the black community the breakthrough in courage came in April 1963, when Sam Boynton, the durable champion of the civil rights cause, died of heart problems. He had known his health was beginning to fail, and he told his wife that he didn't mind dying, but he didn't want his life to be in vain. "I want you to see," Amelia Boynton remembered him saying, "that all Negroes are ready to vote."

Remembering those words, Mrs. Boynton was receptive when she was approached by Bernard Lafayette, a former freedom rider and now an organizer with SNCC. Lafayette had come to Selma in 1962 to help with the voting rights campaign, and the Boyntons were impressed with his physical courage—his calm confrontations with Selma's white leaders, including Sheriff Jim Clark—and his respectful dealings with the black leadership, including themselves.

When Sam Boynton died, Lafayette proposed a community gathering to honor his life, a funeral service that would also double as a voting rights rally. Mrs. Boynton agreed, and Lafayette went immediately to one of the bravest ministers in town, the Reverend L. L. Anderson, and asked to hold the meeting at his church. Anderson was happy to grant his permission, but some of his deacons were not so sure. They knew what had happened in Montgomery and Birmingham—how the Klan had bombed churches sympathetic to the movement—and the deacons understood that it could happen in Selma.

They had long been proud of Tabernacle Baptist, with its stately columns and stained glass windows that gave it such a holy aura on Sundays. They simply didn't want to put the building at risk.

Anderson listened with mounting frustration, for how could a building compare with being free? Finally, he shrugged and told the deacons he understood their concerns and there would be no meeting within the walls of the church. Instead, he said, they would hold it outside, on a strip of ground just beyond the church property, and if anyone asked him about his reasons, he would tell them that the leaders of the church were afraid.

Thus shamed, the deacons relented and the historic rally went forward inside. The night could hardly have been more tense, with police lights flashing, an overflow crowd, and an angry white mob gathering in the street, shouting their racial slurs and smashing car windows, while sheriff's deputies looked on in approval.

Sheriff Clark himself stalked into the church, a large, heavy man with a menacing presence, but the people seemed to be unafraid. In the months after that, voter registration lines at the courthouse began to grow even longer, and the desperation of white officials became more intense. Finally, in July 1964, a local judge by the name of James Hare issued an injunction against any "assembly of three or more persons" even to *talk* about civil rights. The injunction was clearly unconstitutional, but in Selma, Alabama, it was rigidly enforced, and the movement dwindled for the next several months.

There were, in fact, only eight black leaders who continued to meet, the "courageous eight," as they were known in the African American community, and they sometimes gathered at Amelia Boynton's house. At one of those meetings in December 1964, they decided it was time to pull out the stops. They drafted a letter to Dr. Martin Luther King Jr., asking him to bring his movement to Selma.

For King it was an offer he could not refuse. He had great respect for the Boynton family, knowing their long history with the movement, and if Amelia Boynton wanted him to come, there was simply no way to tell her no. On January 2, 1965, a cold winter Saturday, King held his first mass meeting in the town.

The Selma movement was about to begin.

What to See

As this book goes to press, the Boynton home at 1315 Lapsley Street is no longer occupied and has drifted into a state of disrepair. But the National Voting Rights Museum has plans to restore it, thus preserving a crucial piece of history. At 1431 Broad Street just a few blocks away, Tabernacle Baptist Church, with its handsome columns and yellow brick walls, still stands proudly on the main street of town. A historical marker records its story and tells of the night in 1963 when a watershed meeting occurred within its walls.

The Courthouse and Sheriff Jim Clark

The Site

The Dallas County Courthouse is a handsome presence on the corner of Lauderdale Street and Alabama Avenue in Selma. In the 1960s, it was also the domain of Sheriff Jim Clark, who became legendary for his harsh

ANOTHER BOYNTON IN HISTORY

Sam and Amelia Boynton were not the only members of the family to make civil rights history. Their son, Bruce Boynton, who grew up in Selma and later returned as a civil rights lawyer, had been a forerunner of the sit-in movement. In December 1958, he was on his way home from Howard University law school, returning to Selma on his Christmas break.

His Trailways bus made a stop in Richmond, Virginia, and in those days of rigid segregation, Boynton stepped from the bus and entered the terminal. What he saw, he remembered years later, was "a clinically clean white restaurant and an absolutely filthy black café. I was really insulted that someone would expect me to eat in the black restaurant in that kind of condition. I went over and sat in the white restaurant. Even though I didn't expect to be served, I expected something like, 'It's not me. It's the law.' But the white waitress called the manager who put his finger in my face and said, 'Nigger, move.' That crystallized what I was going to do. I did not move."

The police were summoned, and Boynton spent the weekend in jail, studying for his law school exams. On Monday, he was taken to city court and fined ten dollars. It was a minor penalty, and Boynton could easily have let it go. But he decided instead to appeal his conviction all the way to the U.S. Supreme Court. In an opinion written by Justice Hugo Black, a former U.S. senator from Alabama, the high court issued a landmark ruling, declaring that bus terminals, as well as the buses themselves, must be desegregated.

The purpose of the freedom rides in 1961 was to test that decision and to demand its implementation in the South. But even before the Supreme Court ruling that bears his name, Bruce Boynton's courage, as he staged his personal sit-in in Richmond, became a part of civil rights lore—and another inspiration for the sit-in movement of the 1960s.

encounters with a wide variety of voting rights protesters. Unwittingly, in the end Clark succeeded only in reinforcing the determination of Dallas County's African American citizens to add their names to the voting rolls.

The Story

Amelia Boynton's confrontation was one of the first. On January 19, 1965, she assumed her place near the front of the line in a march on the Dallas County Courthouse. On the Alabama Avenue side of the building, Sheriff Jim Clark was waiting at the steps, and as usual he seemed to be in a rage. The day before, Dr. Martin Luther King Jr. had led a demonstration

Foreground, left to right: Civil rights leaders Fred Shuttlesworth, Martin Luther King Jr., Ralph Abernathy and Andrew Young attend a January 1965 voter registration drive at the Dallas County Courthouse in Selma. *Birmingham News.*

in which a group of nearly four hundred protesters had waited all day at the courthouse door. They were not allowed to register to vote, but instead of accepting that verdict they were back again on the following morning. In Clark's mind, they were creating a nuisance and getting in the way of courthouse business.

Clark ordered them to disperse, and when they didn't he grabbed Amelia Boynton from the front of the line and shoved her roughly in the direction of jail. As the news quickly spread, the black community of Selma was appalled, for Mrs. Boynton was not an ordinary citizen. For more than thirty years, she and her husband, Sam, had been Selma's leading voting rights activists, and her shabby treatment at the hands of the sheriff seemed to add a new intensity to the protests.

Dallas County Sheriff James Clark orders African American voting demonstrators to leave the Dallas County Courthouse in Selma on January 19, 1965. Photograph courtesy of the Library of Congress, Prints and Photographs Division [LC-USZ62-135700].

Three days later, a Selma teacher named F. D. Reese—another of the town's most respected black leaders—led a teachers' march on the courthouse. As Reese understood, this was a step that carried great risk. Black teachers could be fired by Dallas County's all-white school board, and most had worked hard at building their careers. But on the afternoon of January 22, dozens of them began to march two abreast down Alabama Avenue. Soon they were joined by cheering students and weeping parents, people caught up in the powerful emotions of this winter afternoon.

When the demonstrators arrived at the courthouse entrance, Sheriff Clark was again there to block their path. With his billy club, he shoved Reese and A. J. Durgan, another teacher at the head of the line, down the steps to the sidewalk below.

"What shall we do?" said Durgan, turning toward Reese.

"We are going back up the steps," Reese replied.

Two more times he and Durgan, followed by the others, climbed the stairs toward the courthouse door, and two more times Clark and his deputies shoved them back down. Reese decided finally that the point had been made, and the teachers turned and headed back quietly to the black side of town.

But the courthouse demonstrations continued, and the sheriff's outbursts became more intense. On January 25, he grabbed Annie Cooper, an outspoken Selma activist who had already been fired from her job in retaliation for her support of the movement. When Clark pulled her by the collar from the line, Mrs. Cooper wrenched free and told him angrily: "Don't jerk me like that."

Clark hit her in the back of the head with his hand, and Mrs. Cooper said later she felt something snap. "I went to fighting him," she admitted. She flailed away with roundhouse blows until one of Clark's deputies hit her with his billy club in the eye and then continued the beating as she lay on the sidewalk. A few minutes later, as Clark and his deputies

Selma sheriff's deputies arresting a demonstrator at a SNCC voter registration demonstration in front of the Dallas County Courthouse.

Photograph © 1978 Matt Herron/Take Stock.

dragged her away, Mrs. Cooper began to sing through her pain "Jesus, Keep Me Near the Cross." The whole episode quickly transformed her into one of Selma's grassroots heroes.

But perhaps the most dramatic confrontation of all came on February 16, when the SCLC organizer C. T. Vivian faced off verbally against Clark and his troopers. Vivian had been a freedom rider, and though he was resolutely nonviolent, he was known throughout the civil rights movement for his fiery disposition and courage. On this particular day, he began speaking passionately to a small group of deputies, urging them not to follow Jim Clark, proclaiming that the day of reckoning would come.

Clark decided suddenly he had heard enough. He stepped forward angrily and hit Vivian squarely in the mouth with his fist. The sheriff said later he didn't remember the punch, but it was hard enough to break a bone in his hand and knock Vivian down the steps to the sidewalk. But Vivian simply rose and continued with his sermon. "We are willing to be beaten for democracy," he said. "You can't turn away."

Some of the newsmen watching that day predicted when they talked about it later that the events in Selma were about to explode.

What to See

The Dallas County Courthouse stands directly across from the federal building on Alabama Avenue. There are two entrances to the county building, one on Alabama and the other on Lauderdale Street. The most dramatic confrontations occurred at the steps on Alabama Avenue.

Dallas County Courthouse, 105 Lauderdale Street.
Photograph courtesy of Jimmy S. Emerson.

MALCOLM X IN SELMA

As tensions in Selma continued to grow, national dignitaries began to stream into town, offering their moral support for the voting rights movement. In February 1965, one of the most controversial of those visitors was Black Muslim leader Malcolm X, who made his first trip south of the Mason-Dixon line to speak on behalf of Martin Luther King Jr. (On that same trip, he also spoke at Tuskegee Institute.)

With King himself in a Selma jail, his wife, Coretta, shared the podium with Malcolm when they spoke that evening at Brown Chapel AME Church. King's associates, especially James Bevel and Andrew Young, were worried about what Malcolm might say, fearing the possibility of violence. Earlier in his career, Malcolm had criticized the nonviolent movement, and even in 1965 he demanded black liberation "by any means necessary." But on his February 4 visit to Selma, he sought to be reassuring. As Mrs. King remembered it later, "He seemed rather anxious to let Martin know he was not causing trouble or making it difficult, but that he was trying to make it easier. He seemed sincere."

For his own part, Malcolm declared: "I think people in this part of the world would do well to listen to Dr. Martin Luther King and give him what he's asking for and give it to him fast, before some other factions come along and try to do it another way."

Less than three weeks later, Malcolm X was dead, murdered in Harlem, apparently by black nationalist rivals.

Malcolm X, 1964. Photograph by Marion S. Trikosko, courtesy of the Library of Congress, Prints and Photographs Division [LC-U9-11695-5].

The Edmund Pettus Bridge:
Bloody Sunday and Beyond

The Site

The Edmund Pettus Bridge, which towers over the Alabama River, is still one of the most dramatic symbols of the civil rights years. At this site, on March 7, 1965, peaceful marchers setting out from Selma to Montgomery were attacked by a combination of Alabama State Troopers and the mounted posse of Dallas County Sheriff Jim Clark. This moment of infamy—which soon became known as Bloody Sunday—only added intensity to the voting rights struggle in the Alabama Black Belt, in which the river town of Selma was the center of the storm.

Edmund Pettus Bridge, Selma. Photograph courtesy of Marcia Jones Media.

The Story

In the early winter of 1965, John Lewis walked alone through the streets of Selma, certain that history was about to be made. There was a light snow falling as he strolled along the river past the Edmund Pettus Bridge, and Lewis knew that later in the day Martin Luther King would be speaking in the town. Lewis always looked forward to that. As an Alabama native, his own involvement in the civil rights movement had been inspired in part by the eloquence of King. But he knew that things were complicated now.

By 1965, the movement had grown, and slowly, but surely, it was splitting into factions. Lewis himself, a former freedom rider and sit-in veteran, was currently the chairman of the Student Nonviolent Coordinating Committee, the most militant wing of the movement in the South. Since 1962, SNCC organizers had been working in Selma, helping to bolster the courage of hometown activists. Some of the SNCC workers were unhappy about the arrival of Dr. King. They considered him to be a headline grabber, blowing into cities and towns around the South, speaking to rallies, maybe leading a march, and then moving on.

The SNCC workers, on the other hand, took up residence in the communities they served, which were often the most dangerous places in the South. They regarded Selma as one of those places, with its swaggering and violence-prone sheriff, Jim Clark, and along with the local activists in Selma they lived with the risk and the fear every day. They were bitter at having their work upstaged.

For his part, John Lewis understood their resentment toward King and his organization, the Southern Christian Leadership Conference. But Lewis also knew that Selma's black leaders had invited King in, and Lewis was determined to minimize the rivalry. On January 18, 1965, he and King led local activists in a march to the courthouse, SNCC and the SCLC side by side. The demonstrations gained strength over the next several weeks, as word began to spread to neighboring counties. In Perry

County especially, there were major protests leading to more than seven hundred arrests. And on the night of February 18, police shot and fatally wounded Jimmie Lee Jackson, a young demonstrator in the town of Marion (see chapter 4).

Back in Selma, James Bevel, an organizer for the SCLC, led the movement's chorus of outrage. His first idea—suggested to him, some say, by Marion activist Lucy Foster—was to march to Montgomery with Jackson's body and lay it on the doorstep of George Wallace. But over the next several days the idea was refined, toned down just a little for the sake of propriety, and a new plan emerged: to march by the thousands from Selma to Montgomery, demanding equal access to the ballot.

Their first attempt came on Sunday, March 7. The demonstrators gathered, as they had many times in the past several months, at Brown Chapel AME Church, a brick sanctuary just north of downtown. They began their march in silence, two by two, led symbolically by John Lewis and Hosea Williams, representatives from SNCC and the SCLC. At the summit of the Edmund Pettus Bridge, they slowed their pace, many of them startled by the spectacle that was waiting for them at the bottom.

It seemed as if every law enforcement officer in the state was waiting on U.S. Highway 80, blocking their path on the road to Montgomery. The Alabama State Troopers were dressed in blue; Sheriff Clark and his men, in khaki. Hosea Williams looked down at the Alabama River swirling a hundred feet below.

"Can you swim?" he asked John Lewis.

"No," answered Lewis.

"Well," said Williams, forcing a smile, "neither can I, but it looks like we might have to."

Instead, they continued down the slope of the bridge, and stopped in front of the line of state troopers. The officer in command, Major John Cloud, gave them two minutes to disperse, but the attack began after barely a minute. "Troopers, advance!" the major commanded, and in the words of the March 8 *New York Times,* "The troopers rushed forward, their blue uniforms and white helmets blurring into a flying wedge as they moved."

Amelia Boynton, one of the local leaders in Selma, was standing just behind John Lewis when one of the troopers hit her with his club. When she didn't fall, he hit her again, and this time, she crumpled to the pavement unconscious. Sometime later in the bloody aftermath, people told her what had happened next—how the trooper continued to pound her with his club, screaming as he did it, "Get up, nigger! Get up and run."

Everywhere, it seemed, people were screaming and running from the bridge, as a mounted posse chased them down, cursing and clubbing, while a cloud of teargas hung in the air. Even people who made it back to the church were attacked at they tried to clamor inside. On national television that night, ABC was showing *Judgment at Nuremberg,* a film about Nazi persecution of Jews, and when the network switched to footage from Selma, there were viewers who thought it was part of the film.

Martin Luther King Jr., who was preaching in Atlanta, rushed immediately to Selma and put out a national call for volunteers. Within a day, people by the thousands poured into the town, and on the following Tuesday, March 9, King led another march. Troopers once again were blocking the highway. There was no attack this time, as King and the marchers turned around and went back into town. But that night, a small group of marchers, including James Reeb, a white Unitarian minister, went to eat dinner at Walker's Café, a little soul food place on Washington Avenue.

When they had finished, they turned the wrong way as they left the restaurant and found themselves headed toward the Silver Moon, another café just a few blocks away that was known to be a hangout for the Klan. As the marchers approached, the Klansmen began to jeer and taunt. One of them picked up a club and hit Reeb in the head, cracking his skull.

John Lewis, leader of the Student Nonviolent Coordinating Committee, is attacked by a state trooper during the attempted march on the state capitol, March 7, 1965. Photograph courtesy of the Library of Congress, Prints and Photographs Division [LC-USZ62-127732].

The young minister was rushed by ambulance to Birmingham, where he died less than two days later—a thirty-eight-year-old martyr to the cause. But it was nearly always the case in the civil rights years that the violence only made the movement stronger. Among other things, President Lyndon Johnson chose this occasion to deliver a powerful address to the nation, calling Selma "a turning point in man's unending search for freedom."

"Because it is not just Negroes," the president said, "but really it is all of us, who must overcome the crippling legacy of bigotry and injustice. And we shall overcome."

Marchers on the Edmund Pettus Bridge during the Selma to Montgomery march in 1965. Photograph courtesy of the Alabama Department of Archives and History, Montgomery, Alabama.

On March 21, two weeks after the attack on Bloody Sunday, Martin Luther King Jr. once again led a group of marchers who set out for Montgomery, protected this time by the National Guard. When they arrived at the capitol on the fifth day, King delivered one of the most powerful speeches of his career.

"I know," he said, in a cadence that had become familiar through the years, "that some of you are asking, 'How long will it take?' I come to say to you this afternoon, however difficult the moment, however frustrating the hour, it will not be long, because truth pressed to earth will rise again. How long? Not long, because no lie can live forever. . . . How long? Not long, because the arc of the moral universe is long, but it bends toward justice."

The march from Selma to Montgomery, March 1965. Photograph by Peter Pettus, courtesy of the Library of Congress, Prints and Photographs Division [LC-USZ62-133090].

Annie Cooper, one of the veteran foot soldiers from Selma, remembered thinking in the crowd that day that King was better than she had ever seen him. "His eyes were just a'twinklin'," she said. It was a moment, she added, when it was easy to believe that the day of democracy might be at hand.

What to See

The Edmund Pettus Bridge still stands on the bluffs of the Alabama River where U.S. Highway 80 comes into Selma. At both ends of the bridge, monuments, murals, and historical markers tell the story of what happened there. A half block away at 1012 Water Avenue, the National Voting Rights Museum tells the story also in a powerful, immediate, and grassroots way.

The Old Depot Museum on the corner of Water Avenue and Martin Luther King Jr. Street has exhibits recalling the whole history of Selma,

More than twenty thousand civil rights marchers crowd Dexter Avenue in front of the Alabama state capitol in Montgomery on March 25, 1965, as the Selma to Montgomery march ends. Photograph courtesy of the Library of Congress, Prints and Photographs Division [LC-USZ62-135689].

including the civil rights years. Outside the museum, a monument honors the martyrdom of James Reeb.

Another marker paying tribute to Reeb stands on the street where he was killed, Washington Street, not far from Walker's Café where he ate his last meal. That café, located at 118 Washington Street, is now Towns Family Restaurant.

Brown Chapel AME Church, where the marches began, is located at 410 Martin Luther King Jr. Street, adjacent to the George Washington Carver Housing Project. Historical markers at the chapel record its story. First Baptist Church, also important in the Selma movement, is located three blocks away on the corner of Martin Luther King and Jeff Davis Avenue.

Selma University: Cradle of Heroes

The Site

Selma University, founded in 1878, sits on an unimposing thirty-five-acre, twelve-building campus on Lapsley Street. In the course of its distinguished history, it has produced more than three thousand liberal arts graduates and several thousand African American ministers. Included in that number are some of the heroes of the civil rights years.

The Story

When William McKinley Branch set out for Selma, he didn't know he would one day become the preeminent civil rights leader in his county. He was simply a young man called to preach, and he thought he needed some more education. One day early in the 1940s, before he had even graduated from high school, Branch left his Greene County home and headed for Selma.

He caught a milk truck to the town of Demopolis, paid the driver a quarter to take him another twenty miles down the road, and walked the last thirty miles to Selma. He spent the night at a local juke joint and the following morning appeared at the door of William Dinkins, the president of the school. Dinkins was a dark-eyed man of great erudition, a graduate of Brown University, class of 1912, and the son of C. S. Dinkins, who had served as Selma's president from 1893 to 1901.

From 1927 to 1950, William Dinkins devoted his life to a college that had been so much a part of his family. Founded in the days of Reconstruction, it began holding classes at what later became First Baptist Church, one of the stalwart institutions of the civil rights years. Nurtured by the church, the school grew slowly into a training ground for African American ministers. Many of them were people like Branch, young men of ambition who came from the hamlets of rural Alabama, determined to try to make something of their lives.

DR. SULLIVAN JACKSON'S HOUSE

During the Selma voting rights campaign, Dr. Martin Luther King Jr. set up a kind of informal headquarters at the home of Dr. Sullivan Jackson, an African American dentist in Selma. Widely known for his courage, Jackson was one of the movement's most prominent supporters. His home at 1416 Lapsley Street was one block from Sam and Amelia Boynton's house, where King also spent time in Selma, and about an equal distance from Selma University, another important center of leadership.

In March 1965, King and other SNCC and SCLC leaders held strategy sessions at the Jackson house, and King met with Assistant Attorney General John Doar to negotiate plans for the Montgomery march. Perhaps the most dramatic moment came on a Monday evening, March 15, when President Lyndon Johnson addressed a joint session of Congress. King was watching the speech on television, huddled with his aides in Jackson's living room, when the president issued his lofty call.

"Rarely," Johnson said, "in any time does an issue lay bare the secret heart of America itself. . . . The issue of equal rights for American Negroes is such an issue. And should we defeat every enemy and should we double our wealth and conquer the stars and still be unequal to this issue, then we will have failed as a nation."

When Johnson ended his speech with the words "We shall overcome," King's lieutenant C. T. Vivian looked across the Jackson living room and saw a tear glistening on Dr. King's cheek. Nobody in the room had ever seen King cry. They had seen him worried, fretful, sometimes depressed, but more often they had watched him lead with humor and courage, his emotions always carefully in check. On this night, as they sensed that the voting rights victory was near and as the president of the United States seemed to be adopting their cause as his own, King finally let his feelings flow.

CHURCH AND STATE

One block north of the Dallas County Courthouse, on the corner of Selma Avenue and Lauderdale Street, Saint Paul's Episcopal Church has earned a designation on the National Register of Historic Places.

First consecrated in 1843, the church was burned by Union forces during the Civil War and then rebuilt on its current spot in 1875. Throughout its history, the handsome brick building has provided a Sunday morning sanctuary for some of Selma's most prominent white citizens. But in 1965, at the height of tensions over the issue of civil rights, the Saint Paul's congregation was plunged into discord. In March, Jonathan Daniels, an Episcopal seminarian who had come south for the Selma to Montgomery march, began taking integrated groups to Saint Paul's, forcing the church membership to confront its long history of racial segregation. On the first two Sundays, the interracial groups were turned away, but under Daniels's leadership they kept returning, and the church's rector, Frank Matthews, preached about the need for reconciliation. By August 1965, small integrated groups were attending services at Saint Paul's regularly. On August 20, however, Jonathan Daniels was murdered in the neighboring town of Hayneville by a segregationist enraged by his support of civil rights (see chapter 4).

President Dinkins was impressed with William Branch. His gumption alone was enough to make the educator take notice. "Finish high school," Dinkins told him gently. "Then come back."

Branch followed that advice, and after studying for the ministry in Selma, he returned to Greene County, where he started a chapter of the NAACP and helped lead the voting rights struggles of the 1960s. But he was not the most famous alumnus of the school. In the civil rights years, that distinction belonged to Fred Shuttlesworth, the fiery leader of the Birmingham movement (see chapter 2). Shuttlesworth was drawn to Selma because of its emphasis on classical education, and because President Dinkins provided him a job working in the vegetable garden of the college and milking the university-owned cow.

When he left the school in 1949, he was armed not only with an education but also with a sense of the possibilities of his people. The same was true of Autherine Lucy, who overlapped with Shuttlesworth at Selma and went on from there to become the first black student at the University of Alabama (see chapter 5). And in the realm of civil rights pioneers, Selma was also the place where Juanita Abernathy came of age.

A native of the Black Belt community of Uniontown, Mrs. Abernathy attended a high school operated by the college, before sharing in the civil rights journey of her husband, Ralph. Like her friend and fellow Alabamian, Coretta Scott King, Mrs. Abernathy accepted the dangers of that journey with grace. On January 10, 1957, a bomb exploded on the porch of her Montgomery home, just a few feet from the bedroom, and she could only assume that divine intervention had saved her life and the life of her child.

But it wasn't just the close brushes with death. During the Montgomery bus boycott, Mrs. Abernathy said, segregationists used other tactics as well. "The White Citizens Council hired a woman to call and cuss all day long," she remembered. "She'd stop at seven and a man would start and go till one in the morning, at which time I would take the receiver off the hook. This went on the whole year of the boycott."

Throughout those trials, Mrs. Abernathy and others in the civil rights movement drew strength from the institutions black citizens had established—the churches and schools that were the legacies of former slaves. And for many of the students who came through its doors, none was more important than Selma University.

What to See

Selma University is located at 1501 Lapsley Street. One of the school's handsomest buildings is Dinkins Memorial Chapel, which carries the name of two of Selma's presidents. At the time of the university's founding, it was nurtured by the city's black First Baptist Church, located at 709 Martin Luther King Jr. Street. It was known originally as Alabama Baptist Normal and Theological School, and First Baptist Church was Saint Phillips Street Baptist Church.

Alabama's First Black Congressman

The Site

Selma's Old Live Oak Cemetery is located near the corner of King Street and Dallas Avenue just west of downtown. It is a place of unexpected beauty, with Spanish moss draped from the live oak branches, and many of its graves are among the most historic in the state. One of those graves, located on the far eastern side of the grounds, belongs to Benjamin S. Turner, who, in 1870, became the first black Alabamian elected to the U.S. Congress. Though he served for only one term, the tone he set in his short career foreshadowed, in many ways, the reconciling spirit of the civil rights years.

The Story

During the Civil War, it fell to Benjamin Turner to manage the St. James Hotel, one of the finest facilities in Selma. The hotel, which has been restored and is still operating on Water Avenue, was built in 1837 and at the time of the war it was owned by Dr. James T. Gee. When Gee went off to fight for the Confederacy, he left his hotel in the capable hands of Ben Turner, his literate slave.

Then thirty-five, Turner was born into slavery in North Carolina; as a teenager, he moved with his owner to Dallas County. Somewhere along the way he had learned to read, and when freedom came in 1865 he set out to improve the fortunes of his people. While he was successfully running the St. James Hotel, he had built his own livery business on the side, and the U.S. census of 1870 lists him as one of the wealthiest freedmen in the state, with a personal fortune of more than twelve thousand dollars.

He used his own money to create a school for black children in Selma and in 1868 was elected to the city council. Two years later he ran successfully for Congress. While in Washington, Turner spoke out strongly for the rights of black Americans. He called for reparations for former slaves, helped secure pension payments for blacks who had fought in the Union army, and opposed a cotton tax that hurt black farmers.

But he set out to represent his white constituents as well. "The people of Selma have been magnanimous toward me," he said, "and I intend to stand by and labor for them in their need and desolation." He sought funds to rebuild Saint Paul's Episcopal Church, a place of worship for Selma's white citizens burned by the Union army during the war. And Turner called for amnesty for Confederate veterans, including leaders in the cause. General Edmund W. Pettus, a Confederate hero for whom the Edmund Pettus Bridge is named, praised Turner's efforts and called him "a man of brains and will."

In 1872, Turner lost his bid for reelection when another black candi-

Benjamin S. Turner, date unknown. Photograph from the Brady-Handy Photograph Collection, Library of Congress, Prints and Photographs Division [LC-BH83-2344].

date ran against him and split the black vote. But he continued to support education for black children and remained a successful businessman in Selma until the Panic of 1877. He returned to farming after losing his business in that recession and died in poverty in 1894.

Turner was buried in an unmarked grave, but in 1985 a biracial group in Selma erected a grave marker to celebrate his life—paying final tribute to a man who wanted freedom for his people and reconciliation with his white neighbors.

What to See

To find Benjamin Turner's gravestone, turn left after entering the Old Live Oak Cemetery and go to the last row of markers on the east.

Shaded by the branches of an oak, a marble monument bears a simple inscription: "Benjamin S. Turner, March 17, 1825–March 25, 1894." A slab that covers the grave itself offers the following tribute: "BORN A SLAVE IN HALIFAX COUNTY, NORTH CAROLINA, B. S. TURNER BECAME IN 1870 THE FIRST SELMAN ELECTED TO THE U.S. HOUSE OF REPRESENTATIVES AND THE FIRST BLACK CONGRESSMAN FROM ALABAMA. HE FOUGHT FOR AMNESTY FOR CONFEDERATE LEADERS, CIVIL RIGHTS FOR BLACKS, AND EDUCATION FOR ALL."

The St. James Hotel, which Turner operated during the Civil War, is still in business just east of the Edmund Pettus Bridge on Water Avenue. Turner's story is told at two of Selma's most important institutions, the National Voting Rights Museum and the Old Depot Museum, both of which are on Water Avenue. And finally, Selma's first-rate public library maintains an extensive file on Turner's life and career.

Selma: City of Museums

The Site

This river city of twenty thousand people, which, in the nineteenth century, produced a vice president of the United States, suffered major destruction during the Civil War, and later became the site of civil rights protests, has become a place that takes its history seriously. No fewer than five museums in Selma document the city's heritage and the complicated history of the area around it.

The Story

When former civil rights leaders in Selma were looking for a home for

Benjamin S. Turner's gravestone, Old Live Oak Cemetery. Photograph courtesy of Susan Finch.

the National Voting Rights Museum and Institute, they turned to a row of brick buildings on Water Avenue. There on the bluffs of the Alabama River, just a stone's throw from the Edmund Pettus Bridge, they found a storefront with a disconcerting history.

In the 1950s, when the White Citizens Council expanded from Mississippi to Alabama, the organization came first to Selma. This infamous white supremacist group set up shop at 1012 Water Avenue, and by 1956 it had become a force in racial politics, holding massive rallies to oppose the Montgomery bus boycott. Also in that year, one of the council's young supporters from Selma, Leonard Wilson, helped lead the resistance, which quickly turned violent, to the desegregation of the University of Alabama (see chapter 5).

Such was the white supremacist legacy emanating from the Water Avenue storefront. But the space seemed perfect for a small museum, and in 1993, the National Voting Rights Institute chose that site for its celebration of civil rights.

The grassroots facility not only repudiates the legacy of white supremacy but also documents the gradual expansion of American democracy from the Fifteenth and Nineteenth Amendments (which granted, respectively, former slaves and women the right to vote) through the Voting Rights Act of 1965.

One whole room in the small museum records the history of Reconstruction politics in the 1870s, a time when African Americans from eight Southern states were elected to the U.S. Congress. Three of those representatives came from Alabama, and the National Voting Rights Museum tells the stories of Benjamin Turner and Jeremiah Haralson, both from Selma, and James Thomas Rapier of Lauderdale County.

But arguably the museum's most powerful exhibits deal with events in the twentieth century. The "I Was There Wall" immediately across from the institute's entrance features written testimonials from participants in the tumultuous demonstrations of the 1960s. Mary Liuzzo Ashby, daughter of civil rights martyr Viola Liuzzo (see chapter 4), has penned one of the most poignant inscriptions of all: "For my mother. She came, she marched and she died for what she believed in." Immediately adjacent to the Liuzzo remembrance is a simple acknowledgment from Tom McElroy who was on the other side of the battle: "I was a state trooper in 1965." According to museum staff members, McElroy wrote the note as his personal gesture of reconciliation, which is part of the museum's larger purpose.

The institute also pays special tribute to the late J. L. Chestnut, a Selma native and one of Alabama's leading civil rights lawyers.

National Voting Rights Museum and Institute, 1012 Water Avenue.
Photograph courtesy of Susan Finch.

What to See

All the museums on Water Avenue are within walking distance of each other, and most visitors find that the National Voting Rights Museum is the best place to start. Both the Vaughan-Smitherman and the Sturdivant Hall sites are a five-minute drive away. At 1410 Water Avenue, the Slavery and Civil War Museum records the history of the international slave trade from its beginnings in the 1400s through the Dred Scott decision in 1857 (see chapter 7) and the Thirteenth Amendment to the U.S. Constitution, ratified in 1868, that ended the slave system once and for all.

Farther to the east, the Old Depot Museum on the corner of Water Avenue and Martin Luther King Jr. Street covers some of the same historical ground with a more direct focus on Selma.

Near the museum's entrance, there is a portrait of William Rufus de-

Slavery and Civil War Museum, 1410 Water Avenue.

Photograph courtesy of Susan Finch.

Vane King, a Selma cofounder and the thirteenth vice president of the United States, serving under President Franklin Pierce. At the time of his death in 1853, only thirteen weeks after being sworn in, King was known as a southern moderate—a defender of slavery, but an opponent of secession by the southern states. Not far from his portrait hangs another painting, this one of Benjamin Sterling Turner, Selma's first U.S. Congressman and the first black Alabamian to hold that office.

Two other museums record parts of Selma's antebellum heritage. The Vaughan-Smitherman Museum at 109 Union Street is a three-story Greek revival house that has also served as a school, courthouse, and hospital. Now a museum, the building features artifacts from Selma's long history, including a replica of the office of Joe T. Smitherman, the town's white mayor during the civil rights years.

As this book goes to press, a similar exhibit is planned for Selma's first African American mayor, James Perkins, elected on September 12, 2000.

And finally, Selma's antebellum past—with its elegant foreshadowing of a turbulent future—is further preserved in the Sturdivant Hall Museum at 713 Mabry Street.

Old Depot Museum, 4 Martin Luther King Street.
Photograph courtesy of Susan Finch.

Vaughan-Smitherman Museum, 109 Union Street.
Photograph courtesy of Susan Finch.

REVOLUTION IN THE BLACK BELT

After the Selma to Montgomery march and the impending passage of the Voting Rights Act of 1965, activists in the Black Belt—those rural Alabama counties named for their fertile soil—intensified the push for voter registration. In Lowndes County and those nearby—Wilcox, Greene, Perry, Dallas, Marengo, and Hale—African Americans by the hundreds who had never tried to vote made their way to their local courthouses, demanding to add their names to the roles.

The resistance to that demand was sometimes deadly. In Lowndes County, on the night that followed the Montgomery march, a civil rights supporter named Viola Liuzzo was murdered by members of the

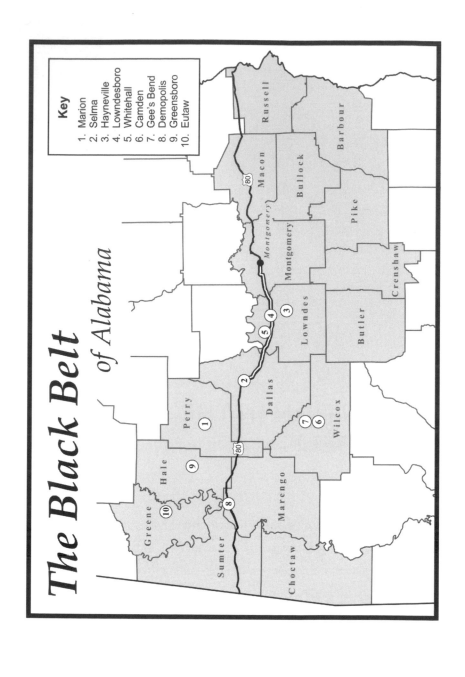

The Black Belt
of Alabama

Key
1. Marion
2. Selma
3. Hayneville
4. Lowndesboro
5. Whitehall
6. Camden
7. Gee's Bend
8. Demopolis
9. Greensboro
10. Eutaw

Russell
Barbour
Macon
Bullock
Pike
Montgomery
Montgomery
Crenshaw
Lowndes
Butler
Dallas
Wilcox
Perry
Hale
Greene
Marengo
Sumter
Choctaw

Ku Klux Klan. The following August in the county seat of Hayneville, a white Episcopal priest named Jonathan Daniels was gunned down near the courthouse square.

Meanwhile, many black farm workers who had dared to register were evicted from the cabins they rented from whites. Tent cities sprang up in Lowndes and other counties, and despite the inevitable hardships of the moment, these temporary communities became symbols of a newfound dignity and pride. African Americans understood that the ability to vote in local elections would have profound—even revolutionary—implications for their lives. As one black demonstrator in Greene County put it, "It made a big difference who the sheriff was."

Steadily, between 1965 and 1970, African Americans took control of the governments in these rural counties, and in the process they broke the old cycles of fear and disrespect. And although rural poverty was still a major problem, as it is even now, black citizens established credit unions, farmer's co-ops, and other cottage industries—including, most famously, the Freedom Quilting Bee (FQB) in Gee's Bend—that offered still greater hope for the future.

Lowndes County: Two Martyrs and the Vote

The Site

On a rise overlooking U.S. Highway 80, about halfway between Selma and Montgomery, a small monument marks the spot where Viola Liuzzo was killed. In 1965, Mrs. Liuzzo, a mother of five, drove down from Detroit to participate in the Selma to Montgomery march. On March 25, after the march, she was murdered by members of the Ku Klux Klan. Less than five months later in the town of Hayneville, Jonathan Daniels, another civil rights worker, was shot and killed by a white supremacist near the courthouse square. The murder of Liuzzo helped lead to the

Jonathan Daniels,
Selma, 1965.

passage of the Voting Rights Act of 1965, and the killing of Daniels eight days after the act was passed added urgency to the push for voter registration.

The Story

Early on the night of March 25, Viola Liuzzo had just dropped off her first load of marchers and was headed back to Montgomery for her second. Three weeks earlier at her home in Detroit, she had been horrified by the images coming out of Selma—the terrible attack at the Edmund Pettus Bridge in which peaceful demonstrators were beaten by police and run over with horses while a cloud of teargas hung in the air. She had immediately informed the members of her family that she was going to Alabama to do what she could.

Her primary role during her week in the state was to ferry marchers to Selma from the nearest airports. She had driven from Michigan in her 1963 Oldsmobile, and the organizers of the Montgomery protest were grateful to have the use of the car. On the day that the marchers arrived at the capitol, Mrs. Liuzzo had been in the crowd and had marveled at the powerful speech of Dr. King. But as soon as it was over, the organizers were faced with the task of transporting hundreds of people back to Selma.

Liuzzo, again, was happy to help. After delivering her first carload, she turned around and headed back to Montgomery to see if there were others still needing a ride. About 8:00 P.M. near the outskirts of Selma, a car full of Klansmen began to give chase. For more than twenty miles, the two cars raced along Highway 80, reaching speeds of a hundred miles per hour, until finally the Klansmen were able to pull alongside. On a desolate stretch of road just east of Whitehall, one of the white men fired two shots, killing Mrs. Liuzzo at once. Leroy Moton, a black teenager riding with her, survived the shooting and subsequent wreck of the car by playing dead until the Klansmen drove away.

Later, in court, Moton would describe the eerie last moments of Liuzzo's life. Apparently resigned to her fate, he said, she was softly singing "We Shall Overcome" at the time that the fatal bullets were fired.

The nation was horrified by the killing and even more so by the trial that followed. The crime had not been a hard one to solve, for there was an FBI informer riding with the Klansmen. Within hours of the shooting, Gary Thomas Rowe called his handlers at the Bureau and identified the killer as Collie Leroy Wilkins, a twenty-one-year-old recruit, eager to prove his mettle to the Klan.

Wilkins was arrested, and in early May he went on trial in the county seat of Hayneville. The weather was suffocatingly hot. Roberta Gamble, one of the people in the courthouse gallery, remembered later how the room was overflowing with Klansmen, their leader wearing a white trench coat, even though the temperature was stifling. Everything about the scene was surreal—from the armies of reporters from all over the world to the defense attorney who wore a Klan button and came to court every day with his guns.

But Roberta Gamble was more concerned about her husband, whose job that week was to prosecute the crime. Arthur Gamble was a respected attorney and politician whose family had deep roots in central Alabama. He was not a supporter of the civil rights movement, but he had no use for the Ku Klux Klan with its peddling of hate and its inclination to murder. He knew that his case this time was airtight, with an eyewitness to the killing who was on the payroll of the FBI. But he also knew that the issue was emotional and the jury, all-white, and he knew that defense attorney Matt Murphy would try to stir racial feeling in the courtroom.

Murphy was always a flamboyant figure. In his closing arguments, he stood before the jury and made little reference to the guilt or innocence of his client. Instead, he talked about segregation. "I'm proud to be a white man," he declared. "I'm proud to say I'm for white supremacy. . . . The Communists are taking us over. I say *never!* Gentlemen, we shall die before we lay down and see it done."

Prosecutor Gamble, in his rebuttal, tried to be as rational as Murphy was extreme. Drawing himself up to his impressive height of six-foot-three, Gamble reminded the jury that Mrs. Liuzzo had done nothing wrong. "She had every right to be here on our highways," he said, "without being shot down in the middle of the night."

The jury deliberated for a day, with ten of its members favoring a conviction. But there were two who insisted on acquittal, regardless of what the evidence might reveal, and the jury in the end was unable to agree. The case ended in a mistrial.

From his vantage point in Washington, D.C., President Lyndon Johnson was appalled by the verdict and urged Congress immediately to pass the Voting Rights Act of 1965. It was a bill with teeth, which, among other things, would bring federal registrars into the South to make sure that all black citizens could vote.

The legislation passed quickly as Johnson had hoped, and on August 6, 1965, he signed it into law. "The vote," said the president, "is the most powerful instrument ever devised by man for breaking down the walls of injustice."

Civil rights activists were inclined to agree. Even before the Voting Rights Act, workers from SNCC had decided to focus on Lowndes

County. Symbolically, it was the county through which the marchers had passed on their way to Montgomery and the county where Viola Liuzzo had died. But more concretely, as of the spring of 1965, it was a county with no black voters at all.

Its population was 80 percent black. But the white minority had clung desperately to power, and white supremacists had put out the word that an African American who even attempted to register might be risking his life in the process. Such was the climate of fear in the Black Belt.

Now, however, with the Voting Rights Act, the door to democracy was suddenly thrown open, and despite the euphoria that went with that fact, the SNCC people knew that the hard and dangerous work had just begun. Two organizers, Bob Mants and Stokely Carmichael, took up residence in Lowndes County. They were supported in their voter registration work by an Episcopal priest named Jonathan Daniels. Daniels was twenty-six years old, a New Hampshire native who had come south for the Selma to Montgomery march. But like the SNCC workers, he saw the march as nothing more than a dramatic first step. He decided to stay in Alabama for a while, doing whatever he could to be of help.

In Selma, he had made an impression on the black community, especially the young people, whom he befriended with good humor and kindness. He took them for ice cream, gave them rides on his back, and made them feel a little safer in the world. JoAnne Bland, a young Selma activist who tended to view white people with suspicion, recalled her amazement when Daniels came to town.

"Jonathan was white," she said, "and he was also nice."

In neighboring Lowndes County, Daniels played a more serious role. He offered his support to the SNCC organizers, often driving them to the distant reaches of the county, where they urged black citizens to register and vote, and to come to the organizing meetings every Sunday.

On August 14, Daniels was arrested following a demonstration in the town of Fort Deposit. He spent the next six days in the Lowndes County jail, along with a white Catholic priest named Richard Morrisroe and a small group of blacks. On August 20, when they were released, the two priests and two young women, Ruby Sales and Joyce Bailey, walked up the block to a local country store to buy soft drinks.

Tom Coleman, a Lowndes County white man, was waiting with a shotgun. When he raised it to fire, Daniels pushed Ruby Sales to the side, probably saving her life, before the bullets tore through his chest. He died on the spot.

Father Morrisroe was seriously wounded, but survived. Tom Coleman turned himself in, and despite the eyewitness testimony of Bailey and Sales, he was tried and acquitted by an all-white jury. It was a bitter moment for the civil rights movement, a reminder that despite the Voting Rights Act and the recent signs of progress, the struggle in the Black Belt was likely to be both ugly and long.

What to See

The monument to Viola Liuzzo, marking the spot where she was killed, stands on the south side of U.S. Highway 80 between the towns of Lowndesboro and Whitehall.

In the county seat of Hayneville, the courthouse where her killer was tried, along with the killer of Jonathan Daniels, still stands in the square at the center of town. There is also a monument to Daniels in that square, erected by his graduating class at Virginia Military Institute.

The jail where Daniels and his compatriots were held is no longer in use, but the old building still stands—unmarked—less than a quarter of a mile from the courthouse. So does the store where Daniels was killed, though it too is no longer in use.

There are also markers for lesser-known heroes—three African Americans, David Hall, Robert Gardner, and Rosa Steele who made their farms available as campsites for the march. As the highway passes by Whitehall, a new interpretive center operated by the National Park Service records

Clockwise from top left:

Jonathan Daniels Memorial marker, Hayneville. Photograph courtesy of Frye Gaillard.

Viola Liuzzo Memorial, Highway 80, Hayneville. Photograph courtesy of Susan Finch.

Historical marker for the Robert Gardner farm where civil rights marchers camped during the Selma to Montgomery march. Photograph courtesy of Susan Finch.

HIGHWAY 80: THE ROAD TO FREEDOM

No other Alabama highway is more historic than U.S. 80 between Selma and Montgomery. This was the route of the Selma to Montgomery march, a five-day trek in pursuit of black voting rights in the South. Historical markers abound on this rolling, fifty-mile stretch of blacktop, including the Liuzzo Memorial between Lowndesboro and Whitehall.

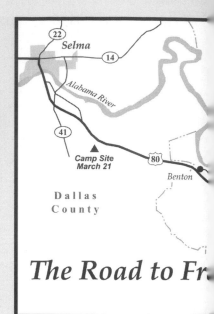

The Road to Fr

not only the events of the march but also the entire civil rights struggle in the Alabama Black Belt. The center itself is built on the site where black tenant farmers put up a tent city in 1965 after being evicted from their homes by white landowners. Their offense was registering for the vote.

One frigid night in the dead of winter, a young black woman, Josephine Mays, gave birth to a baby in one of those tents. Bob Mants, a former SNCC worker who remained in Lowndes County and assumed a leadership role in the community, said the courage of such rural people made him think sometimes of runaway slaves—people whose dogged will to survive offered a legacy of strength on which the movement could draw.

But there is also, along Highway 80, a record of senseless tragedy and violence. One marker near Lowndesboro, for example, tells the story of Elmore Bolling, a thirty-nine-year-old black man who was lynched in 1947 simply because of his success in business. Bolling ran a small trucking company that hauled cattle from Lowndes County to Montgomery

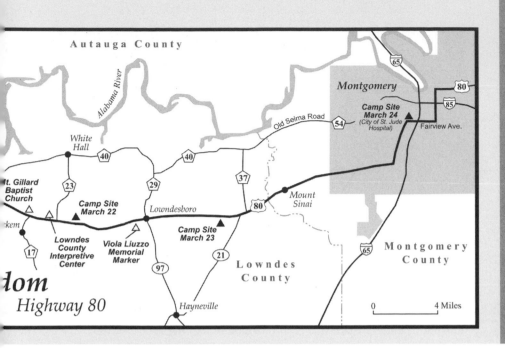

Lowndes County Interpretive Center, Highway 80, Whitehall. Photograph courtesy of the National Park Service.

Lowndes County Black Panther Party sign, used in the 1966 elections.
Photograph © 1978 Matt Herron/Take Stock.

and was regarded by whites, in the words of one local, as "too successful to be a Negro." On December 4, 1947, Bolling's body was found riddled with shotgun and pistol shots just a few yards from his general store.

The Black Panthers

The Site

On U.S. Highway 80 near the community of Trickum, the Mount Gillard Baptist Church stands on the northern side of the road, a reminder of the most dangerous days of the movement. In 1965, when the voting rights struggle came to Lowndes County, some of the earliest organizing meetings occurred in this church, and those who were present understood the risks. There were no registered black voters in Lowndes County at the time, and the white minority, which held political and economic power, was determined to crush any hint of revolt. The blacks, however, had other ideas, soon forming their own political party, which adopted the provocative black panther as its symbol.

The Story

John Hulett, who would become Lowndes County's first black sheriff, grew up in the darkest days of segregation. The grandson of a slave, he remembered the times when he was still a young man and would walk sometimes along a back road at night and see in the distance the head-lights of a car. Whenever that happened, he said, "You better hit the ditch. It could be the sheriff. More than one time, I've laid down to hide. I ain't gonna lie. Those were some pretty sad times, you know."

The civil rights activist Stokely Carmichael distributes literature for the Lowndes County Freedom Organization in 1966.

For a young man growing up in the 1940s, it was a time when it seemed as if nothing would change. Hulett moved away for a while, taking a factory job in Birmingham and becoming involved with the NAACP. But in 1959 he moved back to Lowndes County, partly to take care of his ailing father and partly to see if African Americans could build a civil rights movement there. It took a while to get things rolling, but by the spring of 1965, when the Selma to Montgomery march passed through, blacks in the county were beginning to meet and to talk about the issue of political power.

The numbers suggested that power was there for the taking. Blacks made up 80 percent of Lowndes County's population, and if they registered to vote they could take over the government. But they were also afraid. There had been so much violence for so many years, including in 1965, when Jonathan Daniels and Viola Liuzzo were murdered. But at the time of the Selma to Montgomery march, something fundamental was changing in the county. A small group of SNCC organizers, led by Stokely Carmichael and Bob Mants, took up residence and began to work with local leaders, including John Hulett.

Slowly but surely the voting rights movement in Lowndes County began to gain momentum. In 1965, on the first Tuesday in March, a group of three dozen African Americans gathered at the courthouse to register to vote. They were turned away by a white registrar who dismissed their aspirations as "dumb." Two weeks later another group returned, even larger than the first, and this time John Hulett and the Reverend J. C. Lawson were added to the rolls, becoming the county's first black voters in more than half a century.

That summer, President Lyndon Johnson signed the Voting Rights Act of 1965, which, among other things, sent federal registrars to southern states, and African Americans began to register by the thousands. In the elections of 1966, they formed their own political party, the Lowndes

County Freedom Organization, and as its symbol they chose a black panther. "A panther," explained John Hulett, "won't bother anybody, but push it into a corner, and it will do whatever it takes."

More than nine hundred African Americans from every corner of Lowndes County voted in the local elections of 1966. For the vast majority, it was the first time they had ever voted for anything, and in the minds of the local SNCC organizers there was a fundamental triumph in that fact. In a county where white supremacy had ruled, blacks had proclaimed their basic rights as citizens and in that moment had redefined their own humanity.

All seven of their candidates were defeated that year, but their struggle became a national news story. Out in California, angry young African American militants formed the Black Panther Party for Self-Defense,

Lowndes County Courthouse, Hayneville. Photograph courtesy of Kenny Shackleford.

adopting the symbol of the Lowndes County movement as their own. Meanwhile, John Hulett and other local leaders vowed to keep fighting, and in the elections of 1970 Hulett led a full slate of candidates to victory.

He promised that as sheriff he would be color blind, treating whites and blacks with equal respect, and trying to heal the deep wounds of the past.

What to See

Mount Gillard Baptist Church is located on U.S. Highway 80 near the intersection with Route 17. The Lowndes County Courthouse where African Americans lined up to register for the vote, thus changing the balance of power in the county, is located at the downtown square in the county seat of Hayneville.

The First Baptist Church, a small wooden building on Pine Street in Hayneville, was the county's first polling place for blacks.

The Martyrdom of Jimmie Lee Jackson

The Site

On the night of February 18, 1965, a group of demonstrators gathered at Zion United Methodist Church across from the courthouse square in Marion. Led by grassroots activist Albert Turner, they assembled in support of organizer James Orange who was then locked away in the county jail. Before the night was over, a young serviceman named Jimmie Lee Jackson lay mortally wounded after trying to rescue his grandfather from police. Though other martyrs have received more attention—both from the national media at the time and from historians in more recent years—none were more important than Jackson. His death inspired the Selma to Montgomery march.

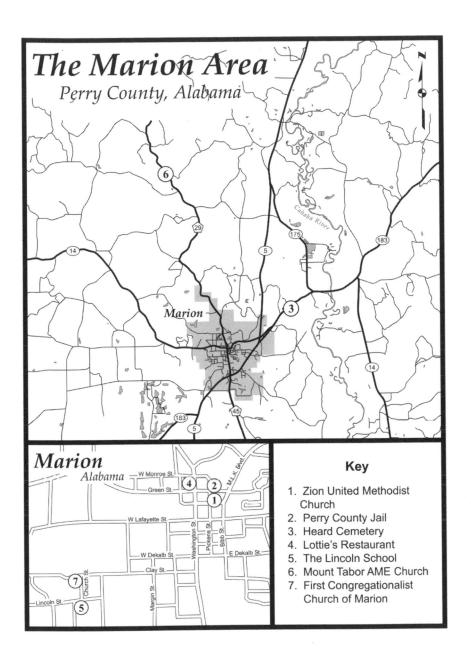

The Marion Area
Perry County, Alabama

N

Cahaba River

Marion

Marion
Alabama

W Monroe St.
Green St.
W Lafayette St.
W Dekalb St.
E Dekalb St.
Clay St.
Lincoln St.

M.L.K. Blvd.
Washington St.
Pickens St.
Bibb St.
Margin St.
Church St.

Key

1. Zion United Methodist Church
2. Perry County Jail
3. Heard Cemetery
4. Lottie's Restaurant
5. The Lincoln School
6. Mount Tabor AME Church
7. First Congregationalist Church of Marion

The Story

By the winter of 1965, the voting rights struggle that was centered in Selma had begun to spread to other parts of Alabama. One of the new hotbeds of activism was Perry County, where Albert Turner, Alabama's field secretary for the Southern Christian Leadership Conference, became the driving force in a round of winter protests.

He was joined in the county seat of Marion by James Orange, another SCLC staffer toughened by his participation in the Birmingham demonstrations of 1963. Orange, an organizer still in his twenties, spent time with many of the young people of Perry County, teaching them their rights and duties as citizens. By mid-February, the students had begun to march, and during one demonstration more than seven hundred of them were arrested.

They were driven like a herd of cattle to a high-walled stockade where they slept together on a concrete floor and got their drinking water from a trough. A short time later, on February 18, Orange himself was arrested and jailed, charged with contributing to the delinquency of a minor. The charges were serious, the kind that could lead to hard prison time, and there were rumors circulating in the black community that Orange might never even make it to trial. The Ku Klux Klan was planning to lynch him.

Albert Turner called for a protest march on the night of the arrest. The people would gather at the Zion United Methodist Church, a downtown chapel less than two blocks from the Perry County jail, and they would sing freedom songs in support of Orange. Turner invited C. T. Vivian, a fiery orator from the SCLC who had recently faced off against Dallas County sheriff Jim Clark (see chapter 3), to deliver the message at the church that night.

Vivian had deep misgivings from the start. He knew that a nighttime march could be dangerous, for the darkness most often belonged to the Klan. It was a time when otherwise law-abiding men might be tempted to become part of a mob and do things for which they would later be ashamed. But despite the dangers, Vivian made the short drive from Selma to Marion, where he delivered a powerful address and then stepped aside to let the people march.

One of the demonstrators, Theresa Burroughs from neighboring Hale County, remembered how the police were waiting just up the street. "The white people shot out the streetlights," she said, "and then everything broke loose."

The mayhem began when Marion police chief T. O. Harris ordered the marchers to stop. They had made it less than half a block from the church when they confronted massive numbers of police—the small force from Marion, buttressed by Alabama State Troopers and even some deputies from other parts of the state, led by Dallas County Sheriff Jim Clark.

When the marchers were ordered to return to the church, one of the local leaders, James Dobynes, knelt for a moment to pray, and one of the troopers hit him in the head. Other troopers followed with a full-scale assault on every marcher they could get to, and in the *New York Times* the following day, reporter John Herbers described the scene this way: "Negroes could be heard screaming, and loud whacks rang through the square."

Some marchers ran for the safety of the church; others found themselves cut off as the police continued the beatings in the street. Cager Lee, an eighty-two-year-old farmer who hoped to become a voter before he died, fled to a little café behind the church, but the troopers followed him inside. His daughter, Viola Jackson, tried to protect him, and when the policemen began to beat her too, the old man's grandson, Jimmie Lee Jackson, stepped in to intervene.

Jimmie Lee was twenty-six years old, an army veteran and the youngest deacon in his small Baptist church—an upstanding member of his community. When he rushed to the aid of his mother and grandfather, one of the policemen shot him in the stomach, and the young man lay for nearly half an hour in a slowly widening pool of his own blood. Finally, he was taken to the Good Samaritan Hospital in Selma, where he died on February 26.

Soon after Jackson's death, James Bevel of the SCLC came up with a dramatic idea in response. African Americans by the thousands, he said, should march from Selma to Montgomery, carrying the casket of Jimmie Lee Jackson, which they would lay symbolically at the doorstep of George Wallace. Eventually, the idea was toned down. Blacks would march, but Jimmie Lee's body would be buried with dignity at the Heard Cemetery just outside of Marion.

On the first attempt to march—March 7, 1965, which would soon become known as Bloody Sunday—Perry County's Albert Turner was one of the leaders, a gesture of respect for his role in the movement. The marchers were attacked and beaten that day (see chapter 3), and Turner was caught in the middle of the chaos. But two weeks later, they began the triumphant journey to Montgomery, and one of the honored members of the group was Cager Lee, the grandfather of Jimmie Lee Jackson.

Zion United Methodist Church, 3087 Pickens Street, Marion.
Photograph courtesy of Susan Finch.

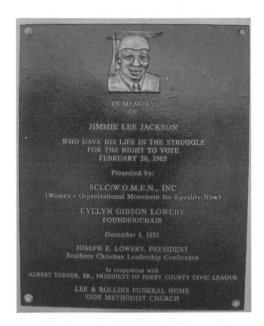

Jimmie Lee Jackson Memorial marker, at Zion United Methodist Church, Marion.
Photograph courtesy of Frye Gaillard.

Jimmie Lee Jackson's gravestone, in a cemetery on Highway 14, near Marion.
Photograph courtesy of Frye Gaillard.

Less than five months after the march, President Lyndon Johnson signed the Voting Rights Act of 1965, and over the next several years blacks by the thousands in rural Alabama were able to register for the vote. As the people of Perry County often said, Jimmie Lee Jackson didn't die in vain.

What to See

Zion United Methodist Church stands across from the town square in Marion at the corner of Pickens Street and Highway 14, which has been renamed the Martin Luther King Memorial Parkway.

A Civil Rights Freedom Wall graces the small front lawn of the church, engraved with the names of local "freedom fighters." Behind the church in the parking lot of what was formerly Mack's Café—the place where Cager Lee sought shelter—there is a plaque in honor of Jimmie Lee Jackson, erected by the Women's Organizational Movement for Equality Now, a committee of the Southern Christian Leadership Conference.

In front of the Perry County jail at 206 Pickens Street, less than two blocks from the church, the SCLC has placed markers in honor of James Orange and Albert Turner.

On the other side of the courthouse square, Lottie's Restaurant, which serves some of the best home cooking in rural Alabama, is owned and run by the Turner family. It is named for Lottie Turner, who was Albert's mother and a supporter of the movement in her own right. Her portrait welcomes visitors to the restaurant. As this book goes to press, the manager of Lottie's is Byron Turner, Albert's nephew and son of civil rights attorney Robert Turner. Albert Turner himself died in 2000, but his son Albert Turner Jr. is a Perry County commissioner.

Finally, on Highway 14 about four miles east of Marion, Jimmie Lee Jackson is buried in a small, oak-shaded cemetery, his gravesite visible on the south side of the highway.

Good Samaritan Hospital, where Jackson died, is located in nearby Selma on Broad Street just north of Jeff Davis Avenue. The hospital also

Martin Luther King Jr. and Coretta Scott King. The couple was married on June 18, 1953, in Heiberger, Coretta Scott's hometown. Photograph by Herman Hiller, courtesy of the Library of Congress, Prints and Photographs Division [LC-USZ62-116775].

treated the wounded on Bloody Sunday and was the place where Selma's first black mayor, James Perkins, was born.

Coretta Scott King: First Lady of the Movement

The Site

Perry County, in addition to being known for the events in Marion, was also the birthplace of Coretta Scott King. The revered "first lady of the civil rights movement" grew up in the rural community of Heiberger, where her family's home place and church still stand. She also graduated first in her class at the historic Lincoln School in Marion.

Mount Tabor AME Church, Highway 29, Perry County.

Photograph courtesy of Frye Gaillard.

The Story

Mount Tabor AME Church, built in 1886, stands on a hill on a small country road, and among other things it was the home church for Obediah Scott and his family.

The Scotts lived next door on a patch of land where Obie, as most people called him, coaxed out a living with the help of his wife and three children. During the Depression, they picked cotton together in the fall and raised truck crops, and eventually Obediah built his own sawmill.

In the community of Heiberger, Scott was known by people black and white as a resourceful, hard-working man, determined to build a decent life for his family. His younger daughter, Coretta, was a gifted child who, as a teenager, attended high school nine miles away in the village of Mar-

Lincoln School, Church Street and Lincoln Street, Marion. Photograph courtesy of Susan Finch.

ion. In 1945, she graduated first in her class at the Lincoln School, one of the most respected black institutions in the South.

In 1867, a group of nine former slaves came together to establish the school, and in 1868 they turned to the American Missionary Association for support. The AMA, once an abolitionist organization tied to the Congregationalist Church, took a leading role in supporting black schools in the years just after the Civil War. Among others, the AMA helped established Atlanta University, Fisk University, and Talladega College (see chapter 7).

In 1868, the AMA bought land for the school in Marion, and the following year established a Congregationalist Church and sent in a minister to run both the church and the school. The institutions grew, and Lincoln School operated both as a college, with an emphasis on preparing black teachers, and as a primary school for black children.

In 1887, the college was moved to Montgomery and eventually became Alabama State University. But the primary school remained in Marion and continued to grow, led at the beginning of the twentieth century by Mary Elizabeth Phillips, a former professor at Talladega College. By the time Coretta Scott King attended high school there, Lincoln School had earned national renown.

Coretta was one of many students who left Lincoln in pursuit of a college degree. Her studies took her first to Antioch College in Ohio, where her older sister, Edythe, had broken the color barrier, and then to the New England Conservatory of Music. While in Boston, she met Martin Luther King Jr., and on June 18, 1953, they were married on the porch of her family home in Heiberger.

She shared the civil rights goals of her husband and endured the turbulence that went with the movement, including the bombing of their Montgomery home. On the night of January 23, 1956, she heard a noise on the parsonage porch and quickly grabbed their infant daughter, Yolanda, and carried her to the back of the house. The dynamite exploded, tearing a gash in the cement porch, but Coretta and the baby were unhurt (see chapter 1).

Her husband, speaking that night at a civil rights rally, rushed home to find them shaken but calm. As historian Taylor Branch later wrote, "King took his wife aside and emotionally thanked her for being such a soldier. She was deeply moved to hear that King, with all his strength, needed her."

With the death of her husband in 1968, Coretta Scott King assumed a more public role in the civil rights movement and supported its goals for the rest of her life. In her later years, she sought to broaden the definition of civil rights to include equal rights for women, the alleviation of poverty, and opposition to apartheid in South Africa. She also supported equal rights for lesbians and gays, including gay marriage.

"Homophobia," she said, "is like racism and anti-Semitism and other forms of bigotry in that it seeks to dehumanize a large group of people, to deny their humanity, their dignity and personhood."

Coretta King died on June 30, 2006, at the age of seventy-eight.

Scott's Grocery, owned by Coretta Scott King's family, Perry County.
Photograph courtesy of Frye Gaillard.

What to See

A statue of Coretta Scott King stands in a small garden area outside Mount Tabor AME Church on County Highway 29 about ten miles north of Marion. Her father's cinder block store, no longer in operation, is still next to the church, and the family home where she and Martin Luther King Jr. were married on the porch stands next to the store.

Phillips Auditorium, the last remaining building of the Lincoln School, which closed its doors in the 1960s, is located at the corner of Church and Lincoln Streets in Marion. A marker in front of the school recounts its history and, among other important details, lists the names of the nine former slaves who created it. These founders are James Childs, Alexander H. Curtis, Nicholas Dale, John Freeman, David Harris, Thomas Lee, Nathan Levern, Ivey Pharish, and Thomas Speed.

A block from the school, on the corner of Church and Clay, the First Congregationalist Church of Marion, which provided the first principal of the Lincoln School, still stands. The pastor of the church in the 1950s was a young seminary graduate named Andrew Young, who began to study the writings of Gandhi while he was in Marion and soon became a friend of Martin Luther King Jr.'s and a leading strategist in the civil rights movement.

In 2008, efforts were under way to restore the small frame church in which Young had pastored, a building closely tied ever since its construction in 1869 to the quest for equal opportunity in the South.

The Quilts of Gee's Bend, Wilcox County

The Site

Gee's Bend is an isolated rural peninsula, a "river island" tucked into a deep bend of the Alabama River. Officially called Boykin since it got a post office in 1949, it is across the river from Camden, the Wilcox county seat. The Gee's Bend community, referred to in the 1930s as "an Alabama Africa," is best known today for the style of quiltmaking that has developed since slavery times. The recognition and respect the quiltmakers eventually gained from the art world came as a result of their participation in the civil rights movement.

The Story

There is only one road into Gee's Bend, an undulating two-lane blacktop lined with forest on both sides. As soon as you turn off of Alabama Highway 5 onto the rough pavement of Wilcox County Highway 29, you are in the woods. If you make the seventeen-mile trek and miss the last ferry, you'll be driving back out the same way. So consider a pit stop before your journey to Gee's Bend.

Most of the people of Gee's Bend are descendants of slaves who remained on the land their ancestors had worked. The slaveholder name Pettway still prevails. At least one slave, given the name Dinah Miller, remembered being brought from Africa at the age of thirteen. As a child,

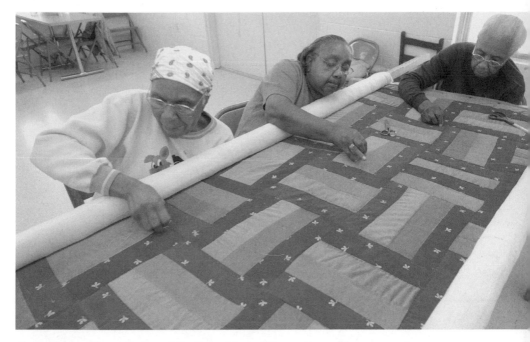

Gee's Bend quilters. *Left to right:* **Lucy Marie Mingo, Nancy Pettway, and Arlonzia Pettway.** *Birmingham News.*

quiltmaker Arlonzia Pettway listened to Dinah tell family stories. "My great-grandmother came from Africa," she says. "I was real small when she told me the story, but it startled me, so I kept it."

After emancipation, the freed slaves stayed to work as sharecroppers. In the late 1960s Gordon Wright of Camden explained his ancestors' plight to a reporter: "They were still slaves but they were free slaves. They were unfree slaves before the Civil War, and free slaves after." Eugene Witherspoon had also heard about the Reconstruction days: "The first Depression was right after they come out of slavery. Those were some mighty bad times."

Bad times got worse in the early 1930s when the price of cotton plunged. The widow of a merchant who had extended credit to people in Gee's Bend decided to call in the debts. Armed henchmen showed up to

Cable ferry between Camden and Gee's Bend, 1939. Photograph by Marion Post Wolcott, courtesy of the Library of Congress, Prints and Photographs Division [LC-USF33-030356-M4].

repossess furniture, farm equipment, livestock, even sweet potatoes and corn. They loaded the goods onto the ferry and left sixty-eight families completely destitute. Quiltmaker Nettie Young, a small child at the time, remembers, "We lived a hard life. We lived near 'bout a starvation life."

They survived by hunting and gathering. As they always had done, the women of Gee's Bend stitched together quilts to shield their families from the cold river mist. They used whatever old scraps they could find, such as fertilizer sacks and clothes that "weren't half worn out, they were worn out." Georgianna Pettway recalls women going from house to house to help each other quilt. "Those old folks would quilt the quilt, they sung the song, they prayed the prayer, they ate what they could eat around the quilt," she said. "That was really their daily occupation."

Gee's Bend made it through the 1930s with the help of the Red Cross. Then the New Deal brought home ownership and an economic cooperative program, which helped ensure the survival of Gee's Bend as a community, but the people still struggled with poverty and the oppression fostered by Jim Crow.

The civil rights movement of the 1960s brought deeper changes. Martin Luther King Jr. visited Gee's Bend on a late February night in 1965 to preach at Pleasant Grove Baptist Church, a church the Gee's Benders founded near the site where their slave ancestors had worshipped in brush arbors. "I've come to tell you that you are God's children," King preached. "You are as good as any white person in Wilcox County and you've got to believe that."

Quiltmaker Mary Lee Bendolph listened to every word King preached that night and rode the ferry with him to Camden the next day. Gee's Benders began crossing into Camden regularly to pray and sing and try to register to vote. They were harassed, tear-gassed, and jailed, sometimes while singing to Sheriff Lummie Jenkins, "Lummie, you never can jail us all." Quiltmaker Nettie Young was in jail for nearly a week. Once, as the protesters knelt on the sidewalk in prayer, police pulled cars up close and blew exhaust into their faces. People suffered evictions and lost their jobs because they tried to register to vote.

To punish the people even further, white officials took away the ferry. Now it was more than an hour by car to get to Camden, at a time when there were very few cars in Gee's Bend. Highway 29 would not even be paved until 1967. Sheriff Jenkins said, "We didn't close down the ferry because they were black. We did it because they forgot they were black."

Martin Luther King holds a special place in the hearts of the people of Gee's Bend. They once tried to rename their town after him but a judge turned down their request. When King was killed, they sent a pair of mules to pull his casket through the streets of Atlanta.

In 1966, Episcopal priest Francis X. Walter of the Selma Inter-religious

Project arrived in Gee's Bend. The Reverend Walter saw some quilts hanging on a line, and their minimalist, colorful compositions reminded him of op-art he had seen in New York City. With a seven-hundred-dollar grant from the Episcopal Society of Cultural and Racial Unity, he spread the word that he would buy quilts for ten dollars each. When he arrived, he remembered, "From Highway 5 in Alberta down to Gee's Bend, there really were quilts piled up on the side of the road and people standing there waiting and I handed out ten dollar bills."

After friends in New York helped auction off the quilts, the Reverend Walter brought the money back to Gee's Bend and asked the women what they wanted to do with it. Remembering their cooperative experiences from the New Deal era, they decided to form another cooperative. They named it the Freedom Quilting Bee and elected Estelle Witherspoon, a natural leader, as president.

The purpose of the quilting bee was economic stability, not creative expression. Quickly, they realized that to thrive in the marketplace they would need to get large contracts and create standardized products. The women found it empowering to work together and use their skills to earn their own checks. Scraps from the Freedom Quilting Bee, such as jewel-toned Sears corduroy, found their way into the personal quilts the women were making their own way, on their own time, at home.

Making quilts their own way meant improvising freely with original ideas. Old patterns they called housetop, hog pen, and lazy gal were continually reinterpreted depending on available materials and the vision of the quiltmaker. It is the personal quilts made at home that caught the attention of art historian William Arnett in 1997. At first the quiltmakers thought he must be crazy. "Bill told us we had artwork," said Arlonzia Pettway. "We didn't know what artwork was."

Quiltmaker Annie Mae Young, who did not work for the quilting bee because her stitches were sloppy, is hailed as a genius now. Best known for her blue denim quilt with mustard and red center medallion featured on the cover of *The Quilts of Gee's Bend,* she explains, "I didn't know how to make no fancy quilt so I just did it my way."

Through his organization the Tinwood Alliance, in 2002, Arnett and Houston's Museum of Fine Arts organized an exhibit of Gee's Bend quilts that then traveled to major cities. Many of the Gee's Bend quilters have lived to see their creations hanging on the walls of art museums. In 2003, they formed the Gee's Bend Quilters Collective.

Ferry service to Gee's Bend was restored August 18, 2006. Also in 2006, the U.S. Postal Service honored the quilters with a set of stamps featuring twelve of their designs. In 2008, Tyree McCloud painted the same twelve quilts onto plywood murals, placing each near the home of the woman who made it, to create the Gee's Bend Quilt Mural Trail.

The women of Gee's Bend still quilt their quilts and sing their songs and pray their prayers. After all, "prayer changes things," says Nettie Young. "See now what the Lord done done for the Gee's Bend women."

Loretta Pettway agrees. "God worked miracles," she says. "Now my last days will be my best days."

What to See

The Gee's Bend Quilt Mural Trail begins on Alabama 5 in Alberta and goes all the way down Highway 29, following signs to the Gee's Bend Ferry. The Freedom Quilting Bee is located at 4295 Highway 29, Rehoboth. As you leave Rehoboth you will see the building labeled FQB on the left. Continuing south on Highway 29, when you come to a T, turn right for the ferry; turn left for the Gee's Bend Quilters Collective at 14570 Highway 29, and the rest of the mural trail.

Just after the Gee's Bend Quilters Collective, a dirt road branches off to the left. This road takes you to Pleasant Grove Baptist Church where Martin Luther King preached in 1965. Continuing in the same direction will bring you back to the main road and more quilt murals.

Marengo County: Reclaiming the History

The Site

Marengo County, bounded on the west by the Tombigbee River, occupies land the Choctaws ceded to the United States in 1816. Demopolis, "the people's city," was founded on an outcropping of Selma chalk called the White Bluff. In 1817, French exiles stayed just long enough to leave the name Marengo. Americans brought slaves to establish cotton plantations, giving Marengo one of the highest slave populations of any county in the nation. From then until now, black people have been in the majority, but white people have dominated the scene. A century after emancipation, it took a combination of local activism and federal intervention to get Marengo's black majority onto the voter rolls. On November 4, 2008, the county's voters supported Barack Obama for president in a historic turnout. Now residents are developing a museum that will honor the true diversity of Marengo's people.

The Story

While the black population in Marengo County has diminished since the days of slavery, proportionately it has never dipped below half. Yet throughout most of the twentieth century, African Americans were not only systematically denied their right to vote but also were so hampered by the constraints of segregation that they had no political or economic power. Nevertheless, black culture progressed, and there were individual successes. Civil rights leader Ralph Abernathy (see chapter 1), businessman A. G. Gaston, and courageous college student Autherine Lucy (see chapter 5) all had roots in Marengo County.

Aware of developments on the national scene, the local civil rights movement gathered momentum in 1964 with marches and boycotts intended to challenge the segregated commercial district of downtown Demopolis. During one of these demonstrations, angry white hecklers

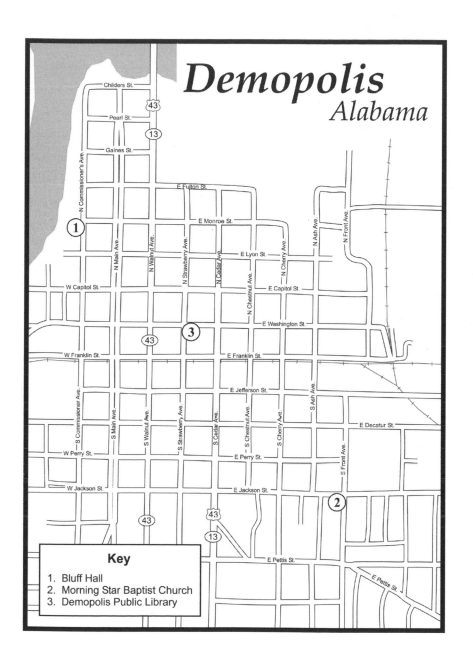

Demopolis
Alabama

Childers St.

Pearl St.

Gaines St.

E Fulton St.

E Monroe St.

E Lyon St.

W Capitol St.

E Capitol St.

E Washington St.

W Franklin St.

E Franklin St.

E Jefferson St.

E Decatur St.

W Perry St.

E Perry St.

W Jackson St.

E Jackson St.

E Pettis St.

E Pettis St.

N Commissioner's Ave.

N Main Ave.

N Walnut Ave.

N Strawberry Ave.

N Cedar Ave.

N Chestnut Ave.

N Cherry Ave.

N Ash Ave.

N Front Ave.

S Commissioner Ave.

S Main Ave.

S Walnut Ave.

S Strawberry Ave.

S Cedar Ave.

S Chestnut Ave.

S Cherry Ave.

S Ash Ave.

S Front Ave.

Key
1. Bluff Hall
2. Morning Star Baptist Church
3. Demopolis Public Library

called the marchers Communists. Local civil rights leader Henry Haskins Jr., a hip young cement finisher, stopped the march, thrust his hands into the air, and said mockingly, "Communist? Why, six months ago, I was only a nigger. I must be moving up in the world!"

By the spring of 1965, the Southern Christian Leadership Conference had shifted its efforts toward voting rights, including educating potential voters to pass literacy tests so they could register to vote. A project called SCOPE, Summer Community Organizing and Political Education, focused on Alabama's Black Belt counties. In Demopolis, Morning Star Baptist Church was the center of movement activity, with some SCOPE workers of both races housed across the street with the Haskins family. Julia Mae Haskins Foster remembers her mother cooking for visiting movement leaders, including Martin Luther King, Albert Turner, James Orange, Andrew Young, Julian Bond, and SCOPE director Hosea Williams. "Dr. King loved my mother's collard greens," she recalled.

Foster, a lifelong educator, was in college the summer she volunteered with SCOPE. She went to Dixon's Mill in southern Marengo county to help potential voters improve their literacy skills. Patiently, she sat with rural community elders who had lived with such deprivation that she was the first person to ever teach them to sign their names.

In March, President Johnson denounced literacy tests, saying that "every device of which human ingenuity is capable" had been used to deny blacks the right to vote. "There is no Negro problem," Johnson said. "There is only an American problem." Understanding that "the history of this country in large measure is the history of the expansion of the right [to vote] to all of our people," Johnson promised to prevent "systematic and ingenious discrimination." If states would not register voters, then federal officials would do it. SCOPE kept working on voter preparation all summer. In August 1965, Congress passed the Voting Rights Act.

Federal registrars took over the task of registering voters in Marengo County. Flyers showed up in the black part of town full of legalistic language that few understood. Demopolis native Charlie Saulsberry created a simpler flyer telling people they could register to vote in the back of the post office. Saulsberry's own mother said she still wouldn't register because the Ku Klux Klan had announced that they planted live rattlesnakes behind the post office. That threat turned out to be just another white bluff, and most of Marengo's eligible blacks did register to vote. In 1966, they shifted their efforts toward integrating schools and the library.

Bobbie Mitchell wasn't yet born when these events took place. She has heard stories from her parents and others about their participation in the movement, and she has read *If White Kids Die: Memories of a Civil Rights Movement Volunteer* by Dick J. Reavis, a white Texan who spent his SCOPE time in Demopolis. Reavis's book contains vivid accounts of

Bluff Hall, Demopolis. Photograph courtesy of the Marengo County Historical Society.

the arrests, beatings, jailings, tear gas, and subterfuge the local people suffered in Marengo County's voting rights struggle. Reavis and others have compiled clippings about the time period that are now on file at the Demopolis Public Library.

Mitchell works at Bluff Hall, an antebellum house perched atop the White Bluff. Because she is African American, people sometimes ask her if it bothers her to work in a "slave house." But Mitchell feels a spiritual calling to understand the deeper nuances of history. She smiles warmly, "Actually, my ancestors built this house, and it is some of the finest architecture in America. Black people ran this place, too. Let me tell you about Fanny Smoot." She shows a picture of the slave woman who did the cooking at Bluff Hall. Mitchell may view antebellum history differently than the previous generation of museum docents, but she knows this is her story, too. The labor and intelligence of slaves created antebellum wealth.

Bluff Hall holds a wine cellarette designed and built by the slave craftsman Peter Lee. This piece of furniture is so exemplary that it travels to other museums. Peter Lee's accomplishments went beyond fine furniture to architecture. At least three of his buildings are listed on the National Register of Historic Places. Lee supervised the building of Prairieville's Saint Andrews Episcopal Church in the carpenter gothic style, directing the crew of slaves who did the work. And at the Faunsdale Plantation, two slave dwellings he built are still standing.

Professional genealogist and historic preservationist Mary Jones-Fitts is the leading expert on the slave population of the Faunsdale Plantation. While researching her own family history, she found the Plantation records surprisingly intact because Faunsdale has stayed in the same family since 1843. In 2005, Jones-Fitts organized a Faunsdale reunion, inviting people from all over the country whose ancestors had been slaves at Faunsdale and persuading the current owners to host them for a tour. "You wouldn't believe how nervous I was," said Shepard Sims, who shares the old family home with her sister Charlotte Byrd, but they rose to the occasion, and "we were so glad we did it." The women who own Faunsdale may be white, but slavery is part of their history, too.

Now Jones-Fitts is presiding over a major new project, the Marengo County History and Archives Museum. Housed in a building donated by the Rosenbush family, the "people's museum" will feature collections representing the Choctaws, the French, the plantation culture, and the Jews of Demopolis. The museum's most comprehensive archives and displays will relate to the county's African American population, with special emphasis on nineteenth-century slavery and school integration in the 1960s because the majority of Marengo County's history is black history.

A personal note: My work on this chapter has been informed in part by knowing that I am a direct descendant of slaveholding members of Marengo County's plantation elite. Mary Jones-Fitts has determined that my ancestor owned her grandfather. —JANE DeNEEFE

What to See

Morning Star Baptist Church is at 614 East Jackson Street. Members of the Haskins family still live across the street.

The Rosenbush Building is downtown on South Walnut Avenue, not far from Bluff Hall, which overlooks the Tombigbee at 407 North Commissioner's Avenue. The Demopolis Public Library is also downtown at 211 East Washington Street.

For buildings associated with slave craftsman Peter Lee, travel east on Highway 80. Turn north on County Road 69 to see Saint Andrews Episcopal Church off to the left across from the large brick Gallion Baptist Church.

Morning Star Baptist Church, 614 East Jackson Street, Demopolis. Photograph courtesy of the Marengo County Historical Society.

Rosenbush Building, Demopolis. Photograph courtesy of the Marengo County Historical Society.

JAMES HASKINS, 1941–2005

James Haskins, arguably Alabama's most prolific author, was born in Demopolis and grew up on East Jackson Street across from the Morning Star Baptist Church. Even though rigid segregation laws kept him from entering the Demopolis Public Library, Haskins developed a love of reading in his childhood that helped determine his life's direction. The Haskins family valued literacy, so his mother found ways to get him the books he needed. Access to magazines like *Ebony* and *Jet,* and the nation's most widely circulated black newspaper, the *Pittsburgh Courier,* kept him abreast of the achievements of black people in the world outside Demopolis.

When Haskins became a teacher in New York City, the lack of appropriate books for his students inspired him to write nonfiction for youth. His biographies introduced readers to real-life role models, people who had overcome poverty and racial adversity to excel in fields like sports, science, music, and more. After his death, one colleague reflected, "Jim Haskins created a canon of literature, particularly for children, that is a resource for anyone studying black history." Now children of all races can check out his books at the Demopolis Public Library.

Haskins published more than 150 works of nonfiction in his lifetime. Here are just a few: *Andrew Young: Man with a Mission* (Lothrop, 1979); *Bayard Rustin: Behind the Scenes of the Civil Rights Movement* (Hyperion, 1997); *Carter G. Woodson: The Man Who Put "Black" in American History* (Millbrook, 2000); *Freedom Rides: Journey for Justice* (Just Us Books, 2005); *Thurgood Marshall: A Life for Justice* (Henry Holt, 1995).

Continuing east on Highway 80, turn south onto Alabama 25 and then west on County Road 54 to find Faunsdale Plantation. Two dwellings built by Peter Lee will be on the left. Farther down the road to the right you'll see the cemetery with two historic markers. The marker on the road mentions Peter Lee. A short walk brings you to the second marker, which commemorates Faunsdale's slave cemetery.

Hale County's Safe House

The Site

The Safe House Black History Museum is tucked away on a back street in the Hale County town of Greensboro. It's a brightly painted shotgun house that in the early spring of 1968 may have saved the life of Dr. Martin Luther King Jr. Today it offers a kind of grassroots record of the civil rights years, lovingly put together by its founder and director Theresa Burroughs, who is herself a veteran of the movement.

The Story

The neighborhood most often is quiet, old dogs sleeping in the bare front yards, much as they might have done in years past. But there was a night in 1968 when these hidden back roads held the imminent possibility of violence.

It was a cool March evening, and Martin Luther King Jr. had paid a visit to Greensboro, speaking at Saint Matthew AME Church, a handsome brick structure in the heart of town, where the pastor, A. T. Days, was a strong supporter of the civil rights movement. Theresa Burroughs, one of the people in the crowd that night, thought Dr. King was splendid as always. But almost as soon as he finished speaking, movement leaders received a disturbing piece of news: The Ku Klux Klan was out on the prowl.

Safe House Black History Museum, 2402 Davis Street, Greensboro.
Photograph courtesy of Frye Gaillard.

Their purpose, apparently, was to kill Dr. King, and they were cruising the highways in and out of town, blocking his departure. Theresa Burroughs, among others, had seen her share of such dangers before. Though still a young woman, she had been an activist for more than a decade, having traveled to Montgomery in the 1950s to offer her support for the bus boycott. And when the movement came to rural Alabama, confronting issues that ranged from police brutality to the right to vote, Burroughs most often was on the front lines.

She had gotten to know Dr. King through the years, and on an evening when his life was potentially in danger, she offered her property as a place of refuge. She owned a rental house that was now standing empty, hidden away in a black neighborhood, and she urged King and his assistant, Bernard Lee, to spend the night there.

A contingent of her neighbors, meanwhile, gathered in the shadows outside the house, most of them armed, and all of them determined to protect Dr. King. Late that night, a fleet of Klan cars passed by the house, cruising lights-off and bumper to bumper through the darkened side streets. They did not notice the people standing guard. "The night was black and so were we," Theresa Burroughs explained.

When the sun came up the following morning, Dr. King was safe. On this particular occasion the Klan failed to find him, but in less than a month he was felled by an assassin's bullet in Memphis. Burroughs, among many others, was determined to keep his memory alive, and as a part of that goal she turned the Safe House into a memorial.

"This is a grassroots museum," she says. "This is where the rubber hits the road."

The sign in front of the yellow-painted house offers a simple summary of its purpose. "The Safe House Black History Museum: We Cannot Let the Dream Die." Inside the well-designed four-room structure are photographs and artifacts from the civil rights years, ranging from an authentic Klan robe on a mannequin to photographs of the funeral procession of Dr. King. In one of those shots, Alabama activist Albert Turner is leading the mule-drawn caravan; the mules were sent from the Black Belt village of Gee's Bend.

Another whole wall is covered with photos—many of them police mug shots—of foot soldiers in the Alabama movement. Pictured with them are the grassroots leaders—Burroughs herself; and Thomas Gilmore, who would soon become the first black sheriff of neighboring Greene County; and Lewis Black, a Hale County activist who, among other things, helped put together a farmer's cooperative in southwest Alabama and a people's credit union in his own county.

Many visitors have said that an hour or two spent at the Safe House, surveying the displays and listening to the stories of Theresa Burroughs, can provide a one-of-a-kind re-creation of the years of struggle in rural Alabama.

What to See

The Safe House Black History Museum is located at 2402 Davis Street, just south of Highway 14 and east of Highway 69. For directions call 334-624-4228. Saint Matthew AME Church in Greensboro, where Dr. King spoke in March 1968, is on Morse Street, one block off Main. At the Safe House, Theresa Burroughs can also direct visitors to other black history sites in the area, including a Negro Baseball League field where Hank Aaron and other stars played, and two schools for black children, set up with help from the Rosenwald Fund (see chapter 6).

In developing the Safe House, Burroughs said she felt fortunate to have the help of her friend the visionary architect Samuel Mockbee, who, before his death in 2001, put a new floor in the building. As founder of Auburn University's Rural Studio Project, Mockbee was motivated by social justice issues when he dedicated his life to creating architecture for impoverished people in the rural South. Rural Studio students have designed and built homes and public buildings that are scattered throughout the Alabama Black Belt. Burroughs added that "Sambo," as she called Mockbee, "even suggested the name 'Safe House.'" His rural studio buildings, she said, including those near Greensboro, are a reminder that the spirit of the civil rights movement survives.

Greene County and Dr. King's Farewell

The Site

Just east of the square in the town of Eutaw, First Baptist Church stands across Highway 14 from a small cemetery. Historical markers on both sides of the road take note of the fact that the church was a meeting place for the civil rights movement in Greene County—and was a place where Dr. Martin Luther King Jr. made one of the final speeches of his life.

The Story

Thomas Gilmore remembers those days as clearly as anything in his life. It was the spring of 1968, and Martin Luther King Jr. had come to rural Alabama seeking support for the upcoming Poor People's March on Washington. Gilmore was a leader in the Greene County movement and would soon become the county's first black sheriff. But on this particular day in March, his job was simply to drive Dr. King from one stop to the next on his tour of the state.

Gilmore knew these were dangerous times. For the past three years, he and other leaders in Greene County, including the Reverend William McKinley Branch (see chapter 3), had been pushing the cause of black voter registration. The Voting Rights Act of 1965 had brought new possibilities, and blacks were determined to take advantage of them.

By 1970, African Americans, who vastly outnumbered whites in Greene County, had seized control of local government. But in the late 1960s, even as they struggled for political power, they were still confronted by the issue of poverty. For Martin Luther King Jr., in the last months of his life, that issue had become his greatest concern.

In the rural South, as well as in the urban ghettos of the North, African Americans and other minorities often struggled to feed their families or find decent jobs. King's goal by 1968 was to unite the poor across racial lines, and along with other Americans of conscience, pursue the goal of economic justice. As King talked about such things in Alabama, first in Eutaw and later in Greensboro and Marion, Thomas Gilmore was struck as always by the civil rights leader's eloquence.

"He was one of a kind," Gilmore remembered.

But in between stops, on the winding back roads that cut through the heart of the Alabama Black Belt, Gilmore thought that King seemed tired. Sometimes he talked about the sickness of the country—the divisions from the war in Vietnam, the backlash against the gains in the civil rights years. And he talked about tensions within the movement itself, the impatience of many young activists who were beginning to reject the philosophy of nonviolence.

According to Gilmore, as evening fell and the conversation ebbed and flowed, their car was caught behind a truck on the two-lane road. Gilmore pulled out to pass, but the truck veered over and ran him off the road and into the parking lot of a store. The white driver of the truck jumped down from the cab and stalked over to the car.

"Nigger," he demanded, "get those lights out of my rearview mirror."

Gilmore, startled by the sudden display of hostility, was not sure exactly how to respond. But King simply leaned in the white man's direction, and to Gilmore's amazement, addressed him in a voice that was calm and even kind. "Young man," he said, "get in your rig and go ahead now. You're starting trouble, and you don't need to do that."

The man stood frozen as he recognized King, then slowly backed away.

Two weeks later, King was dead—murdered on a motel balcony in Memphis—and Thomas Gilmore, in his personal grief, thought about what to do in King's honor. He had already run unsuccessfully for sheriff of Greene County, but he decided to try again in the next election—and if he won, to carry himself in a way that would make King proud.

Gilmore did win in 1969—along with a slate of black candidates running under the banner of the National Democratic Party of Alabama (see chapter 7)—and in his thirteen years as sheriff, he never once picked up a gun. It was his personal tribute to King's nonviolence, and in a rough-and-tumble rural county, Gilmore was surprised at how well it worked. The key, he discovered, was to respect the humanity of the people, black and white, and to soothe the irrationality and the fears that had gotten so inflamed by the issue of race.

He said it was the least he could do for Dr. King.

What to See

Just across from the courthouse square in Eutaw, the William McKinley Branch courthouse building—named for the first black probate judge in Greene County—stands as testament to the success of the voting rights movement.

At the square itself, the people of the county would gather on election night to listen to the returns. The First Baptist Church, where civil rights meetings were often held, and where King spoke about the Poor People's March barely two weeks before his death, is located east of the square on Alabama Highway 14 leading toward Greensboro.

Old Greene County Courthouse, Eutaw.
Photograph courtesy of Ginger Ann Brook.

5

TUSCALOOSA AND THE SCHOOLHOUSE DOOR

The civil rights headlines coming out of Tuscaloosa centered on the University of Alabama. That was especially true in June 1963, when Alabama governor George Wallace made good on a campaign pledge to "stand in the schoolhouse door," if necessary, in order to resist desegregation of the university. With this carefully staged bit of political theater, Wallace transformed himself into a national figure—a presidential candidate who in 1964 and 1968 helped redefine the national debate.

But Wallace was only part of the Tuscaloosa story. Overshadowed by his flair for political drama were the aspirations of African American students, who wanted for themselves and others who would follow the

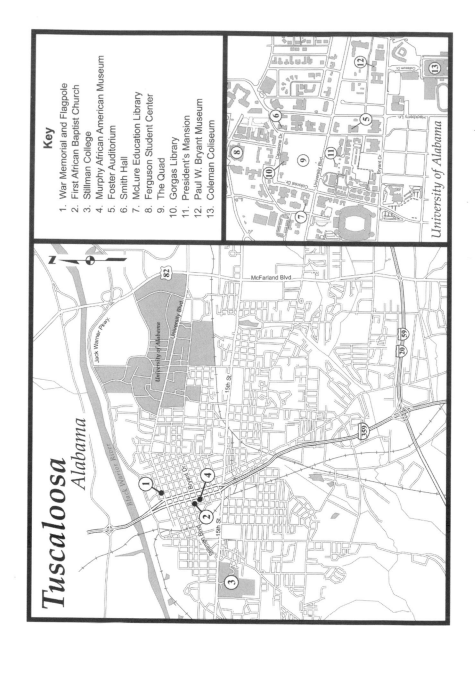

Tuscaloosa
Alabama

University of Alabama

Key

1. War Memorial and Flagpole
2. First African Baptist Church
3. Stillman College
4. Murphy African American Museum
5. Foster Auditorium
6. Smith Hall
7. McLure Education Library
8. Ferguson Student Center
9. The Quad
10. Gorgas Library
11. President's Mansion
12. Paul W. Bryant Museum
13. Coleman Coliseum

same educational opportunities that had long been available to whites. One of those students, whom Wallace tried to bar, was Vivian Malone, a young woman from Mobile who would become, in 1965, the first black graduate of the university.

Throughout her time on the Tuscaloosa campus, Malone continually impressed her classmates with her remarkable air of dignity and poise. The same might have been true for her predecessor Autherine Lucy, if she had not been attacked by a mob in 1956 and expelled from the university by its board of trustees. While the board, and later Wallace, were stubborn in their defense of segregation, there were whites as well as blacks in Tuscaloosa who took courageous stands in favor of progress.

In the end, those moderate attitudes rose to the surface, and even the university's legendary football coach, Paul "Bear" Bryant, whose team was one of the last to desegregate, was praised by his players for treating them fairly, regardless of whether they were white or black.

George Wallace Makes His Stand

The Site

At the University of Alabama a block to the south of University Boulevard, Foster Auditorium—one of the most famous buildings on the campus—stands unobtrusively near a grove of trees. It was here in June 1963 that Governor George Wallace made his famous stand in the schoolhouse door, resisting the enrollment of two black students. Wallace's stand, which made him a national spokesman for the political right, delayed the desegregation of the university for exactly four hours and forty-five minutes.

The Story

George Wallace knew he had no chance of winning. But it was part of

Governor George Wallace stands in the door of the University of Alabama's Foster Auditorium to block black students from entering, 1963. Photograph by Warren K. Leffler, courtesy of the Library of Congress, Prints and Photographs Division [LC-U9-9930-20].

his total transformation from a racial moderate to his state's most ardent apostle of segregation—and finally, as he was beginning to discover, into the kind of charismatic figure who could make some waves at the presidential level.

The improbable odyssey of George Wallace, reaching an apex now at the schoolhouse door, had begun more modestly in the little Butler County town of Clio. The ambitious grandson of a country doctor, Wallace had grown up scrappy and poor, mostly because everybody was poor in that part of Alabama.

For a while, his background made him a populist—an Alabama progressive standing up for his neighbors. After returning home from World War II, he cast his lot with Big Jim Folsom, an Alabama governor who was rumored to be a closet integrationist. During his first term in the 1940s, Folsom had, among other things, appointed voter registrars in Mobile and Macon counties who had the courage to treat black people fairly.

From all indications, Wallace shared Folsom's progressive instincts. During his years as an Alabama circuit judge, he was regarded by many lawyers in the state, including black lawyers, as one of Alabama's most fair-minded jurists. J. L. Chestnut, a civil rights attorney from Selma, would later praise Wallace for his unfailing courtesy. "George Wallace," he said, "was the most liberal judge in Alabama. He was the only judge who called me 'Mr. Chestnut.'"

All of this was back in the 1950s when Wallace tied his political ambitions to a belief in Alabama's racial moderation. He sought, and was granted, a seat on the board of Tuskegee Institute, and when he ran for governor in 1958, he stood before the cameras and declared: "I want to tell the good people of this state . . . if I didn't have what it took to treat a man fair regardless of the color of his skin, then I don't have what it takes to be the governor of your great state."

Wallace's opponent, John Patterson, made no such promises, and in a race dominated by the issue of segregation, Patterson, the hard liner, won a lopsided victory. Shaken to his political core, Wallace promised one of his closest associates that he would never be "outniggered" again. In the years after that, he made good on the pledge, becoming the leading segregationist of his time.

He was elected by an overwhelming majority in 1962, declaring in his inaugural address as governor: "In the name of the greatest people who have ever trod this earth, I draw the line in the dust and toss the gauntlet before the feet of tyranny, and I say segregation now, segregation tomorrow, segregation forever."

And then came the summer of 1963, when three black students were to be admitted under federal court order to the University of Alabama.

Vivian Malone entering Foster Auditorium to register for classes at the University of Alabama, 1963. Photograph by Warren K. Leffler, courtesy of the Library of Congress, Prints and Photographs Division [LC-U9-9928-21].

One of the three, Dave McGlathery, a sharecropper's son from northern Alabama, planned to enroll at the campus in Huntsville. The other two, Vivian Malone and James Hood, were headed for Tuscaloosa, and Wallace decided to honor a campaign promise to "stand in the schoolhouse door if necessary" in order to uphold the laws of segregation.

The issue came to a head on a steamy June morning, when Assistant Attorney General Nicholas Katzenbach arrived on the campus with Hood and Malone. Wallace, as promised, was waiting in the door—specifically the door of Foster Auditorium, the designated site for student registration. It was June 11, 1963, and tensions were high all across the country. The Kennedy Administration was wary, still reeling from events a few months earlier.

In September 1962, two people had died at the University of Mississippi and dozens more were injured in rioting after James Meredith, a black man, was admitted as a student. The Kennedys' wanted no repeat of that violence, and they didn't know what to expect from Wallace. The governor had promised there would be no trouble, and in fact his administration had sent out word to the Ku Klux Klan and other extremists that their presence on campus would not be permitted.

The overall result, instead of a riot, was a choreographed piece of political theater. On the morning of June 11, as Nicholas Katzenbach approached him, Wallace drew himself up and denounced the federal government's interference. And then he simply stood in the door.

President Kennedy had federalized the Alabama National Guard and now he ordered them to the campus. Sometime after 3:00 P.M., a line of infantry took up positions outside the auditorium, and at 3:30 their commander, General Henry Graham, asked George Wallace to step aside "on order of the president of the United States."

Wallace immediately did as he was asked, and the stand in the schoolhouse door was over. That night, President Kennedy made a television speech to the nation, affirming more fully than any president ever had the government's support for the cause of civil rights. The nation, he said, was "confronted primarily with a moral issue. It is as old as the Scriptures and as clear as the American Constitution." And if anyone doubted the reality of prejudice confronting the black man, "who among us would be content to have the color of his skin changed and stand in his place? Who among us would then be content with the counsels of patience and delay? One hundred years of delay have passed since President Lincoln freed the slaves, yet their heirs, their grandsons are not fully free."

Kennedy announced that he was submitting to Congress a civil rights bill that would end discrimination in all public places—hotels, restaurants, theaters, and stores, all those places in the South and beyond where segregation delivered its affront. For many African Americans of

Vivian Malone (*far left*), attending class at the University of Alabama, 1963.

Photograph courtesy of W. S. Hoole Special Collections Library, University of Alabama.

that generation, it was a speech that filled them with a new sense of hope, and Kennedy became a hero in the cause.

George Wallace too went on to greater fame. In Alabama he was widely regarded as David standing up to the federal Goliath, and in the nation as a whole he rode his notoriety into a credible run for the presidency.

Lost in the flurry of political headlines were the aspirations of the two black students. Vivian Malone, a young woman from Mobile, was steady and reserved, an outstanding student at her city's Central High School. She wanted to study personnel management, but there was no such major at Alabama A&M, the black college in Huntsville she initially attended. There was, however, an excellent program at the University of Alabama, and she decided to apply.

James Hood also had been a brilliant student, a star athlete and student body president who had been active in the civil rights movement in Gadsden. He was proud of his role in desegregation, though he did not remain at the University of Alabama, graduating instead from Wayne State University.

Malone, however, went quietly about her studies, winning the respect of her classmates, and in the spring of 1965, she became the university's first black graduate. In a remarkable piece of historical symmetry, commencement that year was at Foster Auditorium, the building where Wallace had stood in the door.

What to See

Foster Auditorium, now on the National Register of Historic Places, stands a half block off University Boulevard between Hackberry Lane and Second Avenue. A small plaque on the door that faces the parking lot takes note of the events of 1963.

Foster Auditorium, site of the stand in the schoolhouse door at the University of Alabama. Photograph courtesy of University Relations Photography.

The Ordeal of Autherine Lucy

The Site

Seven years before Wallace's stand in the schoolhouse door, there was another attempt to integrate the University of Alabama—one that ended in disgrace. In February 1956, a young black woman named Autherine Lucy entered the school under court order. On her second day of classes, she was attacked outside of Smith Hall and again at the Education Library, and was then expelled by the university's board of trustees. Reflecting on the episode later, one student leader concluded with dismay: "The mob won."

The Story

Autherine Lucy did not expect to make the journey alone. When she applied to the University of Alabama and was accepted in 1952, she was one of two black applicants who easily met the standards for admission. The other was Pollie Anne Myers, a supporter of the NAACP who had also worked for the *Birmingham World,* a distinguished African American newspaper.

On September 20, 1952, the two women appeared at the admissions office, where the startled dean told them that "an error has been made." Not having realized that the women were black, admissions officials quickly backtracked and announced that both applications were rejected. Not entirely surprised, Lucy and Myers went immediately to Arthur Shores, an African American civil rights lawyer who agreed to represent them. Shores steered the case patiently through the court system, and in the summer of 1955, U.S. district judge Hobart Grooms ruled that the women had to be admitted.

By February 1956, the university's appeals were exhausted, and Autherine Lucy was accepted as a student. Pollie Anne Myers was not. Investigators hired by the university discovered that Myers had given birth

Portrait of Autherine Lucy in the Ferguson Student Center at the University of Alabama. Photograph courtesy of University Relations Photography.

to a baby only seven months after she was married. They deduced that the baby had been conceived out of wedlock, which in the eyes of the university made Pollie Myers unfit to be a student. Lucy would make the journey on her own.

On Friday, February 3, she arrived on campus for her first day of classes and was relieved when everything went smoothly. There were even a few students who wished her the best. But that same evening the mood turned ugly. A crowd assembled and burned a cross on University Boulevard, then marched on the mansion of University president Oliver Carmichael. Finding that the president had gone out of town, a remarkable decision under the circumstances, the crowd headed west along the boulevard, its leaders carrying a Confederate flag as they marched toward town.

They stopped at the corner of University and Greensboro, where a

Autherine Lucy in 1956, the year she became the first African American to attend the University of Alabama in Tuscaloosa. Photograph courtesy of W. S. Hoole Special Collections Library, University of Alabama.

monument stood in the middle of the street, honoring Tuscaloosa's war dead. One of the students, a Selma native and self-proclaimed white supremacist named Leonard Wilson, climbed the base of the monument and shouted defiantly, "The governor will read about this tomorrow."

There were more demonstrations over the weekend, and a surly crowd, some students, some not, gathered Monday morning between eight and nine, milling restlessly, as they waited for Lucy to arrive on campus. Because the university had refused so far to assign her to a dorm, she was forced to commute every day from Birmingham. On Monday morning, she arrived on time for her nine o'clock class, driven to Smith Hall by H. N. Guinn, one of Birmingham's African American businessmen.

She got out of the car and walked past the waiting crowd of whites, who did not react, as if somehow they didn't think she would come. But once inside, she could hear the crowd grumbling and complaining on the sidewalk. President Carmichael appeared with a bullhorn, urging students to disperse, but his words only seemed to make them angrier.

There were seasoned agitators in the ranks by now, including Robert Chambliss, a Ku Klux Klansman who, seven years later, would plant the bomb that would kill four little girls at a Birmingham church (see chapter 2). Urged on by the Klansman and other ringleaders, the crowd of five hundred outside of Smith Hall soon became a mob chanting slogans of hate: "Lynch the nigger whore" and "keep Bama white."

When the hour had passed and the first class ended, two university officials—Sarah Healy, dean of women, and Jefferson Bennett, a special assistant to President Carmichael—were waiting to drive Lucy to the Education Library, a building diagonally across the quadrangle, where she would attend a lecture on children's literature. The three of them left by the rear of the building, where Healy's Oldsmobile was parked, but the crowd caught up and began to shower them with gravel and eggs.

With Bennett driving, and Lucy in the middle, they drove frantically in a loop around the football stadium and were able to get Lucy into the library. There, she was trapped for more than two hours, until finally they managed to smuggle her off campus, hiding facedown on the floor of a police car.

That night, the university's board of trustees suspended her from school, saying the decision was necessary for her safety. Lucy and her supporters were stunned. As they understood it, the university's leaders, unable or unwilling to control the mob, had simply acquiesced. Arthur Shores and his team of lawyers quickly filed a motion in federal court, accusing the university board of "conspiring" with the mob to resist integration. In retribution, the board expelled Lucy permanently.

Writing about the whole episode, Buford Boone, editor and publisher of the *Tuscaloosa News,* concluded in a Pulitzer Prize–winning column: "As matters now stand, the University administration and trustees have knuckled under to the pressures and desires of a mob. . . . Yes, there's

Smith Hall, where Autherine Lucy was first attacked on the University of Alabama campus. Photograph courtesy of University Relations Photography.

The President's Mansion at the University of Alabama, site of demonstrations to keep the university segregated. Photograph courtesy of University Relations Photography.

peace on the University campus this morning. But what a price has been paid for it!"

What to See

Smith Hall, where Autherine Lucy was first attacked, is a three-story yellow brick building on the corner of Capstone Drive and Sixth Avenue. Diagonally across the university quadrangle, past Denny Chimes, is the McLure Education Library, where Lucy was trapped by the mob later in the morning of February 6, 1956.

Across University Boulevard from the quadrangle is the white-columned mansion with a spreading lawn, where university presidents, including Oliver Carmichael, have lived. On the weekend before the attack on Lucy, an angry crowd of students, urged on by assorted white supremacists, marched on the mansion to demand that the university remain segregated.

From there, the students marched west to downtown Tuscaloosa and assembled on the corner of University Boulevard and Greensboro Avenue. On that corner, a monument still pays tribute to Tuscaloosa's war dead, just as it did in 1956.

Today, on the second floor of the Ferguson Student Center, a portrait of Ms. Lucy hangs above an inscription that reads: "Her initiative and courage won the right for students of all races to attend the University." At the other end of the hall, there is a similar portrait of Dean Sarah Healy, who did her best to protect Lucy from the mob.

And there is a modern footnote to this story of courage. On May 9, 1992, forty years after her first application for admission, Autherine Lucy Foster received her master's degree in education at a commencement ceremony at the university. She was joined that day by her daughter, Grazia, who received her bachelor's degree in finance.

THE MAKING OF A MOB

The corner itself had something to do with it. On the night of February 4, 1956, a crowd of maybe two thousand students, singing "Dixie" and carrying the Confederate battle flag, marched from the campus of the University of Alabama to an intersection in downtown Tuscaloosa. Streaming west on University Boulevard, they stopped at the corner of Greensboro Avenue where a monument stood in the center of the street.

Ostensibly honoring Tuscaloosa's twentieth-century war dead, the monument was also a reminder of something else. As a marker near the intersection recounts, on this same corner in 1865 another group of Alabama students—three hundred Confederate cadets—confronted Union soldiers who were marching on the town. Badly outnumbered, the cadets in the end were forced to retreat, and the Union army took control of the campus and set it ablaze.

Ninety-eight years later, Leonard Wilson, the leader of the students who had gathered near the corner, was caught in the memory of that Civil War history. In his definitive book, *The Schoolhouse Door,* historian E. Culpepper Clark writes about Wilson this way: "[He] was a serious, almost rigid young man, whose conservative values included the racial orthodoxy of white supremacy. . . . He reportedly would sit in the living room, staring for hours at a Confederate flag on the wall, ruminating about the civilization he believed it represented."

It was not uncommon, as the civil rights movement gained momentum in the 1950s, for white Alabamians to share Wilson's views. They felt they were caught in a second Reconstruction, the looming possibility of another lost cause in which powerful forces were invading their state. And, once again, African Americans were at the center of the conflict. For Leonard Wilson, the indignity of it was nearly too much to bear.

On the night of February 4, Harry Shaffer, an economics professor at the university, listened with mingled horror and amazement as Wilson stood on the base of the flagpole, with the Stars and Bars flying just above him, and issued his openly racist appeal. "One listens to Leonard Wilson and wonders," Shaffer wrote soon afterward. "He is telling a 'joke' of thirty monkeys being introduced on a Southern cotton plantation, 'and in a few years they multiplied and became hundreds, and then they passed a law and said we should go to school with them.' And the crowd waves Confederate flags and howls."

But Shaffer's account, which is found in his papers at the university's W. S. Hoole Special Collections Library, offers another image from that night of impending violence. He described Walter Flowers, president of the Student Government Association, mounting the same pedestal of the flagpole, and delivering a message very different from Wilson's: "'I am just as proud of this flag as all of you,' [Flowers] says, pointing to the Stars and Bars waving high above, 'but I believe our forefathers who fought under this flag would not be proud of you tonight. Go home!'"

As Shaffer noted, Flowers was greeted that night with "boos and hisses" as the crowd edged closer to becoming a mob. But the student body president was part of a substantial number of moderates who sought to persuade their fellow students—and the university's leaders—to do the right thing. Later, more than two hundred would sign a petition circulated by two Unitarian students calling for the readmission of Autherine Lucy. But Dennis Holt, another student leader, sadly summarized the basic truth of the matter: "Our university and its trustees," he concluded at a meeting of the Student Government Association, "may well be famous for running away from a fight. They have acquiesced to the mob. Let us face it: The mob is king on the campus today. We must all think a little bit about the fact that the mob won."

FIRST AFRICAN BAPTIST CHURCH

In addition to the national stories unfolding at the University of Alabama, Tuscaloosa, like most Alabama cities and towns, had its local civil rights movement too. Tuscaloosa's mass meetings were held at First African Baptist Church, where the young minister, the Reverend T. Y. Rogers Jr., was a longtime friend of Dr. Martin Luther King Jr. In August 1963, when Rogers became the church's pastor at the age of twenty-eight, King came to deliver the installation sermon, despite the pressures of preparing for the March on Washington, where he delivered his famous "I Have a Dream" speech.

In the spring of 1964, Tuscaloosa protests became heated after

First African Baptist Church, 2621 Stillman Boulevard, Tuscaloosa.

county officials put up "whites only" signs outside the rest rooms of a new courthouse. Angry African Americans formed the Tuscaloosa Citizens for Action Committee under the leadership of Rogers, and the issue reached a violent climax on June 9, 1964. Police attacked a crowd of demonstrators outside the church, forcing them back into the building, then spraying fire hoses and hurling teargas through the church windows. Ninety-one people, including the Reverend Rogers, were jailed. But less than three weeks later, on June 26, a federal judge ordered the "whites only" signs taken down, and that same summer Congress passed the Civil Rights Act of 1964, ending the era of legal segregation.

In the minds of many Tuscaloosa residents, it was appropriate that First African Baptist played a central role in the quest for equal rights. Founded in 1866 in the days just after emancipation, the church had long been a symbol of freedom. Its first pastor, the Reverend Prince Murrell, led the establishment of the new church, many of whose members had previously attended the predominantly white First Baptist Church. In 1878, a statewide meeting of African Americans at First African Baptist voted to establish Selma University, which produced many civil rights leaders in the course of its long and important history (see chapter 3).

In 1907, under the leadership of the Reverend J. H. Smith, the church's current brick structure was built at a cost of fifty thousand dollars. It was designed to be a replica of the chapel at Tuskegee Institute, another important symbol of African American progress and freedom.

First African Baptist Church is located at 2621 Stillman Boulevard at T. Y. Rogers Avenue in Tuscaloosa. Tours are available by appointment.

The church is one of many African American heritage sites in Tuscaloosa, ranging from historic Stillman College to the Murphy African American Museum. For more information on these sites, contact the Tuscaloosa Convention and Visitors Bureau at 205-391-9200.

The end of a mass meeting on June 11, 1964, at Bailey Tabernacle CME in Tuscaloosa. Members of the Tuscaloosa Citizens for Action Committee and others met there after the group's headquarters, First African Baptist Church, was attacked by policemen and members of the Ku Klux Klan two days earlier. Photograph courtesy of the *Tuscaloosa News.*

RFK: A Measure of Change

The Site

In 1968, Senator Robert F. Kennedy, then running for president of the United States, made a triumphant appearance at the University of Alabama. Earlier in the decade, Kennedy had been a pariah in the minds of many Alabamians because of his support for the civil rights movement. He was greeted with hostility on a visit to the state in 1963 to negotiate with Governor George Wallace about his upcoming stand in the schoolhouse door. Five years later, during Kennedy's campaign, more than nine thousand people turned out to hear him at the university's Coleman Coliseum. In the minds of many people that night, it was a dramatic demonstration of a change in attitude.

The Story

His first visit could not have gone much worse. On April 25, 1963, Robert Kennedy flew to Montgomery to meet with George Wallace about the racial confrontation just ahead. Kennedy at the time was attorney general of the United States, and he came to Alabama representing his brother President John Kennedy. The Kennedys were deeply worried about Wallace. They knew he had promised while running for governor to resist every effort at desegregation even if he had to "stand in the schoolhouse door."

Many Alabama journalists who knew Wallace well thought it was simply a moment of hyperbole, when the candidate got carried away with his words. But the promise struck a chord with many white voters, and the Kennedy administration was dismayed. They knew that Wallace could not win, but tensions in the state were running high, and things could easily get out of hand.

When Robert Kennedy arrived at the Alabama capitol for his meeting with Wallace, he found the building ringed with Alabama State Troop-

Robert Kennedy at the University of Alabama, where he appeared on March 21, 1968, as part of the Emphasis guest speakers program. Photograph courtesy of W. S. Hoole Special Collections Library, University of Alabama.

ers. They were there for security, the governor said, but Kennedy thought they seemed like an army, ready to defend their state at all costs. As he made his way toward the entrance of the capitol, one of the troopers jabbed him in the stomach with a nightstick. "The point," said Kennedy, "was to try to show that my life was in danger in coming to Alabama because the people hated me so much."

That was 1963. Less than five years later when Kennedy returned, he came to the University of Alabama itself. The date was March 21, 1968, and Kennedy by then was a candidate for president. In the wake of his brother's assassination, he had picked up the mantel, and run successfully for the U.S. Senate. For the past four years, he had traveled to the most troubled places in the country—to Indian reservations and the Mississippi delta, to northern ghettoes and the desperate mining towns of West Virginia—and had spoken out strongly for the needs of the poor.

By 1968, the issue of poverty had become the new focus of the civil rights movement, and Kennedy was the movement's most visible ally. As a candidate for president, he also worried about divisions in the country, and at the University of Alabama and elsewhere, he set out to deliver a message of healing.

"Our nation is troubled," he declared, "divided as never before in our history; divided by a difficult, costly war abroad and by bitter, destructive crisis at home; divided by our age, by our beliefs, by the color of our skins. . . . But for my part, I do not believe these disagreements are as great as the principles which unite us. . . . History has placed us all, Northerner and Southerner, black and white, within a common border and under a common law. All of us, from the wealthiest and most powerful of men, to the weakest and hungriest of children, share one precious possession: The name American."

There were nine thousand people in the audience that night, many of them students, and to the delight and surprise of Kennedy's advisers, most responded warmly to the candidate's words. Kennedy's staff understood that this was still the heart of the South, still the launching pad for George Wallace, who was himself running hard for the presidency. Wallace still preached a very different message. As he traveled the country, he spoke of urban crime and "the pro-Communist, long-haired hippies" who seemed to be running amok in the streets.

If Wallace appealed to a national backlash against the unrest of the civil rights years, Kennedy spoke of reconciliation, and at least at the University of Alabama, his message seemed to be taking hold. But less than three months after his visit to the campus, Kennedy was murdered on a campaign trip to California. His death closely followed the assassination of Dr. Martin Luther King Jr., and the country reeled once again with division and grief.

In Alabama, a young white man by the name of Dick Holler, a songwriter born in Mobile, sought to capture the moment in a simple set of lyrics. The resulting ballad, "Abraham, Martin, and John," was soon recorded by Dion, and immediately made its way to the top of the charts. Writing about the Kennedys, Abraham Lincoln, and King, the Alabama writer ended his anthem of grief with a question: *Didn't they try to find some good for you and me?*

It was, in a way, the epitaph of an era.

What to See

Coleman Coliseum, a modern-looking brick and glass building on Coliseum Drive (off Bryant Drive), stands apart from the main university campus; it is just across the street from the Paul W. Bryant Museum. In addition to hosting athletic events, it has been the site of visits by dignitaries to the Alabama campus.

The Curious Legacy of "The Bear"

The Site

I remember the day that Bear Bryant died. The editor of the paper where I worked called me in and told me to write his obituary, which was scheduled the following day for page 1. This was not in Alabama, mind you, but in Charlotte, North Carolina, where college football was far less important. But such was the legendary status of the Bear, who at the time of his death in 1983 had won more games than any other coach—most of them at the University of Alabama.

The Story

In doing the interviews for Bear Bryant's obituary, I put in a call to U. W. Clemon, the first black federal judge in Alabama. As a young lawyer in

1969, Clemon had been retained by the Afro-American Association at the University of Alabama to sue Coach Bryant, charging him with racial discrimination for failing to recruit black athletes. The sixties ended and the seventies began without a black football player at the university, making Bryant's teams one of the state's last bastions of whiteness.

At the time of Bryant's death, I didn't know how Judge Clemon would respond. He and the coach had been adversaries, after all. But Clemon was shocked. He had not yet heard the news, and at first he kept saying over and over, "I can't believe it. I can't believe it." Then he began to talk about Bryant and his legacy.

"He was always gracious in our dealings," Clemon said, "always a gentleman. Coach Bryant never acknowledged it to me in so many words, but I think he appreciated the fact that our lawsuit was filed. I never thought he was prejudiced. He never seemed that way. But I believe he felt, initially, he would have to sacrifice some of his immense popularity among Alabama whites if he voluntarily integrated his team."

If Bryant needed the cover that the lawsuit gave him, the issue of segregation was laid permanently to rest in the fall of 1970. Early that season, Alabama lost 42–21 to the University of Southern California, and the star of the game was Sam Cunningham, USC's African American tailback.

"There was no problem with black recruitment after that," said Clemon.

With the team integrated in the 1970s, Bryant coached Alabama to three national championships and an overall record of 107–13. And there was something else as well. At a time when black athletes all over the country were complaining of unfair treatment at the hands of their coaches, there were no such complaints at Alabama. There were, instead, consistent affirmations that the coach was colorblind, and the state's last public symbol of racial segregation became, in the end, a symbol of its opposite.

As Clemon said at the time of Bryant's death, "At a time when Alabama's stature in the eyes of the nation was at an all-time low, he was one person—probably *the* one person—all Alabamians could feel good about."

What to See

The Paul W. Bryant Museum, which is open daily from 9:00 A.M. to 4:00 P.M., is located at 300 Bryant Drive, a block to the south of University Boulevard.

In the museum, the team photos tell an implicit story of racial segregation, ending abruptly in 1971. Beginning with that year, photos of African American stars, including John Mitchell and Sylvester Croom, assume their places amid the memorabilia. Elsewhere in the museum, one of the most prominent exhibits is an oil painting near the entrance, showing Cornelius Bennett, an African American, sacking Notre Dame quarterback Steve Beuerlein in Alabama's first victory over the Fighting Irish.

Paul W. Bryant Museum, 300 Paul W. Bryant Drive. Photograph courtesy of University Relations Photography.

THE TUSKEGEE STORY

In Alabama, there is probably no place more important to the history of African Americans than the college town of Tuskegee. It was there in 1881 that Booker T. Washington brought his dreams of education to the state. Washington was convinced that education and economic advancement were more important to blacks, at least in the early years of their freedom, than securing their full political rights.

With that conviction as his article of faith, Washington set out to build Tuskegee Institute and to make it a symbol of educational excellence. Among other things, he recruited the great African American scientist, George Washington Carver, a Renaissance man of the early twentieth

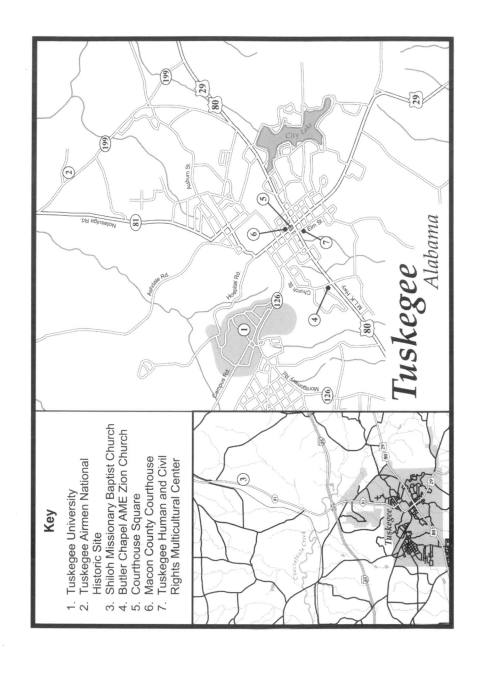

Key

1. Tuskegee University
2. Tuskegee Airmen National Historic Site
3. Shiloh Missionary Baptist Church
4. Butler Chapel AME Zion Church
5. Courthouse Square
6. Macon County Courthouse
7. Tuskegee Human and Civil Rights Multicultural Center

Tuskegee
Alabama

century who was a pioneer in the agricultural sciences, as well as a lover of music and art.

In addition to his efforts as Tuskegee's president, Washington also worked with the Jewish philanthropist Julius Rosenwald to construct more than five thousand schools for black children all over the South. Some of the earliest of those schools were built near Tuskegee, including the Shiloh school in the community of Notasulga.

Tuskegee also became famous during World War II as the home base of the Tuskegee Airmen, America's first black military air corps, who began training in 1941 at the Tuskegee Army Air Field. In addition to proving their courage during the war, the airmen brought fame to Tuskegee at a time of nearly unspeakable injustice—the Tuskegee Syphilis Study, a forty-year experiment, beginning in 1932, in which nearly four hundred black men were left untreated to observe the natural progression of the disease.

And finally, under the leadership of Dr. Charles Gomillion, Tuskegee in the 1950s became a center of voting rights activism and a landmark Supreme Court case that helped black citizens win the right to vote.

Booker T. Washington: Lifting the Veil

The Site

A block from the entrance at Tuskegee University, there is a famous statue of Booker T. Washington that depicts in dramatic, unforgettable fashion Washington's own understanding of his mission. Designed by sculptor Charles Keck and erected in 1922, the bronze likeness shows Washington standing beside an anonymous black man who holds an open book as he crouches near an anvil and plow. Washington is shown lifting a veil, and the inscription below the sculpture explains: "He lifted the veil of ignorance from his people and pointed the way to progress through education and industry."

Statue of Booker T. Washington on the Tuskegee campus. Photograph courtesy of Marcia Jones Media.

The Story

Booker T. Washington came to Tuskegee at a turbulent time. Born a slave in 1856, he began his career as a young educator in an era of deep uncertainty for his people. Their hopes had been raised by emancipation, and during the early years of Reconstruction many African Americans imagined a time when they would assume their rightful place as citizens. The white South, however, had other ideas. In 1870 in Sumter County, Alabama, a black legislator named Richard Burke was murdered by whites who considered him extreme. That same autumn, the Ku Klux Klan broke up a political rally in Greene County, killing four blacks and wounding fifty-four.

In Tuskegee, also, during that season of violence, rampaging white citizens were determined to reassert their political power. On an October night in 1870, white gunmen stormed a meeting at what was then called Zion Negro Church, killing two church members and wounding three more. Established in the earliest days of Reconstruction, Zion Church had become a beacon of black independence. The Republican Party, which supported black suffrage, had held occasional meetings there, and the pastor John Butler wanted to build an institution that was free of white control.

But between 1870 and the end of the century, whites from all over the South used whatever means were at hand—from naked violence to the power of the vote—to curb the freedom of the region's former slaves. There were assassinations, lynchings, and new constitutions that paved the way for the laws of Jim Crow. And more and more as the years went by, white politicians defended with a fierce and unrelenting pride the principles of white supremacy and segregation.

It was into this environment that Booker T. Washington came. He was barely twenty-five when he accepted a daunting new job in Tuskegee. On July 4, 1881, he opened a school on the grounds of Zion Church. Thirty students assembled for the initial classes, held in what was later described as a shanty, and by all accounts they were favorably impressed. Washington had come to Alabama from Hampton Institute, where he had been a graduate and later an instructor to other young teachers.

From the beginning, Washington had high hopes for his fledgling Tuskegee Institute. In 1882, he managed to purchase one hundred acres of abandoned farmland and begin the process of building a campus. Much of the work was done by the students. Under Washington's demanding supervision, they made their own bricks, built classrooms and dormitories and barns, and operated their own college farm. Though most were ostensibly learning to be teachers, Washington wanted them to learn a trade as well, thus assuring a path to economic independence.

He seemed obsessed with the concept of excellence. In building a home for himself on campus, he hired the architect Robert R. Taylor, the first black graduate of MIT. Writing later about The Oaks, as his house became known, Washington summarized his vision this way: "The ac-

Booker T. Washington, sometime between 1890 and 1910. Photograph courtesy of the Library of Congress, Prints and Photographs Division [LC-USZ62-119898].

The Oaks, Booker T. Washington's home in Tuskegee. Photograph courtesy of Marcia Jones Media.

tual sight of a first-class house that a Negro has built is ten times more potent than pages of discussion about a house that he ought to build or perhaps could build."

By the 1890s, Washington had become arguably the most powerful Negro in America. In 1895, he delivered a famous speech in Atlanta outlining his own ideas of racial progress. Understanding clearly the violence of the times, the fears and racial animosities of whites, and the feelings of resentment and defeat among blacks, Washington called for a new understanding. "In all things that are purely social," he declared, "we can be as separate as the fingers, yet one as the hand in all things essential to our mutual progress."

Though he did insist, "It is important and right that all privileges of the law be ours," he also declared that "the wisest among my race understand that the agitation of questions of social equality is the extremist folly." That "Atlanta Compromise" speech, as Washington called it, drew praise from white leaders all over the country, and such great philanthropists as Andrew Carnegie, John D. Rockefeller, and Julius Rosenwald rushed to the aid of Tuskegee Institute. In 1903 President Theodore Roosevelt invited Washington to be his guest at the White House, making him the first African American to be so honored.

But among many blacks, Washington, over time, became a controversial figure. As historian Joel Williamson has noted, race relations in the South continued to worsen in the early years of the twentieth century, causing many African Americans to question Washington's disavowal of "social equality." At the Niagara Falls Conference of 1905, a group of blacks led by W. E. B. Du Bois vehemently denied that "the Negro-American assents to inferiority" or "is submissive under oppression or apologetic before insult. . . . We do not hesitate to complain and to complain loudly and insistently."

As black anger grew in the twentieth century, culminating in the black power movement of the 1960s, Booker T. Washington, though long since dead, became a whipping boy for many young militants—even at the institution he had built. At Tuskegee in 1966, a student activist named Wendell Paris ridiculed publicly the famous sculpture of Washington on campus. "We got this statue out here of that man who's supposed to be lifting up the veil. Man, he's putting it back on."

Such was Washington's controversial shadow. But others have noted as time went by that Washington, through his work at Tuskegee, helped to lay the groundwork for progress. As historian Robert J. Norrell later put it, "Washington had taken a necessary step to secure educational and economic opportunity. From the vantage point of the 1990s, it seemed clear that the attainment of political rights had followed directly from Washington's compromise."

What to See

Reminders of the Booker T. Washington legacy are everywhere on the Tuskegee campus. His elegant residence, The Oaks, is part of the Tuskegee National Historic Site, operated by the National Park Service. Washington's grave is located on the campus in a cemetery near the famous statue that offers such a powerful tribute to his life.

The Tuskegee Airmen

The Site

The Tuskegee Airmen National Historic Site is a tribute to courage and civil rights, and represents another shining moment in the Tuskegee story. Though theirs is a saga not always recounted in textbooks, the Tuskegee Airmen made history as the first black unit of pilots in the U.S. military. Against extreme opposition, these men enlisted in a segregated military where many of their white counterparts valued black failure more than American success. But their refusal to remain passive spoke of a heroism that would reveal itself both on the battlefields of a fascist Europe and the battleground of a racist America.

THE CARVER MUSEUM

One of Booker T. Washington's least controversial decisions was one he made in 1896: his choice of George Washington Carver as head of Tuskegee's Department of Agriculture. For the next forty-seven years Carver devoted his life to Tuskegee, but perhaps even more, to the farmers black and white—but especially black—in rural Alabama. Through his scientific research, Carver discovered literally hundreds of uses for peanuts, sweet potatoes, and soybeans, making those crops as viable as cotton. Farmers, many of them instructed by Carver himself, learned how to rotate their crops, alternating cotton, which depleted the soil, with peanuts, peas, soybeans, and sweet potatoes—all of which enriched it.

For the most part, Carver didn't bother to patent his inventions, and he seemed to care very little about profits. "God gave them to me," he said of his agricultural ideas. "How can I sell them to someone else?" For all his life, he was fascinated by nature. "I literally lived in the woods," he explained. "I wanted to know every strange stone, flower, insect,

George Washington Carver, Tuskegee Institute, Tuskegee, Alabama, 1906.
Photograph courtesy of the Library of Congress, Prints and Photographs Division [LC-J601-302].

bird, or beast." Carver's scientific interests were tempered by his deep appreciation of art. Among other things, he was a skillful painter and a supporter of Tuskegee's Department of Music.

Like Booker T. Washington, Carver is buried on the Tuskegee campus (their graves, in fact, are only a few feet apart), and the building where he carried out his research is now the George Washington Carver Museum. It is operated by the National Park Service.

George Washington Carver's gravestone, Tuskegee. Photograph courtesy of Marcia Jones Media.

George Washington Carver Museum, Tuskegee. Photograph courtesy of Marcia Jones Media.

Some of the Tuskegee Airmen attending a briefing in Ramitelli, Italy, March
1945. Photograph by Toni Frissell, courtesy of the Library of Congress, Prints and Photographs
Division [LC-F9-02-4503-319-07].

The Story

Before they were pilots, the black men who would become the Tuskegee
Airmen were Americans. But they were not ordinary citizens. They were
men who dreamed of serving a country that had never served them. Although all branches of the military in the 1940s shared the same legality
and tradition of segregation that American society did, black Americans

played a significant role in military service during World War II, as they had in all previous American conflicts.

As the war in Europe developed, the black press, continuing an effort begun years before with the NAACP, advocated for blacks to be allowed to train as pilots and fly in the army air corps. After Franklin Roosevelt implemented the draft in the fall of 1940, black leaders lobbied the president to allow black soldiers to serve in a capacity other than support personnel, the only positions then acknowledged as appropriate for Negro soldiers. The military ultimately capitulated, and it was decided that blacks would be included in the army's aviation plans, although there remained a widely held belief that black men lacked the physiological and psychological capacity to be pilots.

Tuskegee was one of six black schools that had previously been included in a nationwide civilian pilot training program. In January 1941, the army air corps announced it would be forming an all-black fighter pilot unit. Largely due to the influence of Eleanor Roosevelt, who visited the Tuskegee civilian pilot school, Tuskegee was chosen as the training ground for the new unit. A group of young black men came from all over the country to the heart of the segregated South. From varying economic backgrounds and diverse life experiences, these young men brought with them not only the desire to fight against fascism abroad but also the passion to combat prejudice at home.

The airmen were housed at Tuskegee University, an atmosphere in which they thrived, experiencing complete freedom and acceptance. Off campus, however, many citizens of Tuskegee had earned a reputation for intolerance. Fearing property values would be adversely affected and the town's social structure would be irrevocably altered by the influx of blacks, the white residents of Tuskegee opposed the implementation of a training program for Negroes in their city. They generated petitions and sent them to Washington, D.C. For the black trainees, the struggle with racism was beginning early.

In July 1941, the first aviation cadet class began. Training and each pilot's first solo flight were conducted on the PT-17. For those pilots who failed to make it through the program or "washed out," segregation, not lack of ability, was often the cause. Because there was only one black unit of pilots and one training ground, there was a de facto quota system. Had those same pilots been white, many would have seen their day in the sky.

On March 6, 1942, the first class of cadets graduated from the flight program at Tuskegee and became U.S. Army Air Corps pilots. In July, they formed the 99th Fighter Squadron. They were assisted both at home and abroad by ground service, line maintenance, and support personnel, all black, all brought in to serve with the 99th because of the military's policy of segregation. But despite the growing need for pilots overseas, the army was averse to using its newly trained black pilots. By the fall of 1942, however, the United States was fighting in both the European and the Pacific arenas. The War Department had little choice but to use all its available pilots.

The 99th Fighter Squadron was deployed to Italy, after having been attached to the 33rd Fighter Group as logistical and administrative support. Because they were black, they were completely isolated. The Tuskegee Airmen, as they had come to be called, saw their first dogfights off the coast of Sicily. The 332nd Fighter Group was the next group of Tuskegee Airmen to be deployed. It was in their performance as close air support for Allied troops storming the beachhead at Anzio, and later throughout Italy, Germany, and eastern Europe, flying side by side with the white pilots they had been designated to protect, that these black pilots, navigators, and bombardiers earned their reputation for bravery and excellence.

In these missions, the Tuskegee Airmen flew P-51 Mustangs, the premier fighter plane of World War II. As escorts for the bombers entering enemy territory, the "red tails," so nicknamed for the red paint they used on the tails of their planes, would pull off to the side, wait for the bombers to hit their targets, and then escort the bombers back home. The Tuskegee Airmen soon became known as the best escorts in the military. As military historians have noted, they amassed "a nearly perfect record of not losing U.S. bombers, a unique achievement."

Despite the glory they achieved in the skies over Europe, the Tuskegee Airmen returned to America to confront the same prejudice that had defined their lives when they left. But for most of the airmen, there was no paradox in using their skills as first-class pilots to defend a country that considered them to be second-class citizens. These black Americans had families, churches, businesses, and communities that were just as much a part of the fabric of American life as they were for white Americans. Although they enlisted in a white military and took their orders from a white commander in chief, they struggled not in the service of a white America but their America, a country they believed to be worth defending, despite the injustices they had suffered at the hands of fellow citizens.

The Tuskegee Airmen went on to receive numerous awards and accolades. Largely because of the airmen's success, in July 1948, Harry Truman signed Executive Order 9981 outlawing segregation in the military. The war was over. Military segregation was no more. But these victories did not ensure equality for the Tuskegee Airmen or for any of America's black citizens. That would be a battle waged for many decades to come. But while the Tuskegee Airmen could not defeat racial inequality in the country they had so courageously risked their lives to defend, they could, and did, forever destroy the notion of black incompetence. Nobody could ever again reasonably question the intelligence, dedication, perseverance, skill, and bravery of black soldiers or black people. This destruction of the old stereotypes would prove crucial in effecting the changes that would one day result in civil rights for America's black population.

Tuskegee Airmen National Historic Site, Moton Field, Tuskegee. Photograph courtesy of Marcia Jones Media.

What to See

The Tuskegee Airmen National Historic Site, administered by the National Park System, is located at Moton Field on Chappie James Avenue in Tuskegee, one mile south of Interstate 85, exit 38. The site includes a temporary visitor center with exhibits, a bookstore, and a theater where historic films are shown. Hangar 1 contains interactive exhibits, period artifacts, and historic airplanes. If you visit on the weekend before Memorial Day, you can watch the annual Tuskegee Airmen Fly-in, which features historic aircraft, military flybys and aviation aerobatics, exhibits, vendors, and visits by Tuskegee Airmen. For more information and for directions, visit the National Parks website at www.nps.gov/tuin/index. htm.

Shiloh: Rosenwald Schools and the Syphilis Study

The Site

Shiloh Missionary Baptist Church sits on a hill outside Notasulga, Alabama, a reassuring presence in the rolling countryside. Though often missed by the steady streams of visitors to Tuskegee, this white frame chapel just a few miles north of the university is one of the most historic sites in the area. A longtime center of community life, it was the place where black citizens, in the early 1900s, built one of the earliest Rosenwald schools. These grassroots centers of education represented the shared vision of Jewish philanthropist Julius Rosenwald and Tuskegee president Booker T. Washington. But there is another side to Shiloh's history. In the 1930s, it was also the place where a public health nurse recruited participants for the Tuskegee Study of Untreated Syphilis in the Negro Male, one of the worst social crimes in American history.

Shiloh Missionary Baptist Church, outside of Notasulga on Highway 81.
Photograph courtesy of Susan Finch.

The Story

In the opening years of the twentieth century, Julius Rosenwald was a strong supporter of Booker T. Washington. Rosenwald himself was a shrewd and ambitious man with a strong social conscience, and he admired those qualities in Washington. Long before he became president of Sears, Roebuck and Company, Rosenwald was the hard-working son of Jewish immigrants. He was born in 1862 just a few blocks from the Illinois home of Abraham Lincoln; as a teenager he moved to New York to learn the clothing trade from his uncles. In the 1890s, Rosenwald's company began to supply men's clothing to Sears, Roebuck, and by 1895 Rosenwald and a partner bought out Roebuck's half of Sears.

In the early 1900s, as Rosenwald made his way up the corporate ladder, he developed an interest in the country's social problems, especially the plight of African Americans. "The horrors that are due to race prejudice," he explained, "come home to the Jew more forcefully than to others of the white race, on account of the centuries of persecution which they have suffered and still suffer."

In 1912, Rosenwald joined the board of Tuskegee Institute, and he and Booker T. Washington began to discuss the need for black schools. Out of those discussions came a remarkable piece of philanthropy—Rosenwald's decision to support the construction of more than five thousand schools for African Americans, mostly in the South. His approach, however, did not take the form of pure charity. Instead, he partnered with black communities, who most often donated labor and land, and the schools became a source of community pride.

That was certainly the case with the school in Notasulga. Sometime between 1914 and 1922, the Shiloh Missionary Baptist Church donated two acres of land, and members of the congregation built the three-room structure with their own hands. It was nothing fancy, just a sturdy, wood-frame building, heated initially with pot-bellied stoves. But it served the community for more than forty years, and as this book goes to press an

Julius Rosenwald.
Photograph courtesy of the
Library of Congress, Prints
and Photographs Division
[LC-B2-4552-18].

organization of local citizens, both black and white, has begun a restoration project. Their goal is to transform the old school building—the basic components of which are still sound—into a museum and community center.

Elizabeth Sims, an educator and longtime Notasulga resident, is president of the Shiloh Community Restoration Foundation, which has emerged from a strong sense of history among local residents. Among other things, members of the community are deeply proud of the Shiloh church. It traces its roots to former slaves, who decided as soon as they were free that they wanted to worship in a church of their own. Their spirit of independence transferred easily to the Shiloh school.

Then, on a Sunday in 1932, something terrible and unexpected happened. Eunice Rivers, a U.S. Public Health Service nurse, came to Shiloh and promised the men in the congregation free treatment for "bad blood" in exchange for their participation in a study.

Elizabeth Sims's grandfathers accepted the offer (one of them later went blind), and even today she shares her community's chilly disbelief that such a thing could have happened. In the course of the Tuskegee Syphilis Study, which lasted forty years, 399 African American men who suffered from the disease—many of them poor and illiterate sharecroppers—were given no treatment for it at all. When the study began, those treatments were iffy and sometimes deadly. By 1947, however, penicillin had become the standard remedy, safe, effective, but deliberately withheld from the Tuskegee patients.

Down the hill from the Shiloh church, there is a graveyard filled with men from the study. "Some of them died from the disease," said Sims. "Some went crazy." One of the most prominent cemetery stones is that of Charles Pollard, a study participant who testified before the U.S. Senate in 1973, the year after a government whistle-blower finally revealed that the study had occurred. In the book *Tuskegee's Truths: Rethinking the Tuskegee Syphilis Study*, author Susan Reverby quotes a part of Pollard's congressional testimony:

Senator Kennedy. What were the shots for, to cure the bad blood?

Mr. Pollard: Bad blood, as far as I know of.

Senator Kennedy: Did you think they were curing bad blood?

Mr. Pollard: I didn't know. I just attended the clinic.

Senator Kennedy: They told you to keep coming back and you did?

Mr. Pollard: When they got through giving the shots, yes. Then they gave us that spinal puncture.

Senator Kennedy: Did they tell you why they were giving a spinal puncture?

Mr. Pollard: No.

Senator Kennedy: Did you think it was because they were trying to help you?

Mr. Pollard: To help me, yes.

Senator Kennedy: You wanted some help?

Mr. Pollard: That is right. They said I had bad blood and they was working on it.

In 1974, civil rights attorney Fred Gray secured a $10 million settlement for Pollard and other survivors of the study. By that time, twenty-eight participants had died directly from untreated syphilis; one hundred had died from related complications; forty of the subjects' wives had been infected; and nineteen of their children had been born with congenital syphilis. On May 16, 1997, President Clinton issued a formal apology on behalf of the government to the study volunteers and their families. "We can look you in the eye," Clinton said, "and finally say on behalf of the American people what the United States government did was shameful, and I am sorry."

What to See

Shiloh Missionary Baptist Church is located on Alabama Highway 81 about three miles north of Interstate 85, exit 38. In 2009, the building that housed the Rosenwald school, also located on the grounds of the church, was being restored. About a quarter of a mile south of the church, at the intersection of Highway 81 and Pistol Range Road, the Shiloh Cemetery contains the gravestones of as many as twenty-five participants in the Syphilis Study.

Charles Pollard, whose hilltop grave is shaded by a small cedar tree, became the lead plaintiff in the class action lawsuit *Pollard v. U.S.* The attorney in the case, Fred Gray, who would later become the first African American president of the Alabama Bar Association, handled other landmark cases in the course of his career. Among the most notable were *Browder v. Gayle,* which led to the desegregation of Montgomery buses (see chapter 1), and the voting rights case of *Gomillion v. Lightfoot* (see next page).

Charlie Pollard's gravestone in the
Shiloh Cemetery on Highway 81.
Photograph courtesy of Susan Finch.

Dr. Gomillion and the Vote

The Site

Located on the corner of North Church Street and Martin Luther King
Highway, Butler Chapel AME Zion Church is important to the history of
Tuskegee in several ways. Established in 1865 and named for its founding pastor, John Butler, it was one of the earliest institutions for African
Americans who had been freed in the Civil War. Then on July 4, 1881,
Booker T. Washington opened school in a shanty on the church's current
grounds. That school would grow into Tuskegee Institute. Finally, in the
summer of 1957, Butler Chapel made history once again. On June 25,
several thousand black citizens gathered there in a ground-breaking protest, demanding equal access to the ballot. They were led by Dr. Charles
Gomillion, a professor of sociology at Tuskegee, and supported by the
Reverend Kenneth Buford, the church's outspoken minister.

The Story

When Charles Gomillion came to Tuskegee in 1928, he was twenty-eight years old and had only recently graduated from college. He grew up in Johnston, South Carolina, where the only school for African Americans was closed nine months out of every year. His father was an illiterate janitor, but his mother, Flora, valued education as the key to the future—an opinion that was soon absorbed by her son.

Gomillion's path to a college degree was a long one, involving delays to support his parents, but by the time he joined the faculty at Tuskegee, he was committed to the life of a citizen-scholar. He shared Booker T. Washington's belief in education and economic advancement, but in the 1930s, Gomillion became part of a group of professors who thought it was time to take the next step. Among other things, they believed that Tuskegee's black middle class, consisting mostly of highly educated people, should pursue the right to vote—with all the power and responsibility it held.

They formed an organization known as the TCA, the Tuskegee Civic Association, to push the cause of voter registration, and slowly in the 1940s and 1950s, they began to make some progress. They knew there were obstacles to be overcome. Throughout Alabama, particularly in places with a black majority, which included Tuskegee, white officials went to great lengths to keep black voter registration to a minimum. Registrars had one standard for whites, another for blacks, and they used instruments ranging from the poll tax to subjective interpretations of the U.S. Constitution to keep most African Americans off the voting rolls.

But in December 1949, Gomillion wrote a letter to Governor Jim Folsom declaring that "all law-abiding citizens . . . have the right, and should have the opportunity, to participate in self-government." As Gomillion discovered, it was the perfect approach to take with the governor, a populist (and some even said, "a closet integrationist") who was happy to court the sympathy of black voters.

Charles Gomillion, 1974. Photograph courtesy of the Penn State University Libraries, Special Collections Department, The Jack Rabin Collection.

Folsom called an old friend, a Macon County farmer by the name of Herman Bentley, and asked him to serve as a voter registrar. Bentley was a white man, a tall, thin, weather-beaten Methodist who had taken his Sunday school lessons to heart. He believed quite simply that all men were equal in the eyes of God, and in a two-year period, he registered more than five hundred blacks—easily enough voters to change the balance of power in Tuskegee.

Indeed, by the middle of the 1950s, African Americans represented more than 40 percent of the electorate. It was then that the white city fathers fought back. Under the leadership of Sam Engelhardt, a state senator and ardent segregationist, they pushed through a bill in the Alabama legislature redrawing the boundaries of the town and intricately excluding the black neighborhoods. Tuskegee, which had once been a perfect square, was now an all-white metropolis with twenty-eight sides.

Charles Gomillion could hardly believe it. For more than a decade, the African American community had been so patient in its quest for the vote—persistent, yes, but civil, dignified, and understanding, and now it was confronted with an act of bad faith. At Gomillion's urging, on June 25, 1957, more than three thousand people gathered at Butler Chapel AME Zion Church, having agreed that sterner measures were required. As the community cheered, Gomillion called for a boycott of white merchants—those, at least, who had supported the gerrymandering of the town.

"We are going to buy our goods and services," he proclaimed, "from those who help us, from those who make no effort to hinder us, from those who recognize us as first-class citizens. Soon the time will come when they have to respect us. They may hate our guts, but they will respect us."

In his own quiet way, Gomillion cut a striking figure as he spoke. He was a slender, well-dressed man with high cheekbones and closely cropped hair—the very portrait, some people said, of a black intellectual. "He was the epitome of what I wanted to be," remembered Charles Hamilton, who was then a young sociologist at Tuskegee. "He had all the virtues—civility, intelligence—and he was a scholar." But Hamilton and others also detected a simmering rage at Gomillion's core, as if he regarded segregation as a deeply personal affront.

All those qualities were on display at the church as Gomillion recalled the example of Montgomery—the bus boycott victory from six months before, when blacks refused to ride segregated buses and also filed a federal lawsuit seeking definitive relief from the courts. In Tuskegee, Gomillion and his followers chose the same dual path, boycotting white merchants and filing a lawsuit.

On November 15, 1960, after the landmark case of *Gomillion v. Light-*

foot made its gradual journey up the line, the U.S. Supreme Court ruled the gerrymander unconstitutional. In February of the following year, the original boundaries of Tuskegee were restored.

In the quest for black voting rights, the community of Tuskegee played a watershed role. It represented, in a sense, the eastern front in a long-running struggle as another showdown loomed across the state—Selma (see chapter 3).

In the end, according to many historians, equal access to the ballot proved to be the most revolutionary achievement of the civil rights era.

Butler Chapel AME Zion Church, 1002 North Church Street, Tuskegee. Photograph courtesy of Susan Finch.

What to See

At the Tuskegee Institute National Historic Site, operated by the National Park Service, little if any attention is paid to the accomplishments of Charles Gomillion and his followers. But the visible reminders of those achievements—and the historical context in which they occurred—can be found at the Butler Chapel AME Zion Church, an impressive brick structure on the crest of a hill on North Church Street, overlooking Martin Luther King Highway.

SNCC and the Killing of Sammy Younge Jr.

The Site

At the center of the courthouse square in Tuskegee, a Confederate monument towers over the grounds, as is often the case in small southern towns. During a time of anger in the civil rights years, this tranquil, tree-shaded place became the site of bitter demonstrations after a SNCC activist named Sammy Younge Jr. was gunned down by a white man. The killing was merely the most brutal manifestation of hardening racial attitudes in the town—wounds, some say, that have never quite healed.

The Story

Organizers from the Student Nonviolent Coordinating Committee came to Tuskegee in 1964, urging the students to stand up and be counted. Leading the effort were Bob Mants and Stokely Carmichael, both of whom were involved in voting rights drives in some of the roughest areas of the South. Carmichael, especially, was moving toward a more militant stance, challenging the assumptions of the nonviolent movement, and over the next two years he would become a leading proponent of black power.

At Tuskegee, he found some willing activists—brilliant students eager to play a role. There was George Ware, a graduate student in chemistry, who would soon emerge as a leader in SNCC, fearless in his confrontations with authority. There was Gwen Patton, Tuskegee's student body president, who was always more of a scholar-activist, preparing herself for the day when the movement would win, and when students like herself, steeped in notions of racial equality, would take their places in the life of the country.

And there was Sammy Younge Jr.

Like many young people who attended Tuskegee, Younge had grown up in an academic community, graduating from an eastern prep school before he entered college. In the spring and summer of 1965, he became deeply involved with civil rights. On March 10, he participated in a tense demonstration supporting the Selma to Montgomery march. Tuskegee students had made the trip to the capital and found themselves in a sullen face-off with the Montgomery police. They blocked the sidewalks in front of the capitol and refused to move for the rest of the day.

When they returned to Tuskegee, the students began a series of local

Sammy Younge Jr., 1965. Photograph courtesy of H. Councill Trenholm State Technical College Archives, Gwendolyn M. Patton Papers.

demonstrations that lasted all spring, and Sammy Younge Jr. was square-ly in the middle of it. He was beaten one Sunday at a white Method-ist church where he and other blacks were denied admission. As anger among the students increased, Younge was one of the most militant of all. He directed his rage not only at whites but also at older black leaders such as Charles Gomillion, the Tuskegee sociology professor, who took a dim view of the student protests.

For more than two decades, Gomillion had crusaded for the right to vote and dreamed of the day when blacks and whites working side by side would assume the governance of their community. Now that dream was coming apart, destroyed, it was true, primarily by the white racism that had been laid bare by the student protests. But Gomillion thought the students shared some of the blame. With the civil rights movement on the threshold of victory, the younger activists, ironically, were being swept away by their militancy and rage, and racial polarization was the result.

By 1965, many SNCC leaders were rejecting the tenets of nonviolence. Having faced bigotry and violence on the front lines of the struggle, they had grown indifferent to the goal of reconciliation. "The black people have nothing to prove to the whites," wrote Stokely Carmichael. "The burden is on whites to prove that they are civilized."

In Tuskegee, Sammy Younge shared Carmichael's rage, and it erupted on the night of January 3, 1966. About ten o'clock, Younge left a party at the SNCC "freedom house" and stopped at a service station downtown. According to later testimony in the case, he asked the owner Marvin Seg-rest to tell him where the "damn bathroom" was. The two of them began to argue, and before it was over Segrest, an aging supporter of the White Citizens Council, had pulled a gun and shot Younge in the head.

When Segrest was tried the following December, he was quickly ac-quitted by an all-white jury, prompting an angry march of more than fifteen hundred students. When they arrived at the courthouse square in Tuskegee, one of the demonstrators climbed the Confederate monument, and as historian Robert J. Norrell later wrote, "painted the soldier's face black and put a yellow stripe down his back. Inscribed at the base of the statue were 'black power' and 'Sam Younge.'"

The demonstration lasted until 4:00 A.M., with protesters starting fires near the square and throwing rocks at downtown stores. Eventually, the violence subsided, but race relations in Tuskegee were strained. For many whites as well as blacks, there was simply too much anger and mistrust.

Mab Segrest, the daughter of Sammy Younge Jr.'s killer, moved away from Tuskegee and became a crusader against racial intolerance. In her

Macon County Courthouse, Tuskegee. Photograph courtesy of Ken Blackwell.

autobiography *Memoir of a Race Traitor* she wrote these words: "I was born to a town of white folks willing itself to die, a world in which love and beauty mixed inextricably with hatred and pain. How to grieve for what should not, did not, deserve to last?"

What to See

Tuskegee's Confederate monument, scene of demonstrations after the death of Sammy Younge and the trial of his killer Marvin Segrest, is located at the center of the town square adjacent to the Macon County courthouse.

Sammy Younge Jr.'s story is also told at the Tuskegee Human and Civil Rights Multicultural Center at 104 South Elm Street. Serving as both a museum and an official visitor center for Tuskegee and Macon County, this tax-exempt, nonprofit facility, one of the best of its kind, offers a more complete account of Tuskegee's history than either the Tuskegee Institute or Tuskegee Airmen National Park Service sites. The multicultural center's exhibits trace the history of Macon County from prehistory to the contemporary era. The mission of the center is "to recognize the human and civil rights contributions of Native Americans, European Americans, and Americans of African descent." For more information, visit the center's website at www.tuskegeecenter.org.

A TRANSFER OF POWER

By the time of the 1966 elections, African American voters outnumbered whites in Tuskegee and surrounding Macon County. In a sense, that fact represented a triumph for Charles Gomillion and his allies, as blacks began taking their positions in government.

In a heralded election in 1966, an African American Korean War veteran named Lucius Amerson became the new sheriff of Macon County, the first black to hold that position in the South since the days of Reconstruction. It was a welcome change for rural African Americans, who, like their counterparts all over the region, were tired of the caprice and occasional brutality of white sheriffs.

In 1972, Johnnie Ford, a twenty-nine-year-old federal antipoverty administrator, became the first black mayor of Tuskegee, completing the transfer of political power. For Charles Gomillion, the change was bittersweet. Throughout his public life, he had dreamed of an interracial democracy—whites and blacks working together for the betterment of the community. Many whites in Tuskegee had long resisted that vision, and by the mid-1960s the same, ironically, was becoming true of many blacks.

Student militants led by SNCC had become active in the voter registration effort, and many were influenced by the black power theories of SNCC leader Stokely Carmichael. In his book *Black Power*, written with former Tuskegee professor Charles Hamilton, Carmichael concluded that whites were not interested in sharing power, and in communities where blacks represented a majority they should accept that reality and simply seize control.

By all accounts, Gomillion was saddened by that kind of militancy and the rejection of his interracial ideals. In 1974, he left Tuskegee and moved to Washington, D.C. But shortly before his death, perhaps sensing that the end was near, he returned to the town where he had lived and worked for nearly fifty years. In 1995, he died in a hospital in nearby Montgomery at the age of ninety-five.

Tuskegee, meanwhile, had become a very different place. As African Americans gained political power, many white citizens simply moved away. By the time of Charles Gomillion's death, Tuskegee's population was more than 97 percent black.

"INVISIBLE MAN"

Gwen Patton, a student leader and activist during SNCC's heyday at Tuskegee, recalled her personal struggles to maintain a balance between the competing demands of the movement and the classroom. Fortunately, she said, there were places where the two overlapped. In her English classes, she read the novel *Invisible Man,* written by Tuskegee alumnus Ralph Ellison. Ellison, an Oklahoma native, had entered the college in 1933 to study in its renowned school of music. He was deeply influenced by department chair Charles Dawson and piano instructor Hazel Harrison, but he found himself spending more and more time in the Tuskegee library poring over the work of contemporary writers. He was especially taken with T. S. Eliot's poem *The Waste Land,* which helped shape his own decision to write.

For Gwen Patton, who would later emerge as a civil rights archivist and scholar at Trenholm State Technical College in Montgomery, Ellison's *Invisible Man* was as influential as the writings that Ellison himself had discovered at Tuskegee. The idea of blacks as invisible in the eyes of white America resonated with Patton, as it did with other Tuskegee activists during the civil rights years. But the literary power of Ellison's novel was a reminder of the importance of academic work, which could have been pushed aside by the movement. Years later, Patton would say she was happy she managed to maintain a balance. Meanwhile, the civil rights archives at Trenholm State are some of the strongest in Alabama.

7

THE BURNING BUS AND THE
ALABAMA HILLS

In the Alabama hill country near the town of Anniston, the image that defines the civil rights years is the freedom riders' bus set aflame. In May 1961, when the integrated group headed west across the Alabama line, their Greyhound bus was attacked near Anniston by a mob of Klansmen. Its tires slashed, the bus limped to a halt on U.S. Highway 78, where the mob broke the windows, set the interior of the bus ablaze, and tried to keep the riders from escaping.

In the years that followed, the horror of that moment hovered over Anniston, prompting many local leaders, black and white, to work toward some kind of reconciliation. The issue came to a head in the sum-

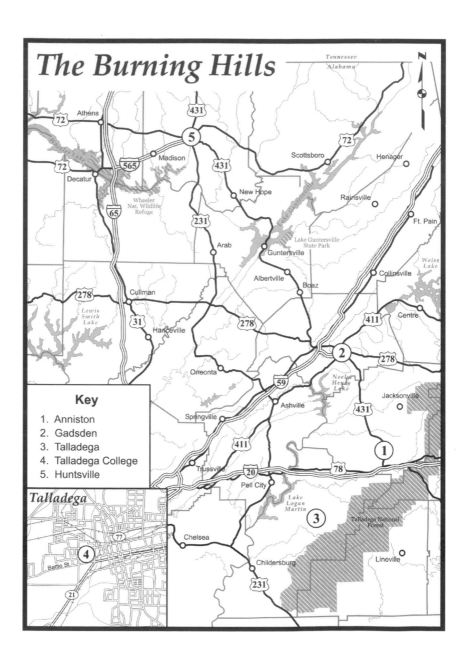

The Burning Hills

Key

1. Anniston
2. Gadsden
3. Talladega
4. Talladega College
5. Huntsville

Talladega

mer of 1963, when two prominent African American ministers tried to visit Anniston's previously all-white public library. They too were attacked and beaten by supporters of the Klan. But the following day, an integrated group returned to the library, serving notice to the racists—and also to the decent members of the community—that the Klan didn't speak for everybody in town.

The drama was equally intense in small industrial city of Gadsden, about thirty miles northwest of Anniston. There, also in the summer of 1963, law enforcement officials used cattle prods—apparently for the first time in Alabama—on a group of African American demonstrators. But in these same Appalachian foothills, just outside the town of Talladega, there was a different kind of story unfolding, one that centered on the oldest, private black college in the state.

Founded in 1867 by two former slaves, Talladega College has been a kind of living monument to the best of black history—to art and education, as well as the preparation for the long and difficult quest for equal rights. The same was true in Huntsville, where two historically black colleges—Alabama A&M and Oakwood College—played their critically important roles in the movement.

Anniston: The Library and the Bus

The Site

On a lonely, two-lane stretch of highway outside of Anniston, there is a little-noticed marker that stands at the site of an infamous crime. This particular road, now a side street, was once the main route to Birmingham, and it was the road on which a Greyhound bus was burned by a mob of Ku Klux Klansmen. The date was May 14, 1961, and the bus was carrying nine freedom riders who had set out to test a Supreme Court ruling ordering desegregation of interstate travel. The Anniston attack

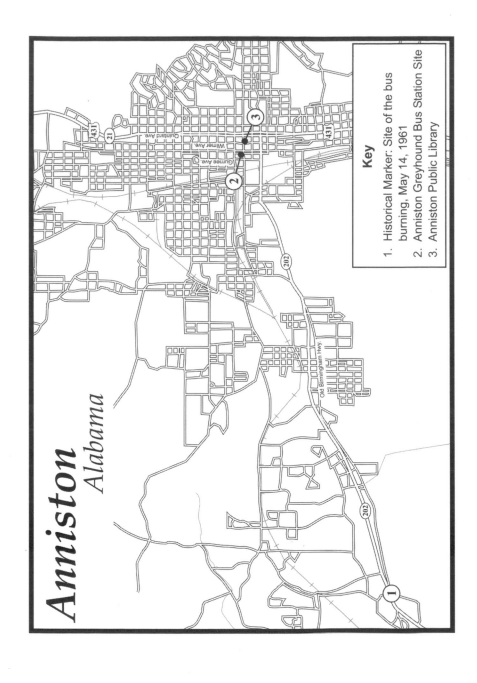

Anniston
Alabama

Key

1. Historical Marker: Site of the bus burning, May 14, 1961
2. Anniston Greyhound Bus Station Site
3. Anniston Public Library

was merely the first that the freedom riders would endure, and more racial violence in Anniston would follow.

The Story

Anniston had always been a tough town. When Alabama native Nat King Cole was attacked in Birmingham in 1956 (see chapter 2), the perpetrators were white supremacists from Anniston. And on more than one occasion, black students from nearby Talladega College had endured harassment and sometimes worse from members of the Anniston Ku Klux Klan.

Even so, the violence against the freedom riders was shocking. It was Mother's Day 1961 when the Greyhound bus pulled into the station. The riders had started their journey in Washington, D.C., where leaders of the Congress of Racial Equality had set out to test the *Boynton* decision. That 1960 U.S. Supreme Court ruling had been triggered by a young Alabamian, Bruce Boynton of Selma, who was arrested after taking his seat in an all-white Trailways terminal in Richmond (see chapter 3).

Represented by Thurgood Marshall, Boynton appealed his trespass conviction, which had carried only a ten-dollar fine. The principle, he thought, was worth much more, and the Supreme Court agreed. In a decision written by Hugo Black, a veteran justice who had once been a senator from Alabama, the court affirmed that bus terminals and interstate buses must be desegregated immediately. But in the spring of 1961, everyone knew that southern states had ignored that decision, and the freedom riders set out to call attention to the issue.

At the Anniston terminal a mob of maybe two hundred people was waiting, and as the Greyhound pulled slowly to the rear of the station they began to attack. At first they tried to board the bus, but E. L. Cowling, an Alabama undercover policeman who was a passenger, managed to keep them at bay. The mob then began slashing the tires as the bus driver restarted the engine and desperately tried to make it out of town.

Freedom riders sit by the side of the road as their bus burns; it was fire-bombed by a mob outside of Anniston, May 14, 1961. Photograph courtesy of the Birmingham Civil Rights Institute.

But within a few miles, the tires went flat and the bus limped helplessly to a stop.

The attackers now began smashing windows, somebody threw a fire-bomb, and the riders began to choke on the fumes. Now the mob, which had tried at the station to break through the door, began to hold it shut, refusing to let the passengers escape. People might have died at that point, but Officer Cowling, who had radioed for reinforcements, drew his gun and forced the mob to back away from the doors.

The violence subsided when Alabama State Troopers arrived on the scene, and the freedom riders were taken to the Anniston Hospital. Soon, however, they found themselves surrounded again by the mob. In Birmingham, some sixty miles away, civil rights leader Fred Shuttlesworth received word of their plight and dispatched a caravan to rescue them.

Leading the expedition was a battle-toughened civil rights veteran named Colonel Stone Johnson, who had once discovered a dynamite bomb smoldering outside of Shuttlesworth's house. Johnson and another civil rights supporter, Will Hall, grabbed the dynamite and threw it into a nearby ditch just a few seconds before it exploded. Because of such courage, Shuttlesworth was happy to trust Johnson with the rescue mission.

The heavily armed convoy made the drive to Anniston in less than an hour, where they took the marauding Klansmen by surprise. "We walked right between those Ku Klux," Johnson remembered. "Some of them had clubs. There were some deputies too. You couldn't tell the deputies from the Ku Klux."

Johnson and his fellow rescuers gathered up the freedom riders and rushed back to Birmingham, where the riders were taken to places of safety. But if their terrible adventure in Anniston was over, the memory of it hovered over the town. For a few white citizens, whether they were supporters of the civil rights movement or not, the whole episode became a source of embarrassment and shame. Phillips Noble, minister at Anniston's First Presbyterian Church, was one of the most outspoken white leaders, and he soon began meeting with two of his African American counterparts, N. Q. Reynolds, who was a Baptist minister, and William B. McClain, a United Methodist.

The preachers urged the creation of an interracial commission, to help bridge the chasm of race. Nothing much happened until Mother's Day 1963. But on that second anniversary of the attack on the freedom riders, a group of white hoodlums—probably members of the Ku Klux Klan—fired shots into the homes of several black citizens. For respectable white leaders it was finally too much. Miller Sproull, a city commissioner, called Noble and told him: "It's time to establish the interracial commission. I want you to be the chairman."

In the weeks that followed, commission members began meeting with the library board, including its chairman, Charles Doster, an Anniston attorney. Doster agreed that in the pursuit of integration, the library seemed to be a good place to start. "What could be so onerous," he asked, "about letting a black man read a book in the library?" Doster and his board, with the support of Miller Sproull, announced that on Sunday, September 15, 1963, the library would open its doors to all citizens.

In celebration of the board's decision, the two black ministers, William McClain and N. Q. Reynolds, appeared at the library that Sunday. Before they even made it to the building they were confronted by members of the Ku Klux Klan. "They were beaten," remembered Doster. "Beaten with clubs and chains within an inch of their lives. A gun was fired. . . . Fortunately, they survived but Mr. Reynolds was in bed for a long, long time. A week or longer I guess. Mr. McClain was able to get up and move around some."

The events in Anniston were overshadowed by those in Birmingham that same day—the bombing of the Sixteenth Street Baptist Church, which killed four little girls (see chapter 2). But the citizens of Anniston rallied to the cause. The following morning, an integrated group entered the library together, serving notice that the citizens of Anniston would not be deterred by the Ku Klux Klan. Many years later, Phillips Noble, the Presbyterian minister who was part of that group, remembered the barrage of threatening phone calls and the worry every time he started his car that maybe somebody had planted a bomb. But he knew the community was moving forward as it should.

As Charles Doster put it, "Everybody in this town turned against that gangsterism or hoodlumism or whatever you want to call it. . . . This community was *not* going to be run by the Klan."

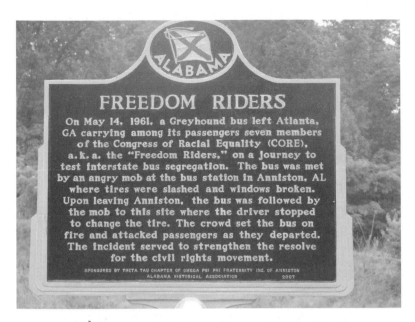

FREEDOM RIDERS

On May 14, 1961, a Greyhound bus left Atlanta,
GA carrying among its passengers seven members
of the Congress of Racial Equality (CORE),
a.k.a. the "Freedom Riders," on a journey to
test interstate bus segregation. The bus was met
by an angry mob at the bus station in Anniston, AL
where tires were slashed and windows broken.
Upon leaving Anniston, the bus was followed by
the mob to this site where the driver stopped
to change the tire. The crowd set the bus on
fire and attacked passengers as they departed.
The incident served to strengthen the resolve
for the civil rights movement.

SPONSORED BY THETA TAU CHAPTER OF OMEGA PSI PHI FRATERNITY INC. OF ANNISTON
ALABAMA HISTORICAL ASSOCIATION   2007

Freedom riders historical marker at the site of the bus bombing.

Photograph courtesy of Susan Finch.

What to See

The historical marker denoting the place where the freedom riders' bus was burned can be found on a knoll on the Old Birmingham Highway west of downtown, two-tenths of a mile beyond the city limits, and approximately three miles from the former Greyhound station. The marker, which was erected by the Alabama Historical Association and the Omega Psi Phi fraternity, can be found near a dead-end spur on the old highway, just off Highway 202. The building where the bus station was located still stands at 1031 Gurnee Street in Anniston. The building is now an Anniston business called Howell Signs.

Anniston's excellent public library has a new building now, but is located on the same plot of land where the Ku Klux Klan attacked Revs. N. Q. Reynolds and William McClain. In its Alabama Room, which features material on Alabama history and genealogy, the library offers in-depth information on the civil rights movement in Anniston. The current library address is 108 East Tenth Street.

Gadsden and the Cattle Prods

The Site

The industrial city of Gadsden was already a town with a violent past when Al Lingo, Alabama's public safety director, decided in the summer of 1963 to experiment with an even more brutal form of repression.

The Story

In his 1965 memoir *I'll Never Forget Alabama Law*, CORE field representative William "Meatball" Douthard summarizes what happened in Gadsden in the summer of 1963: "It was there the 'cattle prod,' a battery-powered instrument used in most stockyards, capable of rendering a shock from 18 to 24 volts, was introduced as a weapon against civil rights demonstrators. It was there the theory of brutally beating Negroes in large numbers as a means of creating a blanket of fear in the community was initiated in the grandest of Southern style."

As one of more than four hundred people arrested on June 18, 1963, Douthard was still in jail the following night when "over 500 Negroes, men, women and children" assembled for a prayer vigil on the grounds of the Etowah County Courthouse. From his cell on the top floor, he recalls, "I saw over 300 law officers of the city, county, and state surround the protestors and begin the systematic beating of all. As Negroes broke and ran they were chased on foot and in cars, overtaken and beaten again." Describing in detail the beating and cattle prodding he received personally from Colonel Al Lingo, Douthard concludes, "This was Gadsden in 1963."

When fire hoses and dogs failed to preserve segregation in Birmingham, Lingo clearly decided that a more intense onslaught of violence was the only way to break the spirit of the civil rights movement. For his next target he chose Gadsden, a city with a violent past.

Gadsden's troubled labor history and ugly Jim Crow traditions suited it uniquely to Lingo's brand of repression. Ever since the city's founding, Gadsden's power elite had been antiunion. A 1937 article in the *Nation*, "Gadsden Is Tough," charged that "the reign of terror which has been maintained in the employer's interest in this small southern town has not been spontaneous or sporadic. . . . Labor organizers have been mercilessly beaten on the streets in the very heart of the city, twice in broad daylight." To suppress interracial cooperation among workers in the steel industry, where more than a fourth of the workers were black, union opponents sought to exploit white racial prejudices. In the late 1930s, police raided a racially integrated meeting of the steel workers union and put all the participants in jail.

The *Gadsden Times* and local civic leaders trumpeted the myth that Gadsden was "a virtuous, peaceful and innocent community lacking internal differences." To preserve this image, union organizers were derided with such emotionally charged labels as carpetbagger, Communist, and outside agitator, because discontent among local people would contradict the Gadsden myth.

This pattern would continue during the civil rights era when black union men shifted their focus to the issue of segregation. Joseph Faulkner was a local steelworker when he filed his first discrimination suit in the early 1960s. Neither he nor his friends were being influenced by outside agitators. They assessed conditions in Gadsden for themselves and, aware of changes afoot on the national scene, they decided it was time to act locally. After being arrested for challenging segregation laws by sitting in the front of a bus, Faulkner and his friends formed the East

Gadsden Brotherhood, a nonviolent civil rights organization. They built a grassroots movement of sit-ins, demonstrations, and mass meetings. They were arrested repeatedly.

By late spring of 1963, the situation in Gadsden had intensified. Everyone knew about the events in Birmingham, the police dogs and the fire hoses and the jailing of hundreds of schoolchildren. James Hood, a Gadsden student who attended the city's Carver High School, had been accepted to the University of Alabama, but no one knew yet what would happen when he got there. When William Moore, a white postal worker on a one-man antidiscrimination march, was murdered on Highway 11 between Gadsden and Attalla, it seemed like the right time to increase the pressure on the Gadsden power structure.

On June 11, in a major civil rights address, President Kennedy informed the nation that he had called in the Alabama National Guard to keep order in Tuscaloosa while the first black students, including Hood, enrolled at the University of Alabama (see chapter 5). Kennedy directed Congress to draft civil rights legislation, and the East Gadsden Brotherhood launched a boycott of white merchants downtown. Field secretaries from SNCC, CORE, and the SCLC arrived to support the local movement.

As CORE field representative Douthard remembers, "From June 11 to August 5, we demonstrated almost daily in an effort to bring the town to recognize the justice in our demands. . . . What we didn't expect was the continuous beatings."

On June 21, Martin Luther King Jr. came to Gadsden to address a mass meeting at the Galilee Baptist Church. "I hear they are beating you. I hear they are cursing you," he told the eager crowd. "Some of you have knives and I ask you to put them up. Some of you may have arms, and I ask you to put them up. Get the weapon of nonviolence, the breastplate of righteousness, the armor of truth, and just keep marching."

Efforts to negotiate with the town failed, and the demonstrations and rough treatment continued. A massive demonstration, the biggest yet, was organized for August 3, 1963.

On that day, the marchers were met on Forrest Avenue by a heavily armed phalanx of state troopers, local police, and a "ragtag posse" composed of every hothead they could find to deputize for the occasion. The marchers did not back down, but they were immediately arrested, beaten, and cattle-prodded into jail until the cells were filled beyond capacity, with women in the city jail and men in the county lockup. Eventually, the overflow of prisoners was forced to line up on the street two by two.

Joseph Faulkner later described Al Lingo directing the action with a bullhorn, his belly hanging over his belt. When Lingo bellowed, "Move 'em out!" one witness wrote that "it was like some TV cowboy on a cattle drive. With clubs swinging and cattle prods burning, the prisoners [were] herded down the street to the Gadsden Coliseum almost two miles away." Remarkably, the marchers stuck to their nonviolent discipline and did not fight back.

At the coliseum, the marchers were forced to lie on the ground. As protester J. D. Cammeron remembered, "Those they thought were from out of town, they beat. They beat me across the legs with billy sticks and cattle-prodded me all over. . . . It made you feel like you were nobody, like you had no rights whatsoever." When he tried to tell them he had lived in Gadsden his whole life, they didn't believe him.

As if to reinforce that they did not consider their prisoners fully human, the police then herded and prodded them onto a fleet of 18-wheel cattle trucks and drove them out of town to a Ku Klux Klan rally where a large cross burned in the night. Almost unbelievably, no one was taken off the truck and physically attacked. They were then taken to an old prison camp where they spent six days crammed into cells with cement floors, inedible food, and no medical treatment for their wounds.

Exhausted and crushed, Gadsden's civil rights protestors backed off for a while, spending the next months in litigation since their arrests had been unconstitutional. While many felt that the Gadsden movement had been a failure, Martin Luther King disagreed. To him, the summer of 1963 "was historic . . . because it witnessed the first offensive in history, launched by Negroes, against a broad front." As a part of this broader effort, Gadsden helped dramatize for a national audience the challenges of the southern freedom struggle.

After all the brutality the people had endured, it is ironic that the most significant civil rights victory to come out of Gadsden turned, as Alabama attorney general Richmond Flowers observed, on a simple point of etiquette. Mary Hamilton, the only female CORE field secretary working in the South, told a prosecutor who had called her by her first name in court, "My name is Miss Hamilton. Please address me correctly." She was jailed for contempt of court, intimidated daily, and told that the abuse would stop if she agreed to answer questions without being addressed as "Miss."

NAACP lawyers appealed, arguing that to omit courtesy titles when addressing nonwhite witnesses violated the equal protection clause of the Fourteenth Amendment. The Alabama Supreme Court upheld her conviction, but in 1964, the U.S. Supreme Court agreed with Mary Hamilton. Their decision in the "Miss Mary Case" established the precedent that all people brought to the bar of justice must be addressed equally with titles of courtesy, regardless of race or ethnicity.

What to See

Galilee Baptist Church, where Martin Luther King Jr. preached, now abandoned, is tucked between two hills below the Forrest Cemetery and behind the new Galilee Baptist Church on Sixteenth Street. Several blocks away, the Etowah County Courthouse and jail are in the 800 block of Forrest Avenue. The buildings have been replaced, but you can see the civil rights–era courthouse in police surveillance photographs available digitally in the Jack Rabin Collection on Alabama Civil Rights and

Southern Activists, an online archives maintained by Pennsylvania State University Libraries. The collection can be viewed at www.libraries.psu.edu/digital/rabin/about.html; click "photos" next to "Demonstrations, sit-ins, surveillance, and arrests."

Talladega College and the *Amistad* Murals

The Site

On a plateau in the hills just south of Anniston, Talladega College is nestled comfortably in a grove of oak trees. The oldest black college in the state, it was founded in 1867 by former slaves Thomas Tarrant and William Savery. Among the school's most striking possessions is a panel of brightly painted murals depicting the *Amistad* rebellion of 1839—an event that led to the nation's first major civil rights lawsuit and, indirectly, to the founding of Talladega College.

Savery Library, Talladega College, Talladega. Photograph courtesy of Susan Finch.

THE MESSAGE OF JERRY "BOOGIE" MCCAIN

Born in Gadsden June 19, 1930, musician Jerry "Boogie" McCain is a lifelong African American resident who understands his town's racial history. As one of the most influential harmonica players in the world, and a prolific songwriter, McCain has won numerous awards including an Alabama Folk Heritage Award in 2007. His songs are admired for their humorous social commentary as well as their innovative harmonica leads.

Now in his eighth decade, McCain has pondered the black history of Gadsden, and he has a deep respect for the people he knows who were in the movement. He bought the book *Without Sanctuary: Lynching Photography in America* for its photographs of the lynching of Bunk Richardson, which took place in Gadsden in 1906. He can point out the trestle where that lynching occurred.

McCain's lyrics sound a warning inspired by growing up black in Gadsden:

> They're gonna have five Rottweilers
> A laser gun and an Uzi on the side
> You know what they say about the long arm of the law
> You can run but you can't hide.

Jerry "Boogie" McCain's home at 807 Henry Street is a museum-like folk art environment, embellished on the front with a glittery 3-D harmonica and collaged inside with ephemera from his career spanning more than half a century. He has welcomed visitors from all over the world. The old train trestle bridge, where Richardson was lynched in 1906, crosses the Coosa River between the two modern bridges in downtown Gadsden.

The Story

The murals are startling in their beauty, six panels of color from the brush of Hale Woodruff. They were installed in 1939, a hundred years after the *Amistad* rebellion, a once-obscure civil rights struggle brought to the nation's attention in a movie by director Steven Spielberg.

The story is this: In the summer of 1839, a cargo of slaves aboard the Spanish schooner *Amistad* broke free from their chains and commandeered the vessel. They spared the lives of two crew members and ordered the survivors to sail the *Amistad* back to Africa. At night, however, while the Africans slept, the crewmen sailed for North America, and on August 26, 1839, the ship and its passengers were taken into custody by the U.S. Navy.

The Spanish crew members told a story of mutiny and murder, and the Africans were jailed and put on trial in Connecticut. They were acquitted on the grounds that the *Amistad* mutiny had occurred on the open seas, not in U.S. waters, and thus the courts had no jurisdiction. But Spain had demanded the return of the *Amistad* and its cargo, including the Africans, and for reasons of diplomacy, President Martin Van Buren was eager to comply.

It was then that abolitionist leaders came to the *Amistad* Africans' defense and sought their freedom through the federal courts, eventually securing a Supreme Court ruling that the Africans deserved to be free. The case had a powerful impact at the time. For one thing, the Africans became celebrities of sorts, making a powerful impression on the people of Connecticut. Their leader Cinque was a charismatic man whose presence on the witness stand was commanding, and one of his lawyers was John Quincy Adams, a former president who brought eloquence and credibility to the proceedings when the U.S. Supreme Court heard the Africans' petition.

In the end, the case helped energize the abolitionist movement, and led to the founding of the American Missionary Association, a Christian organization that supported freedom and equality for blacks. In 1867, the AMA put up money in support of Talladega College and sent teachers to the South to work with newly freed slaves.

All of this is recorded in the Hale Woodruff murals, painted in 1939 for the hundredth anniversary of the *Amistad* rebellion—and for the opening of a new library at the college. Woodruff was the perfect choice for the project. He was a Harlem Renaissance artist, the chairman of the art department at Atlanta University, and a man with a powerful sense of black history.

He understood the story of Talladega College—how it grew out of the dream of two former slaves, William Savery and Thomas Tarrant, who, on November 20, 1865, attended a conference of freedmen in Mobile. The fifty-six former slaves who gathered that day looked to the future with a feeling of responsibility and hope. "We regard the education of our children and youth as vital to the preservation of our liberties," they resolved, "and true religion as the foundation of all real virtue, and shall use our utmost endeavors to promote these blessings in our common country."

Savery and Tarrant came back to Talladega inspired by those collective ideals. A few years earlier, when they were still slaves, the two of them had helped build a Baptist school for white students, and in 1867 they learned the same building was up for sale. They contacted General Wager Swayne, assistant commissioner of the Freedmen's Bureau in Alabama, who in turn persuaded the American Missionary Association to put up half the purchase money. The Freedmen's Bureau put up the rest, and Talladega College was born.

In later years, students would come to revere that history and the legacy of pride and ambition it contained. Lewis Baldwin, an Alabama native and Talladega graduate in the 1960s, who would go on to become a full professor at Vanderbilt University and a biographer of Dr. Martin Luther King Jr., remembered the feeling of purpose when he arrived on campus.

He saw the *Amistad* murals and learned the story behind them during orientation, and it blended easily with the civil rights dramas that were taking shape around him.

"My first semester at Talladega," he said, "I took black history under Dr. Harold Franklin, and he was a major source of inspiration. He was tall and impressive, a dark-skinned man about six-foot-one and a very serious teacher in class. On the first day, he scared the devil out of all of us. But I began to think about what I was learning, and to put it into the context of my own life."

Baldwin was proud of the fact that the school had produced not only educators like himself but also committed activists in the civil rights movement. Perhaps the most prominent of those was Arthur Shores, class of 1927, who was described as "a man among men" by his fellow students, "a fighter, ambitious and verbose." Shores lived up to that advance billing, becoming a civil rights lawyer in Birmingham, fearless in the face of threats on his life and the bombing of his home by the Ku Klux Klan.

Swayne Hall, Talladega College. Photograph courtesy of Susan Finch.

Stained glass windows by David Driskell, in DeForest Chapel, Talladega College. Photograph courtesy of Susan Finch.

Today at Talladega, there is a dormitory named in Shores's honor, one of many buildings on campus that embody their own connection to black history.

What to See

The Savery Library, which contains the *Amistad* murals and is named for William Savery, a founder of the college, stands across the campus green from Swayne Hall, the original building purchased in 1867. The library was completed in 1939 by an interracial work crew, consisting in part of Talladega students. Swayne Hall, with its picturesque columns and antebellum bricks, was named for General Wager Swayne, the federal official who helped lead the Freedmen's Bureau in Alabama and secured initial funding for the college.

The Arthur Shores dormitory, a newer structure less remarkable in appearance than other campus buildings, is located in an open area behind DeForest Chapel, another of Talladega's most treasured sites. Among other things, the chapel contains seventeen stained glass windows by the African American artist and art historian David Driskell, who served on the Talladega faculty during the 1950s.

Huntsville: A History in Pieces

The Site

Huntsville, a progressive community in northern Alabama, is a place where much of the civil rights history has been paved over, as the city has rebuilt its downtown area over the past forty years. There are some scattered historical markers, preserving pieces of the story here and there. (One marker, for example, makes note of the fact that a parking garage has been built on the site of a slave cemetery.) But the force of Huntsville's important contributions to civil rights and black history can be felt more keenly in certain parts of the city, particularly on the campuses of Alabama A&M and Oakwood College, and to a lesser extent, the University of Alabama at Huntsville.

The Story

Back in 1962, Hank Thomas, a former freedom rider then working for CORE, came to Huntsville to try to stir the local black community to action. By all accounts, Thomas was a remarkable young man. The previous year, when he took his place on the freedom rides, he was officially too young to make the trip. CORE, the sponsoring organization for the protests, required every rider to be at least twenty-one or to have parental permission for the journey.

Thomas, who was then nineteen and a student at Howard University,

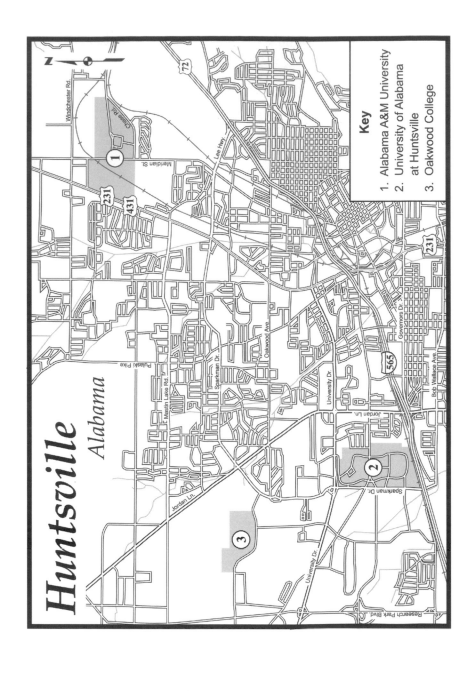

Huntsville

Alabama

Key

1. Alabama A&M University
2. University of Alabama at Huntsville
3. Oakwood College

had simply forged his mother's signature. He had been on the bus that was burned in Anniston, narrowly escaping death, and the following year he returned to Alabama and took up residence in Huntsville. He began organizing other student protesters, including people like Frances Sims, a freshman at Alabama A&M. In January 1962, Sims and a high school student named Dwight Crawford were the first to be arrested in what became a series of Huntsville sit-ins.

As the demonstrations continued through the winter and spring, students from Alabama A&M played a leading role. That was fitting, for this historically black university in northeast Huntsville had long been synonymous with racial progress. It was founded in 1875 by William Hooper Councill, one of the iconic figures in Alabama education, and in the 1960s many A&M students felt powerfully drawn to the cause of civil rights.

They soon found support among more established black leaders, people like John Cashin, a prominent dentist, and his young wife, Joan, who had embraced the philosophy of nonviolence as simply an extension of her own Christian values. The Cashins were friendly with Joseph Lowery, a Huntsville native and African American minister who had become a confidante of Dr. Martin Luther King Jr. On March 19, 1962, with Lowery's encouragement and support, King came to Huntsville and spoke to a crowd of three thousand people at Oakwood College (now Oakwood University).

He predicted "a victory for justice, a victory for freedom," and more than a year before the famous March on Washington, he ended his speech with words that were soon to become immortal: "Free at last, free at last. Thank God Almighty, we're free at last!"

At the time that all of this was happening, Huntsville was home to Redstone Arsenal, a critical ingredient in the space program for a country embarked on a race to the moon. With Redstone as its anchor, Huntsville was clearly a city on the rise, a community of nearly eighty thousand people whose white leaders were proud of its progressive reputation. By the summer of 1962, they had begun to negotiate with the civil rights movement, agreeing to integrate local restaurants and to establish a commission of whites and blacks to consider the other issues that remained.

The next item on the agenda proved to be education. In June 1963, Dave McGlathery, a Huntsville resident and graduate of Alabama A&M, applied to take additional courses at the University of Alabama at Huntsville. On June 12, the day after Governor George Wallace's stand in the schoolhouse door in Tuscaloosa (see chapter 5), McGlathery was admitted without incident to the Huntsville campus.

Another breakthrough came in September. Sonnie Hereford III, a Huntsville physician and a movement stalwart almost from the start, took his young son by the hand and, under federal court order, enrolled him in Fifth Avenue Elementary School, which had been all white. The date was September 9, and Sonnie Hereford IV and three other students—David Osman, Veronica Pearson, and John Anthony Brewton—became the first in Alabama to break the color barrier in the state's public schools.

But perhaps Huntsville's greatest contribution to the movement came in the form of a political party, an integrated group established through the work of Dr. John Cashin. Called the National Democratic Party of Alabama, and chartered in 1968, the purpose of the NDPA was to enfranchise the black and the poor, particularly in the rural parts of Alabama. The fiery Cashin, a successful dentist, financed much of the effort himself, backed by the work of two civil rights lawyers, Charles Morgan and Orzell Billingsley, the former, white, the latter, black.

It took a U.S. Supreme Court ruling to get NDPA candidates on the ballot in 1968, but in the Alabama Black Belt, seventeen of the party's candidates won local elections—five in Marengo County alone—and in Greene County, where candidates were excluded in defiance of the Supreme Court ruling, the NDPA forced a new election in 1969. With that vote, blacks effectively seized control of the county.

By 1970, thanks to a political party created in Huntsville, the State of Alabama suddenly led the nation in the number of blacks who held public office.

What to See

The offices of the NDPA were located in the Grove, an African American neighborhood in Huntsville that has mostly been destroyed by urban renewal. Alabama A&M, whose students were especially active in the Huntsville sit-ins, is located in the northeast part of the city at 4900 Meridian Street. A Branko Medenica statue honoring the university's founder, William Hooper Councill, a former slave, stands in front of the Meridian Street entrance. The University of Alabama at Huntsville, located not far from Redstone Arsenal, takes little note of its role in the desegregation of the state university system. But its first African American student, Dave McGlathery, registered for classes at Morton Hall, which still stands and is the oldest building on campus. Fifth Avenue Elementary School, the first public school in Alabama to desegregate, no longer exists.

Elsewhere in Huntsville, there are markers offering at least a passing tribute to the legacy of civil rights and black history. At 226 Church Street, a marker stands at the site of the boyhood home of Joseph Lowery, friend and ally of Dr. Martin Luther King Jr., who would later become president of King's organization, the Southern Christian Leadership Conference. In January 2009, Lowery gave the benediction at the inauguration of Barack Obama, the nation's first African American president. A half block away from Lowery's house, an empty and unmarked parking lot is all that is left of the old First Baptist Church, site of the first mass meetings in Huntsville.

At the parking deck of the Huntsville Hospital, next to the entrance on Gallatin Street, another marker notes that the deck was once the site of a slave cemetery, dating back to 1818. On the same site in 1820, the first African American congregation in the state established the Huntsville African Baptist Church. The first pastor was William Harris, a slave. In 1872, the congregation moved four blocks north to what is now Williams Street and named the new building Saint Bartley Primitive Baptist Church in honor of the church's revered second pastor, Bartley Harris. A marker at the Williams Street site recounts this story.

Another obscure piece of Huntsville's racial history was recorded in the book *The Agitator's Daughter* written by Sheryll Cashin, a professor of law at Georgetown University and daughter of John Cashin. Soon after the Huntsville movement gained momentum in 1962, the White Citizens Council, an organization formed to resist integration, held a rally in Big Spring Park, an idyllic commons area in the heart of downtown Huntsville. Since the park was a public space, Cashin led an integrated group to the meeting, and much to the consternation of the white supremacist speakers, the blacks stood and offered mock ovations as the segregationists made their points.

DRED SCOTT, LITTLE RICHARD, AND OAKWOOD UNIVERSITY

If much of Huntsville's history has been paved over, Oakwood University is a place where it lives. The historically black Seventh-day Adventist college in northwest Huntsville, where Martin Luther King Jr. delivered an important civil rights speech in 1962, was founded in 1896. It stands on the site of the Peter Blow plantation where, in 1819, Dred Scott was a slave. Scott later filed suit to gain his own freedom in a landmark case decided by the U.S. Supreme Court.

Scott maintained that because he and the members of his family had moved with a new master to the free state of Illinois, they should no longer be considered slaves. In 1857, the court disagreed in a decision written by Chief Justice Roger B. Taney and supported by Associate Justice John Archibald Campbell, a Mobilian at the time of his appointment to the court. The justices ordered Scott returned to his owners, who in turn gave him back to his earlier owner Peter Blow. Ironically, Blow almost immediately granted Scott his long-sought freedom. Scott died the following year in Missouri and is buried in Saint Louis. But his first wife and two children are buried in a slave cemetery at Oakwood.

Dred Scott, wood engraving in *Century Magazine,* **1887.** Photograph courtesy of the Library of Congress, Prints and Photographs Division [LC-USZ62-5092].

Also, at Oakwood there is a slave block near the center of the campus where human beings were bought and sold. A marker at the site reads as follows: "The Oakwood legacy is the transformation from selling slaves to the preparation of people of color for Education, Excellence, Eternity." Nearby on the oak- and magnolia-shaded grounds, stand Moran Hall, named for the first black president of the school, J. L. Moran, and East Hall, a wooden Creole cottage built in 1909. East Hall, which served as home for the university's presidents, is the oldest building on campus.

At Ashby Auditorium, a marker tells the story of Dr. King's historic visit in 1962, noting that "because of conditions existing at the time," the auditorium was the only meeting place in Huntsville that was both available to blacks and large enough to host the event. Throughout Oakwood's history, the school has offered its students a mixture of liberal arts education and religious instruction. One of its most famous students was rock-and-roll legend Richard Wayne Penniman, better known as Little Richard, who was at Oakwood when he was studying to become a musical evangelist.

Visitors to the Oakwood campus will find guards at the main entrance are quite knowledgeable about the university's history.

Slave cemetery at Oakwood University, Huntsville, on the site of a former plantation where Dred Scott lived. Photograph courtesy of Ellen Brady DeNeefe.

MOBILE
City of Progress, City of Backlash

The civil rights movement came early to Mobile, beginning sometime in the 1920s. For more than forty years, the primary leader was John LeFlore, a postal carrier and member of the NAACP who waged his personal, indefatigable campaigns against lynching, disenfranchisement, and racial segregation. He was joined over the years by other strong leaders, including Joseph Lowery, one of the founders and later president of the SCLC, and R. W. Gilliard, an African American dentist who worked through the NAACP.

By the 1940s, LeFlore had also found some white allies, most notably Joseph Langan, a Catholic layman who had fought alongside African

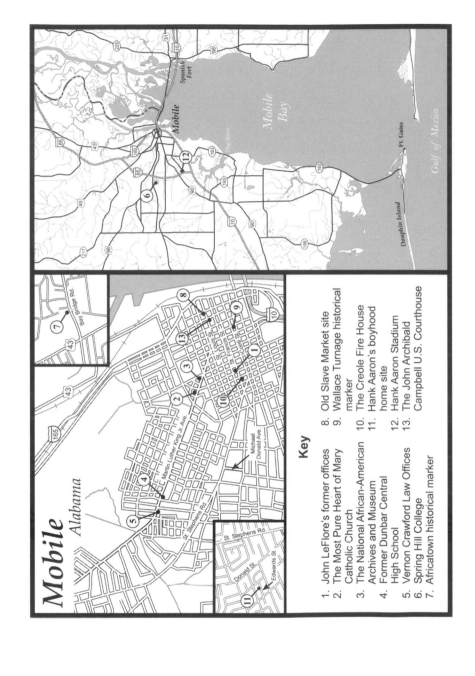

Mobile
Alabama

Key

1. John LeFlore's former offices
2. The Most Pure Heart of Mary Catholic Church
3. The National African-American Archives and Museum
4. Former Dunbar Central High School
5. Vernon Crawford Law Offices
6. Spring Hill College
7. Africatown historical marker
8. Old Slave Market site
9. Wallace Turnage historical marker
10. The Creole Fire House
11. Hank Aaron's boyhood home site
12. Hank Aaron Stadium
13. The John Archibald Campbell U.S. Courthouse

American soldiers during World War II and watched them risk their lives for their country. As a state legislator after the war, Langan worked for equal pay for black teachers and equal access to the ballot for black voters. And as a member of Mobile's city commission, he helped negotiate the desegregation of city buses, the police department, and the public library.

But by the late 1960s, Langan and LeFlore were pushed aside by a new generation of more militant blacks, who in turn confronted a powerful wave of white supremacist backlash. Mobile's racial climate had darkened to such a point in the early 1980s that a black man was lynched by the Ku Klux Klan. Strong leaders emerged in the years after that, determined to restore Mobile's standing as a place of racial progress and fairness.

And there are other ingredients in the Mobile story—the journey, for example, of native son Hank Aaron who encountered threats and racial epithets during his pursuit of Babe Ruth's home run record but managed it all with dignity and grace—completing, in a sense, the journey that the great Jackie Robinson had started.

John LeFlore, Joseph Langan, and NOW

The Site

On the corner of Saint Francis and North Warren Streets, a marker erected on the Mobile African American Heritage Trail stands in front of the building that once housed the offices of the Non-Partisan Voters League, arguably Mobile's most important civil rights organization. Headed by the late John LeFlore, the organization succeeded the NAACP, which was banned in Alabama in the 1950s. The new group continued the dogged efforts of LeFlore, a Mobile postal worker, to secure for himself and his fellow black citizens the rights that every American deserved.

John LeFlore.
Photograph courtesy
of University of South
Alabama Archives.

The Story

It began sometime in the 1920s with a streetcar scuffle involving John LeFlore. Still a teenager at the time, LeFlore took offense when a white man demanded his seat on the trolley. If it had been a white woman or an elderly person of either race, LeFlore would probably have responded differently. But this was an able-bodied man, rude and overbearing, and for LeFlore the offense was simply too much.

When they began to argue and then to scuffle, the police were called and LeFlore was arrested and taken off to jail. The white man was allowed to go free. The patent unfairness of the whole event prompted LeFlore to proclaim to the members of his family that somebody had to overturn segregation and he intended to be the one to do it. "You're talking crazy," his mother said, but a few years later, in 1925, LeFlore organized a chapter of the NAACP. For the next fifty years, he worked every day for the cause of civil rights. He documented lynchings, protested the mistreatment of blacks on buses, and most importantly, battled for greater access to the ballot.

In 1944, after the U.S. Supreme Court ruled that all-white Democratic primaries were illegal in Texas, LeFlore set out to force the issue in Alabama. On May 3, 1944, he organized a group of twelve African Americans who attempted to vote in the Alabama primary. They were turned away from the polls, but after LeFlore secured promises of support from the U.S. Justice Department, the Alabama Democratic Party agreed to allow black primary voting.

There was an immediate backlash, however. A Mobile attorney named Gessner McCorvey, chairman of the state Democratic Executive Committee, urged the Alabama legislature to pass an amendment to the state constitution. Under McCorvey's proposal, known as the Boswell Amendment after its legislative sponsor, registrars could require prospective voters—especially blacks—to interpret the Constitution to the admittedly subjective satisfaction of the registrar. As McCorvey freely admitted, his goal was to limit the number of black voters.

In the legislature, the chief opponent of the Boswell Amendment was another Mobilian named Joseph Langan, who would soon emerge as a staunch ally for the cause of civil rights. Langan, a Roman Catholic, believed that "we are all creatures of God"—a conviction that grew even stronger during World War II. In the Pacific theater, he saw black soldiers fighting for a freedom they didn't fully enjoy, and when he came home to Mobile he was appalled anew by the casual cruelties of segregation.

Once, not long after the war, he boarded a Mobile bus and was shocked as the driver stopped only at corners where the passengers were white. That same afternoon, he wrote a letter to the bus company's executives wondering whether he had "come home to Germany instead of Mobile."

As a state senator at the time of the Boswell Amendment, Langan

Joseph Langan. Photograph courtesy of *Azalea City News* Collection, University of South Alabama Archives.

spoke unsuccessfully against its passage. But he persuaded Alabama governor Jim Folsom to appoint one of his allies, E. J. Gonzalez, to serve on the Mobile County Board of Registrars. When African Americans went to federal court to challenge the amendment, Gonzalez, who would soon become known for his bravery and candor, testified on their behalf. He acknowledged in public what everybody knew—that the amendment was, as its proponents had already admitted in private, part of "the fight for white supremacy in our state."

The courts declared the Boswell Amendment unconstitutional, and as the 1940s drew to a close, black voters in Mobile began to register in record numbers. For the next fifteen years, prodded by Langan and LeFlore, the city became known for its racial moderation. Quietly and steadily, it began to address the most obvious forms of segregation—the buses, the library, the local police. But over time, there were African Americans who became disillusioned, who believed that LeFlore, despite his dedication to the cause, had impeded the growth of a grassroots movement.

LeFlore believed in negotiation, rather than in marches and demonstrations, and in many ways progress was slow. There were, for example, hardly any black clerks in downtown stores or black tellers in banks, and hiring discrimination was the norm. More dramatically, there were neighborhoods that remained so poor that children had to scavenge through garbage for food. Frustrated by that reality, a new organization emerged in the 1960s, a group called the Neighborhood Organized Workers, or NOW.

Some of its leaders were black businessmen like James Finley, co-founder of a chain of pharmacies. But by the late 1960s, the most visible spokesman for NOW was Noble Beasley, a man whom the white community found frightening. Among his other pursuits, Beasley had been a night club owner well known for his toughness. He was also a massive, six-foot bear of a man, so physically imposing at nearly three hundred pounds that there were those who simply withered in his presence. And though he and his organization denied it, there were rumors that Beasley was violent—that he and his most militant supporters were behind a rash of fire bombings, many of them aimed at white-owned stores.

Much more certainly, as the anger of the sixties grew more intense, NOW rode the growing wave of militancy to a new popularity in the black community. Meeting regularly at the Most Pure Heart of Mary Catholic Church, the group developed a grassroots following. But if its leaders were sometimes militant and shrill, many of them raising the cry of "black power," NOW had its share of white followers as well— particularly a group of priests and nuns who sought to reach out across racial lines.

But Mobile was a city now deeply divided. On June 28, 1967, John

LeFlore's house was bombed, shortly after LeFlore had gone to bed. He had been working as usual in his dining room, pecking away on his old manual typewriter and finishing his work sometime around one. The bomb exploded at the window near his chair, and there were reports of a black man running from the scene. LeFlore and Teah, his wife, both escaped serious injury, but the side of the house was reduced to rubble, and speculation spread throughout the city that LeFlore's opponents in the black community had attempted to kill him. Perhaps they hadn't. Perhaps the dynamite had been planted by members of the Klan, who were also active in Mobile.

Whatever the case, tension in the city continued to grow and in the elections of 1969 the divisions cut in multiple directions. With Joe Langan, now a city commissioner, running for reelection with the support of LeFlore, NOW urged blacks to stay away from the polls. Langan's opponent was a white supremacist who ran an openly racist campaign. But Noble Beasley and his followers at NOW wanted to send a message, wanted to say to Langan and LeFlore that they had done too little and done it too slowly. They wanted Langan to go down in defeat, even at the price of electing a racist.

With the unexpected help of Hurricane Camille, the strategy worked. The storm hit the Gulf Coast two days before the Mobile election and almost certainly helped keep voter turnout low. With the NOW boycott, that was especially true in the black community, and Langan was defeated. He never managed to resurrect his political career.

LeFlore, meanwhile, remained an important force in the city. In 1975, he ran successfully for the Alabama House of Representatives but died of a heart attack in January 1976. In the years that followed, there were those who continued to debate his legacy. But even his opponents most often acknowledged that LeFlore and his ally Joseph Langan were patient, courageous champions of progress.

What to See

The Mobile African American Heritage Trail has a marker at 58 Saint Francis Street where LeFlore's offices were located. There is also a marker in front of the Most Pure Heart of Mary Catholic Church where NOW held its rallies in the 1960s. The church, established in 1899 by Mobile's Creole community, whose ancestors were free people of color, is located at 304 Sengstak Street, on the corner of Martin Luther King Jr. Avenue and Sengstak.

There are some forty sites on the African American Heritage Trail, many of them lining Martin Luther King Jr. Avenue. Once known as Davis Avenue (named for Jefferson Davis, president of the Confederacy), the area has long been the heart of Mobile's African American community. At the corner of King Avenue and Congress Street, the National

The Most Pure Heart of Mary Catholic Church, at the corner of Martin Luther King Jr. Avenue and Sengstak Street. Photograph courtesy of Danny Robertson.

African-American Archives and Museum is located in a building that dates to 1931 and was once the only library in Mobile for black citizens. At a vacant lot next door to the archives, a marker denotes the former location of Finley's Drug Store number 3, whose owner, James Finley, was a vice president of NOW.

And finally, at the corner of Martin Luther King Jr. Avenue and Rylands Street, the former Central High School, one of the most cherished institutions in the black community, is now a part of Bishop State Community College. Among the luminaries who attended the high school were baseball star Hank Aaron (though he was expelled for cutting classes); Vivian Malone, who would become the first black graduate of the University of Alabama (see chapter 5); and Sam Jones, Mobile's first African American mayor.

The National African-American Archives and Museum, at the corner of the Martin Luther King Jr. Avenue and Congress Street. Photograph courtesy of Danny Robertson.

Spring Hill College: The First to Integrate

The Site

Spring Hill College, a Jesuit school in Mobile, was the first in the state to desegregate. It began the process in 1947, and graduated its first black student in the spring of 1956, at a time of rioting at the University of Alabama. The only violence at Spring Hill came a few months later when a group of white students chased a band of Ku Klux Klansmen from the campus.

The Story

On an oak-shaded lane at Spring Hill College, Fannie Ernestine Motley took her place with the others. Quietly, without any fanfare on this late spring day, she became the first African American to graduate from a previously all-white Alabama college.

It was May 29, 1956, but the story began nearly eight years earlier. Father Patrick Donnelly, a Jesuit priest and president of Spring Hill, was growing impatient with the laws of segregation—the pattern of injustice that he saw all around him. Everywhere he turned, he heard white leaders making their excuses or at the very least maintaining their silence, and he thought Spring Hill could be a pioneer.

It was, after all, the oldest college in the state, with a history going back to 1830 and a solid reputation for innovation and excellence. "Let Spring Hill break the silence," Donnelly proclaimed, speaking at commencement in 1948. "Let the college that was the first institution of higher learning . . . also light and lead the way to full democracy in Alabama and the Southland. Civil rights? Spring Hill is for them. For ourselves and for every other citizen, regardless of creed or color."

It was clear that Donnelly's were not empty words. The previous year, eight African American nuns had taken summer courses at Spring Hill,

Avenue of the Oaks, Spring Hill College. Photograph courtesy of Spring Hill College.

and then, in 1949, the summer sessions were opened to local black teachers seeking renewal credit for their jobs. These were small but groundbreaking steps, part of a pattern that continued through the years. In 1952, black students were admitted to the school's evening classes, and then in 1954, Spring Hill's new president, Father Andrew Smith, decided it was time to fully integrate.

In a commencement speech on May 25, he praised the Supreme Court's ruling in *Brown v. Board of Education,* handed down on May 17, declaring segregated schools to be unconstitutional. "It is clearly the duty of educators, public and private, to hail the decision of May 17, 1954," he said. "It goes without saying that this historic college, always the champion of social justice, stands ready to play its part."

What Smith didn't say was that ten days before the Supreme

Court ruling, Spring Hill had accepted a black undergraduate, Julia Ponquinette, for admission as a full-time student in the fall. When the term began, Miss Ponquinette was joined by seven other African Americans, who entered the college without any fanfare and took their places in the student body of a thousand. On September 18 the *Mobile Register* learned of their presence and asked Father Smith if such a thing could be true—if the barriers in higher education had fallen and African Americans were now at Spring Hill. "I assume there are some in the classes," said Smith. "We have never asked if they were white or Negro."

For a time after that, the journey to racial equality was intense. In 1953, Smith had hired an outspoken priest named Albert S. Foley to teach sociology, and Foley proved to be a memorable presence. A native southerner, he had read extensively on the issue of race, and he wanted his students to understand it as well. Among other things, he urged his white male students to attend the local meetings of the White Citizens Council, and even on occasion the Ku Klux Klan, and report on what they saw for class credit.

At the Klan rallies, the students recorded license numbers of the cars in attendance, and Foley matched the numbers to vehicle registration records in order to produce a list of Klan members. On the surface, Foley seemed an unlikely candidate to play such a role. He was a balding, avuncular, middle-aged priest, with thick frame glasses and a lopsided grin. But as his students discovered, he was also fearless.

Once, in the spring of 1955, he drove a group of eight students to a sociology conference in New Orleans. Two members of the party, Cecelia Mitchell and Fannie Ernestine Motley, were African American, and they were astonished when Foley pulled into a restaurant in south Mississippi and announced to all eight members of the group: "Let's do an experiment. We'll see how it works out."

Five years before the sit-in movement would sweep through the South, Foley led them quietly into the restaurant and seated them together. When the owner objected, the priest drew himself up and declared with a passion that took the students by surprise: "You're going to serve them today. They are with me, so you're going to serve them." The owner complied, but Fannie Motley, among others, was terrified of what would happen next.

"I was just nearly frightened to death," she recalled, "in Mississippi, in 1955, and the climate like it was. When we left there, I kept looking back because I felt that between there and New Orleans, they were going to do something to us."

In fact, the rest of the trip was uneventful, just one more memory that the students carried with them. And there were others that were far less dramatic. On Homecoming Day in 1955, the college glee club, which was now integrated, sang without incident at the dedication of Walsh Hall, the newest building on campus. A few weeks later, Spring Hill played a basketball game against an integrated team from Xavier University, and the following spring an African American named Marc Chatman suited up for Spring Hill's baseball team. All these things created little stir, and indeed, the rest of the community seemed mostly oblivious until the graduation ceremony of May 29, 1956.

The event was already drawing some attention because of the dignitaries on hand. John Sparkman, one of Alabama's U.S. senators, and Mobile mayor Joseph Langan were scheduled to receive honorary degrees. But the day, in a sense, belonged to Fannie Motley, the first black graduate, who stepped from the portico of Byrne Hall and marched with her peers to the Avenue of the Oaks, the handsome, tree-shaded entrance to the college. The press was there to record the moment, and Motley's story went out across the world.

Among the people who took careful notice were the local leaders of the Ku Klux Klan. There were scattered threats and rumblings for the next several months, and the following winter a caravan of Klansmen attempted to burn a cross on the campus. The date was January 21, 1957, which happened to be during exam week at Spring Hill. Students were up late studying in Mobile Hall, one of the campus dormitories, when they heard the sound of hammering outside.

"The Klan is here!" one student shouted, and as historian Charles S. Padgett later reported: "Once alerted, students streamed from both ends of the building carrying whatever brickbats were handy and put the panicked Klansmen to flight." Adding to the humiliation of the moment, the Klan members abandoned their kerosene-soaked cross, which became a souvenir in the basement of the dorm. Later, students hanged a Klansman in effigy, draping a sheet at the entrance to the college, bearing the inscription, "KKKers are chicken."

For the African American students on campus, who were not involved in the skirmish with the Klan, such displays were encouraging. "From that point on," said former student Moody Law, "I think we felt a little safer about being at the Hill, because the student body itself reacted to these outsiders coming on the campus, telling us what we could and couldn't do."

Not that there weren't scattered moments of disappointment—a few white students who were indifferent or hostile, a handful of teachers who clearly resented the black students' presence. But Fannie Motley among many others remained deeply moved by the whole experience, regarding it, she said, as a part of God's plan. "It prepared me to know," Motley said years later, "that God has good people everywhere."

What to See

Spring Hill College sits on a hill about seven miles west of downtown Mobile. Byrne Memorial Hall, site of the first interracial graduation, is on the western edge of the campus, just south of the main entrance on Old Shell Road. In keeping with Spring Hill's understatement of its role, there are no historical markers calling attention to the integration story, but on the second floor of Byrne, there are photographs from those days.

Mobile Hall, where the Klan attempted to burn a cross, stands just behind and a little southeast of Byrne. The Avenue of the Oaks, perhaps the most beautiful spot on campus, and scene of the historic graduation march, runs past an open lawn just west of Byrne.

Africatown and the Last Slave Ship

The Site

Africatown (originally spelled Africa Town) is the official name of a small community in Plateau near Mobile founded between 1866 and 1868 by the last Africans brought into the United States as slaves. The Africatown settlement was the creation of those who were prevented by economics and practicality from returning to a homeland from which they had only been gone for five years before being given their freedom in a country in which they were neither wanted nor wanted to be. As one historian later wrote, "The creation of Africa Town was an act of self-segregation—the only way to preserve their way of life and protect their community from scorn."

The Story

In the heart of Mobile's industrial center sits the small, economically underprivileged black community of Africatown, one of many such communities in Alabama's bigger cities. Africatown, however, is unique in that it was a settlement conceived and developed not simply by former slaves in the post–Civil War era but by a group of people who grew up free, spent the Civil War in bondage, and then, as historian Sylviane Diouf has noted, "became free again."

In 1860, the last slaver transporting captives directly from Africa sailed into Mobile Bay. Though the import of slaves into the United States had been banned in 1808, there were many captains and businessmen who risked fines and imprisonment for the lure of enormous profit still to be made through human trafficking. One such businessman was Timothy Meaher, one of eight children of Irish immigrants and one of the first sons of Mobile. Meaher had originally come to Mobile from the North as a deckhand. Through hard work and ambition, Meaher eventually became a wealthy captain and ship builder, and he brought in several of his brothers to help him in his business. Having made a bet that he could thwart authorities by successfully smuggling in Africans, Meaher commissioned the *Clotilda,* hired William Foster to captain the ship, and outfitted it in preparation for an Atlantic crossing. The *Clotilda* set sail for Africa on March 4, 1860.

Across the Atlantic, unaware of how irrevocably their lives would soon change, a group of Africans, strangers to one another, lived their last weeks of freedom in the region of Dahomey (in present-day Benin). Despite the distinctiveness of their languages, religions, and cultures, the 110 men, women, and children would be unceremoniously stripped of their diversity and thrown together as human cargo to be transferred to the coast to await the *Clotilda*'s maiden voyage as a slaver.

The Africans would spend less than five years as slaves in the United States before the Union victory in the Civil War would procure for them their freedom. Having had insufficient time to assimilate with the black Americans alongside whom they had worked, the Africans' first thought was to return to Dahomey. However, the money and logistics required for such an undertaking prohibited the realization of that dream. So, through hard work and frugality, the Africans, as a community of people who had overcome their own differences to achieve solidarity by virtue of their common heritage, bought property near Three Mile Creek in Mobile. In keeping with African custom, the land was owned not by individuals but by the community, and it was then divided among the inhabitants. In this manner, the Africans clung to the traditions of their homeland while carving out a niche for themselves in their new land.

Cudjo Lewis. Photograph courtesy of the Erik Overbuy Collection, University of South Alabama Archives.

What allowed the Africans to maintain a tenuous independence in a society that wished for them to fail was their tenacity. Even as slaves, the Africans had demonstrated both the ability and willingness to use whatever means necessary to defend both their lives and their dignity. This fierce independence would serve them well after emancipation. Despite strong opposition, the Africatown settlers built their own school, staffed by a black teacher; built their own church, ministered by a black pastor; and worked together to ensure the economic and social success of all in their small community.

Cudjo Lewis, the last surviving African from the *Clotilda* voyage, died in 1935. Those who knew him said he never really abandoned his hope of going home to Africa. Despite a lifetime lived in America, Cudjo, as well as others among the original group, never quite felt at home. Perhaps the times in which they lived prevented them from ever knowing the possibilities the United States could hold for them. It would fall to their children and grandchildren to preserve the legacy of the Africans while embracing the potential of being Americans.

Although little of the original character of Africatown has been preserved, efforts have been made to do so. Ties to Benin have been strengthened, preservation committees have been formed, but few concrete successes have resulted. The National Park Service has said it cannot identify any site or building of national historical significance in the area. The community, in many ways, is floundering. Descendants of the *Clotilda* passengers have tried to preserve the heritage and dignity of their ancestors but poverty and social difficulties still beset the residents.

Is the settlement a failure because so much hardship exists, or is it a success because of the continued efforts being made despite the hardship? Africatown was an experiment (although the founders probably did not think of it that way) at re-creating a lost life in a society that specialized in assimilating black Africans geographically while marginalizing them socially. Cudjo's grief over his loss never abated, not even with time and age. But Cudjo's grandchildren and great-grandchildren, as well as the descendants of the other original settlers, would live during the heart of the civil rights movement. They would live to see a time in which black Americans could not only survive but also thrive. And most importantly, they would live and work in an era when being of Africa yet in America was something to celebrate not something to mourn.

What to See

Today, Africatown sits amid papermills and lumberyards at the foot of the Cochrane–Africatown USA Bridge. Little remains of the original site except for a chimney of one of the first homesteads, though a welcome center houses a collection of artifacts from the original settlement. A graveyard bearing tombstones from the descendants of the original settlers is intact and well-maintained. The church, though not the original building, sits on the site of the Union Baptist Church built in 1869. The address is 506 Bay Bridge Road.

Outside the church is a plaque detailing the origins of the building. In downtown Mobile, just a few miles from the Africatown settlement, a marker on the corner of Royal and Saint Louis Streets commemorates the Old Slave Market and the landing of the *Clotilda* in Mobile. (Africatown's cargo of slaves, however, was not put up for auction on the site.) Each summer, a Juneteenth Celebration Week is held in Plateau, bringing together business, health, cultural, religious, and economic representatives. Representatives from the nation of Benin also participate in the celebration that honors the history and legacy of Africatown.

Plateau Africa Town Historic Cemetery. Photograph courtesy of Danny Robertson.

WALLACE TURNAGE: "A SLAVE NO MORE"

In the last days of slavery, there was another side to the Mobile story, one rooted in the desperate desire to be free. It was the story, in part, of Wallace Turnage, a teenage runaway who made his fevered dash from slavery with the surreptitious help of the city's free blacks. Ever since colonial times, Mobile had been a haven of sorts for Africans and mulattos who were not the property of any other person. Though it was certainly true that they were not fully free, there were at the start of the Civil War some twelve hundred people in Mobile out of a total population of thirty thousand who were known officially as free people of color. Some were Creoles, or mixed blood residents, who traced their ancestry to French or Spanish control of Mobile, when they enjoyed greater rights. And though they had built their own society and carefully distinguished themselves from slaves, some stood ready to aid runaways.

It was this community to whom Wallace Turnage turned. Already a veteran of four failed escapes before he made his final try, Turnage had been sent to Mobile by his exasperated owner, a cotton planter in southwest Alabama. In the city, he became the property of Collier Harrison Minge, a Mobile merchant and nephew of former president William Henry Harrison. Initially, Turnage was treated more kindly in Mobile than he had been in the cotton fields of the state, but after a verbal altercation with his owners he decided once again that he had had enough. In August 1864, he slipped away and disappeared into the local community of free blacks. After a week, he was captured, taken to jail, whipped, and told in his misery that he had to walk home. Instead, he headed south out of town and into the swamps, infested with snakes, alligators, and Confederate patrols.

These were desperate times in Mobile. The Union Navy under Admiral David Farragut had seized control of the forts guarding Mobile Bay and effectively blockaded the port. Turnage knew that his only possibility for escape—and at this point, survival—lay in making it to the Union lines. He managed to swim across Fowl River, a broad estuary south of the city, and after hiding for a time in the marsh, he made it all the way to Cedar Point, the edge of the mainland. He could see the Union forces now, who had set up garrisons at Fort Powell and Fort Gaines on islands near the mouth of Mobile Bay. Sick and hungry, Turnage continued to hide in the swamps until one day a small and damaged boat drifted up to the shore. Using a piece of board as a paddle, Turnage set out in the flimsy craft, and as he later wrote in his own slave narrative, he was rescued at sea by a Union boat.

Taken first to Fort Powell and then to Fort Gaines, Turnage met the Union commander, General Gordon Granger, who was, as one historian later wrote, "a keen supporter of emancipation and the use of black soldiers in the Union army." Turnage apparently remained with the army until the end of the war when he became, at last, a free man. "I had made my escape with safety," he wrote, "after such a long struggle and had obtained that freedom which I desired so long."

Turnage's poetic and bloodcurdling account of his escape was carefully preserved by members of his family and eventually given to the Historical Society of Greenwich, Connecticut. In 2003, it was read by historian David Blight of Yale University and became a starting point for Blight's widely praised book *A Slave No More.*

A marker noting the location of the Minge home, where Turnage's last owners lived, has been erected in the 200 block of Conti Street beside the Saenger Theater in downtown Mobile. No one knows the exact spot where the young runaway managed to swim across Fowl River, but the scenic estuary with its borders of marsh grass looks much as it did at the time of the escape, with the exception of the houses that now line the shores. Fort Powell no longer exists, but Fort Gaines, where Turnage's safety among Union forces was assured, is a historic site on the eastern end of Dauphin Island.

Wallace Turnage. Photograph courtesy of the Historical Society of the Town of Greenwich, Connecticut.

There is also, in Mobile, an important reminder of the community of free blacks. Creole Fire House No. 1 at 13 North Dearborn Street was home to a volunteer fire company organized in 1819 and was part of the social structure of the city's proud and active Creole community.

Hank Aaron: Completing the Journey

The Site

The boyhood home of Baseball Hall of Famer Hank Aaron has been moved to the minor league field in Mobile that bears Aaron's name. As this book goes to press, the home is being converted into a museum honoring Mobile's baseball legacy. For whatever reason, the city has produced five Hall of Famers—all African Americans—and at least an equal number of All Stars, black, white, and Latino. But of all those players, none were more important than Aaron, who completed, in a sense, the journey begun by the great Jackie Robinson.

The Story

In the summer and fall of 1973, as Hank Aaron closed in on the home run record of the late Babe Ruth, hate mail poured in from many parts of the country. It had been twenty-six years since Jackie Robinson broke the color barrier in the major leagues, and African American stars were now a fixture of the game. But in the minds of some fans, Babe Ruth's record was sacrosanct, the loftiest and most iconic in the game. And Ruth, of course, was a white man.

As Aaron moved closer to the number 714, more than 60 percent of his mail was negative, and some of it contained open threats. "Martin Luther King was a troublemaker and had a short life span," one writer declared. And another wrote more ominously, "My gun is watching your every black move."

Growing up in Mobile before the civil rights movement swept through the South, Aaron had seen his share of prejudice. The son of a shipyard worker, he came of age in the working-class neighborhood of Toulminville. From the beginning he loved baseball, and he was discovered by a Negro League scout in 1951. Though he was completely lacking in polish—he batted cross-handed at the time, his left hand above his right—the scout saw promise and signed him to a contract. The following year,

Aaron left the Negro League to sign with the National League's Milwaukee Braves, and he made it to the majors in 1954.

He hit home runs at a steady pace, never flashy, never commanding the same attention as some of his more charismatic peers—Mickey Mantle, Willie Mays, even his fellow Mobilian Willie McCovey, who hit his prodigious home runs in San Francisco, battling the winds of Candlestick Park. Aaron was a quieter, more slightly built man at six feet, 190 pounds, and he seemed to play the whole game at a glide. Often, his home runs were not the towering flies of Mantle or McCovey but scorching line drives that barely made it to the seats.

But they kept on coming. By 1968, Aaron had crossed the 500 mark and five years later was closing in on Babe Ruth's record. In Atlanta, where he had played since 1966, fan attendance in 1973 was appalling. Despite Aaron's steadily approaching milestone, the opening day crowd was the smallest in the National League, and half of the first ten games drew crowds of fewer than four thousand fans. And there were also the racial slurs. In his highly readable book *Hank Aaron and the Home Run That Changed America,* Tom Stanton tells the story of a cluster of hecklers who came to the park on a late April night.

"Stationed in the outfield stands," Stanton wrote, "a few men yelled that Aaron was no Babe Ruth. . . . They insulted his family. They called him 'son of a bitch.' They called him 'nigger.' The abuse spanned innings. By the end of the game, Aaron, hitless, had taken all he could tolerate. He approached the outfield fence with fists clenched and challenged one man, threatening to kick his ass."

But such outbursts, no matter how provoked, were atypical of Aaron throughout that season. Having always idolized Jackie Robinson, he took it to heart when the great trailblazer told him, "Don't let a few crazy people bother you. Just play hard." For the rest of 1973, Aaron carried himself with the dignity and grace that had marked his career.

As he approached the final game, his home run total stood at 713, just one shy of Babe Ruth's record, and there was suddenly a different feeling in the air. On the last night of the season, more than forty thousand fans crowded into the park, and although Aaron didn't break the record—he got three singles before popping out on his final at bat—the crowd responded with a standing ovation that seemed to go on and on.

"It was the most touching thing I've ever seen in baseball," said Braves announcer Ernie Johnson. Tom Stanton summed it up this way: "If the reaction had come after a home run, it wouldn't have meant nearly as much. . . . But of course this wasn't about home runs. It was about something else . . . his remarkable consistency, his superior talent, his dignified behavior."

The following season, when Aaron broke the record, the applause continued and there were those who said that something fundamental was settled by his feat. A quarter century after Jackie Robinson's arrival, baseball's most celebrated record now belonged to an African American player. From every part of the country, fans of every color idolized the man and his achievement, and his peers respected the way he had done it—how Aaron had, as he put it himself, "played the game as it's supposed to be played."

What to See

A marker erected on the African American Heritage Trail notes the site of Aaron's boyhood home at 2010 Edwards Avenue. The house itself now stands at Hank Aaron Stadium, just east of Exit 1 on Interstate 65. As a museum, it will celebrate Mobile's remarkable baseball legacy in which four other players—Satchel Paige, Willie McCovey, Billy Williams, and Ozzie Smith—have joined Aaron in baseball's Hall of Fame. In tribute to Paige, the road leading to Hank Aaron stadium bears his name, and a marker stands at his Mobile home site. Paige, of course, remains one of the most storied players of all time—a man who, because of his color, was barred from the major leagues for most of his prime. He was forty-two years old when he finally took the field for the Cleveland Indians. It was a measure of his remarkable ability that seventeen years later—at the unheard of age of fifty-nine—Paige pitched three scoreless innings for the Kansas City Athletics.

The Last Lynching, Death to the Klan

The Site
On March 21, 1981, on a dimly lit street in Mobile, the mutilated body of Michael Donald, a young black man, was found hanging from a tree. It was a latter-day lynching committed by members of the United Klans of America, horrifying when it happened, but bringing a kind of grim justice in the end. One Klan member was executed for the crime, and in a civil suit that followed that conviction, the UKA—perhaps the most violent Klan group in the state—was driven into bankruptcy.

The Story
It was like something out of the South's bloody past, a throwback to the days in the late nineteenth and early twentieth centuries when African Americans were lynched at the rate of more than one a week. At the age of nineteen, Michael Donald didn't remember those times. He was just a young man on his way to the store, walking alone on a Mobile street, when two white men pulled up beside him. One of the men pulled out a gun and ordered Donald to get in the car.

As the gunman later testified in court, the white men were members of the Ku Klux Klan, and they had set out that night with murder on their minds. Earlier in the week, a biracial jury in Mobile had failed to convict another black man, accused of murdering a white policeman. The Klansmen were out for revenge, out to make a point, and they decided that any random black man would do.

They were members, as it happened, of one of the most lethal Klan

Michael Donald. Photograph courtesy of the Southern Poverty Law Center.

factions in the country—the United Klans of America, the same group that had beaten the freedom riders in 1961 (see chapter 7) and, two years later, had bombed a Birmingham church, killing four little girls (see chapter 2). Henry Hays and "Tiger" Knowles were too young to be a part of those earlier crimes, but they spent a lot of time at a favored Klan hangout in Mobile, where they often talked about the legacy of hate.

In a superb series in the *Mobile Register*, reporter Michael Wilson described the frequent scenes on Herndon Avenue, a dismal little street only one block long where white and black families, none of them prosperous, coexisted in an uneasy peace. On the western side of the avenue, the Klan's bombastic Mobile leader, Bennie Jack Hays, had divided several houses into apartments in which he and his followers could be found drinking, playing cards, and discussing the business of the Ku Klux Klan.

On the night of March 20, 1981, Henry Hays, the twenty-six-year-old son of Benny Jack, set out with Tiger Knowles on a mission of violence. They left Herndon Avenue and picked up a rope from another Klansman, Frank Cox. As they drove around in Hays's black Buick Wildcat, Knowles carefully braided a hangman's noose, thirteen loops that would soon be used in the murder of a black man.

Around 11:00 P.M., the two men came to Davis Avenue, the main artery through the African American part of town, where they saw Michael Donald walking by himself. Donald had spent the evening with his family, watching the NCAA basketball tournament, and he was then on his way to the corner store, on an errand for his niece. By all accounts, Donald was close to the members of his family. He lived with his mother, Beulah Mae Donald, and was good about helping with chores around the house. He loved basketball and rhythm and blues music, and he was a regular at the weekend dances up the street. But he was also a kid who stayed out of trouble. He worked in the mailroom of the *Mobile Register* and attended masonry classes at a local trade school.

"That's the kind of boy he was," said his mother.

But none of that mattered to the Ku Klux Klan. Donald was black; the streets around him were empty and dim; and Tiger Knowles—a boy about Donald's age—pointed his gun and ordered Michael to get into the car.

They drove around for a while, crossing the causeway over Mobile Bay, while Michael pleaded with the men to let him go. But as Knowles would later testify in court, he and Hays were full of bluster and rage, their hatred fueled by a feeling of power that came from the fact that they were armed.

Around midnight, they stopped in a field near the town of Spanish Fort, a darkened area with a scattering of pine trees. They pulled Donald from the car, and the frightened teenager immediately attacked, fighting for his life. "Hays got the noose, and both of us managed to get it around his neck," Knowles testified. Later, the official autopsy showed that Donald died of asphyxiation, but just to make certain the Klansmen cut his throat and stuffed him into the trunk of their car.

They drove the body to Herndon Avenue, where they showed other Klansmen what they had done; they then tied the remains of Michael Donald to a camphor tree on the east side of the street. According to Knowles, the local Klan head, Bennie Jack Hays, gazed at the body the following morning and muttered to the other Klansmen who were with him, "Isn't that a pretty sight?"

On March 21, the terrible news swept quickly through the town, and Mobilians, black and white, were horrified. Most of them were proud of the fact that their city, for the most part, had escaped major violence during the civil rights era and had certainly never seen anything like this. But despite a widespread sense of urgency, it took the police two years to solve the crime. They were diverted at first by erroneous leads—baseless rumors of a drug deal gone bad and a murder staged to look like a lynching.

Donald's family was sure it wasn't true, and they had the support of community leaders who refused to let the investigation die. Finally, FBI agent Jim Bodman, a self-styled "Mississippi redneck," started pursuing the more obvious possibility—that this was a Ku Klux Klan operation. Working closely with Assistant U.S. Attorney Thomas Figures, an African American, Bodman managed to crack the case, pressuring Tiger Knowles to testify against Henry Hays in exchange for a sentence of life imprisonment.

Hays, meanwhile, was sentenced to death, an execution carried out after multiple appeals, on June 6, 1997. But even more devastating to the Klan was a civil suit filed for Beulah Mae Donald, Michael's mother, by the Southern Poverty Law Center in Montgomery. The center's lawyers contended that the United Klans of America, whose terrorist track record twisted back a generation, should be held accountable for its members' vicious crimes. In 1987, a federal jury agreed, and awarded the Donald family $7 million, effectively driving the Klan into bankruptcy.

The Donalds collected only a fraction of that amount, a little more than fifty thousand dollars, when the Klan was forced to sell its headquarters building outside of Birmingham. Mrs. Donald used the money to buy a new house, a minor consolation for a senseless crime. But for the people of Mobile, there was cold consolation in the reality of justice, the hard sentences handed down by the courts, and the financial ruin of an organization that existed solely for the purposes of hate.

In January 2009, at the dedication of a marker honoring Michael Donald, Southern Poverty Law Center founder Morris Dees offered this summary of the Donald lawsuit: "That precedent has helped us put many other hate groups out of business. That's the legacy of Michael Donald."

What to See

Herndon Avenue, as the street was known at the time, runs north and south for one block between Spring Hill Avenue and Old Shell Road, about a mile west of downtown. There is a marker on the east side of the street at the spot where Donald's body was found, making it part of Mobile's African American Heritage Trail. The street, meanwhile, at the family's request, was renamed Michael Donald Avenue, a tribute to a decent young man whose life was ended far too soon—but whose death destroyed a deadly faction of the Klan.

Southern Justice in Mobile

The Site

On the second floor of the federal courthouse in Mobile, there is a photograph of U.S. district judge Virgil Pittman, who presided in a courtroom there from the 1960s until the 1980s. Pittman was one of the last of his kind, a liberal southern judge called upon to pass judgment on the racial and political realities of his time. One of his most important cases—in a way the capstone of his career—helped transform the politics of Mobile.

The Story

Even before the latter-day lynching of Michael Donald, Mobile had become a deeply polarized city. By the 1970s, African Americans felt more excluded from their local government than they had in the days of legal segregation. Back then at least, there was John LeFlore, the tough, intrepid civil rights leader who found allies in the white community. But in Mobile, the turbulent decade of the 1960s gave way to what seemed a new and sullen calm—a situation in which white politicians paid little attention to the black community.

Their innate indifference was made easier by the form of government Mobile had adopted—a three-member city commission elected at large. The result was that all three members of the commission were white.

In 1975, a local activist named Wiley Bolden was part of a group of African Americans who decided to file a federal lawsuit. They maintained that in their white-majority city, it was simply impossible for blacks to participate in government. As luck would have it, the lawsuit landed on the desk of Virgil Pittman, who had been appointed to the federal bench in 1966. A former special agent with the FBI, Pittman was a native Alabamian, born in the wiregrass town of Enterprise.

He was fifty years old when he ascended to the bench, and he quickly began to assume his place in what, by then, was a southern tradition. Federal judges throughout the region had long been part of the push for basic change. Going back to the 1940s, they had begun to hear cases with racial overtones—school desegregation lawsuits at first and then a broad array of other subjects. Up in Montgomery, U.S. district judge Frank Johnson, ruling on issues from voting rights to bus segregation, had become a hero to some, a pariah to others.

If Johnson was a lightning rod for controversy in the 1950s and 1960s, Virgil Pittman would soon follow in his path. In July 1976, when the Bolden case went to trial, Pittman understood that these were especially difficult times. Four months earlier a group of eight Mobile policemen, all of them white, captured a black robbery suspect by the name of Glenn Diamond. They handcuffed him, tied a hangman's noose around his neck, and looped it over the branches of a tree.

The mock lynching, condemned by the NAACP and openly defended by the Ku Klux Klan, provided a controversial backdrop for the Bolden trial and was clearly on Judge Pittman's mind when he issued his ruling on October 21. "The sad history of lynch mobs, racial discrimination and violence," he wrote, "raises specters and fears of legal and social injustice in the minds . . . of black people. . . . The court concludes that in the aggregate, the at-large election structure as it operates in the city of Mobile substantially dilutes black votes in the city."

Pittman ordered a new form of government—a mayor-council arrangement in which only the mayor would be elected at large, and nine council members would be elected from districts. Predictably, the city's white officials appealed, and as the case was making its way up the line, a group of white citizens calling themselves the Constitutional Crisis Committee took out a newspaper advertisement condemning Pittman under a headline that read: "Impeach! Appeal! Arrest!"

As the controversy swirled, the U.S. Fifth Circuit Court of Appeals upheld Pittman's ruling, but on April 22, 1980, the U.S. Supreme Court reversed it. The high court ruled that the issue was not whether African Americans were excluded from government but whether the exclusion, in fact, was deliberate. The case was returned to Pittman for further deliberation under the court's new standard. Pittman simply refused to let it go.

As new hearings began in 1981, a more ominous cloud hung over the city. There had been an actual lynching this time; a young black man, Michael Donald, had been strangled and his body mutilated by the Ku Klux Klan.

As Mobilians reeled from the horror of the crime, dramatic new evidence was introduced in the Bolden case. The plaintiffs' legal team, led by the civil rights firm of Vernon Z. Crawford, had discovered a 1909 letter in which a Mobile congressman, urging the Alabama legislature to ratify an at-large city government, had written this sentence: "We have always, as you know, falsely pretended that our main purpose was to exclude the ignorant vote, when, in fact, we were trying to exclude, not the ignorant vote, but the Negro vote."

Having been shown the smoking gun of intent, on April 15, 1982, Pittman ruled once again for the plaintiffs. There was no appeal by the city that time. Instead, negotiations began for a new local government—a mayor-council system, implemented in 1985, with a formula for district representation that virtually assured an interracial government. Twenty years later, the face of Mobile politics had changed, and the city—still with a white majority—elected its first African American mayor, Sam Jones, a navy veteran and Mobile native who had been a longtime member of the county commission.

Some local commentators have argued that it might never have happened without Judge Pittman, who represented, like many of his peers, the most progressive side of southern justice.

What to See

The John Archibald Campbell U.S. Courthouse stands on the corner of Saint Louis and Saint Joseph Streets. Pittman's former courtroom, with its wooden paneling and dark green drapes, is located on the second floor of the building. Pittman's photograph hangs outside. There is also a portrait in the downstairs lobby of the man for whom the building was named. John Archibald Campbell was a Mobile attorney appointed to the U.S. Supreme Court just before the Civil War. Living in a very different time, he wrote a concurring opinion in the court's now infamous Dred Scott decision, which was a devastating blow to the cause of abolition (see chapter 7). But Campbell himself was uneasy with the issue. He had freed his own slaves upon being appointed to serve on the court, and he believed that the institution of slavery was doomed.

The law offices of civil rights attorney Vernon Crawford, which are part of Mobile's African American Heritage Trail, are located at 1407 Martin Luther King Jr. Avenue.

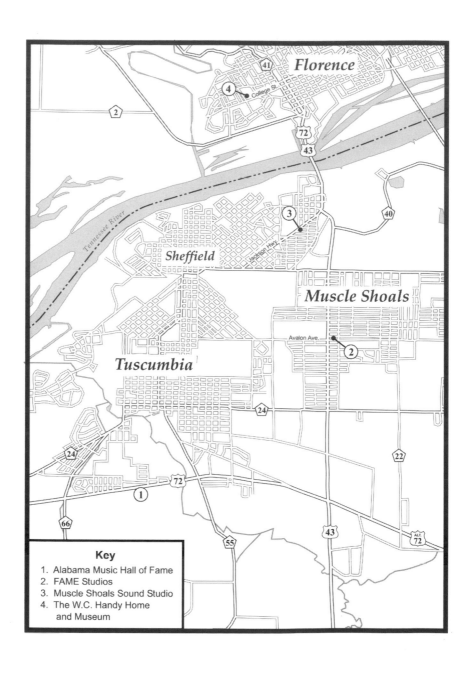

Florence

41

4 • College St.

2

72

43

Tennessee River

Sheffield

3

40

Jackson Hwy.

Muscle Shoals

Avalon Ave. •

2

Tuscumbia

24

24

22

72

1

66

43

ALT 72

55

Key
1. Alabama Music Hall of Fame
2. FAME Studios
3. Muscle Shoals Sound Studio
4. The W.C. Handy Home
    and Museum

OTHER PLACES OF INTEREST

The echoes and legacies of the civil rights movement are scattered throughout the state of Alabama. On the Gulf Coast just south of Mobile, the multicultural fishing community of Bayou La Batre consists of whites, blacks, and Asians—and a small but growing minority of Hispanics—trying to coax a living from the sea. This small village is, in a sense, a microcosm of what the South is becoming—a place of diversity where the broadest lessons of the civil rights years, consciously or unconsciously, are a cornerstone of community survival.

At the other end of the state, near the border with Tennessee, the town of Scottsboro still harbors memories of a trial in the 1930s when nine black men were falsely accused of rape. That original trial and subsequent defense of "the Scottsboro boys" became one of America's earliest civil rights struggles.

In between Bayou La Batre and Scottsboro lie a variety of sites and destinations, including the birthplaces of two sports heroes, Jesse Owens and Joe Louis, whose lives and careers dramatically refuted the notion of white supremacy. In the town of Florence, the W. C. Handy Home, Museum, and Library honors the Alabama-born father of the blues, and nearby the Alabama Music Hall of Fame pays tribute to the musical "desegregation"—black and white artists working together—that has characterized the area since the 1930s.

And finally in Ardmore, which straddles the Alabama border with Tennessee, a lonesome stretch of railroad track offers a haunting and almost forgotten reminder of a night of fear for a group of freedom riders, who were saved by the courage of two old people—anonymous heroes of the civil rights years.

Bayou La Batre: The New Old South

The Site

The fishing village of Bayou La Batre, located about thirty miles south of Mobile, was once a place where African Americans knew they would not be welcome after dark. There are still black residents who remember those days and the unease that came with the setting of the sun. But now, the Bayou, as the local people call it, is a place of diversity where whites, blacks, and Asians—and a new and growing population of Hispanics—live together in peace. Despite hard times for the local economy and the battering of killer hurricanes, Bayou La Batre has come to embody the new face of the South. It is no longer merely biracial; it is a place where multiple cultures come together, where Buddhist temples stand among the Baptist, Catholic, and Pentecostal churches—and where in a special ceremony every May, people of all races gather for the Blessing of the Fleet.

The Story

Nancy McCall remembers the stories that the old people told, how her own ancestors came to the Bayou at the depth of the Great Depression in the South. They had been sharecroppers in south Mississippi, and the life they endured in the 1930s bore an unsettling resemblance to slavery. Most of them lived in primitive cabins, provided by the owners of large plantations, and as one of their neighbors would put it later on, "a black man had no rights at all that a white man felt any need to respect."

Finally, McCall's great uncle, Crate West, decided he just couldn't take it any more. Late one night with the rising of the moon, he and his family slipped away. They knew it was dangerous, for even with slavery more than sixty years dead, white people in that part of Mississippi often restricted the movement of their workers. In making their escape, the Wests relied on a kind of latter-day Underground Railroad, hopping a freight at a place where it slowed down on its way to Mobile. They knew other families had done the same and knew also that some of those who had fled had found steady work in the towns along the coast.

Thus they came to Bayou La Batre and built a home just beyond the city limits. Their white neighbors, they discovered, had been there a while, many families tracing their roots to the founding of the village in 1786. Most of them tended to be good people, and despite the prejudice of the times and the crippling reality of the Jim Crow laws, blacks and whites found a way to coexist. By the 1950s, there were cracks in the walls of racial segregation, neighborhoods where people of both races lived, and where nobody seemed to think much about it. As some of the residents remembered, there was even an integrated baseball team.

But the greatest change in the Bayou community took shape late in the

1970s, when refugees from Southeast Asia began moving into the area in large numbers. These were survivors of war and genocide, and though their language and culture were different, their work ethic was not. They soon took their place in the seafood industry, and despite some scattered tensions early on, the Bayou became a multiracial place.

The community was tested in the next several decades, particularly in the summer of 2005, when Hurricane Katrina pushed its wall of water through the town. Some two thousand people, out of a total population of twenty-three hundred, were forced temporarily from their badly damaged homes, and some of them lost their houses altogether. The people of Bayou La Batre spent the next several weeks at a shelter, and one of the people who stepped forward to help was Regina Benjamin, an African American physician in the Bayou.

Benjamin was a native of the Alabama coast. She had grown up in Daphne, on the eastern side of Mobile Bay, and after she completed her medical training, she returned to the area and opened a clinic in Bayou La Batre. Her patients came from every part of the community, black, white, and Asian, and she developed a reputation as an old-fashioned doctor, making house calls, spending unhurried time with her patients, treating even those who had no insurance.

Her office was devastated by Katrina, but she salvaged what she could and set up shop at the community center, which doubled as a shelter. Grace Scire, one of the volunteers at the center, remembered Benjamin ordering the medicines her patients had to have but couldn't afford after losing nearly everything in the storm. Insulin, antibiotics: whatever it was, Benjamin arranged for nearby pharmacists to fill the prescriptions and then send her the bills. She said her clinic would pay them somehow.

"After the storm," Benjamin recalled, "we saw everybody for free for eight months. People didn't have their co-pays. But they needed care, and they needed their meds."

Such was the spirit of Bayou La Batre. It was a working-class town where people understood—even more clearly in the wake of Katrina—that life on the edge of the continent was hard, and if they were going to make it they had to pull together.

As Benjamin put it just after the storm, "We are all in the same state."

What to See

Dr. Benjamin's office, a symbol of unity in Bayou La Batre, is located on Tapia Street in the heart of downtown. A half block away is Saint Margaret's Catholic Church, home to the annual Blessing of the Fleet, a celebration in early May that underscores the multiracial character of the community. About three blocks east of Saint Margaret's, in an area known as Little Saigon, a Buddhist temple serves the Vietnamese population of the town. Two other temples, for the Laotian and the Cambodian populations, stand a few miles north of downtown. The Laotian Temple is

Buddhist Temple in Little Saigon, Bayou La Batre.
Photograph by Mui Lam © MOC 2007.

on the Irvington–Bayou La Batre Highway, about four miles from Saint Margaret's Church. The Cambodian Temple is the anchor for a strong Cambodian neighborhood on Angkor Road, just off of Padgett Switch Road leading out of town.

About ten miles west of Bayou La Batre, on U.S. 90 in the town of Grand Bay, a historical marker stands at the site of the Grand Bay School for Colored, one of the first schools for black children on this part of coast. Built in 1919 as a Rosenwald school, the five-room building was a symbol of progress for the African American community—and a symbol of cooperation across racial lines. The school was built on land donated by Peter S. Alba, a wealthy white resident of the Bayou area who had fought for the Confederacy during the Civil War. At the time he offered the land in Grand Bay, Alba, who had become known as a turn-of-the-century philanthropist, also donated land in Bayou La Batre for a white school.

The Grand Bay school building no longer survives, but the historical marker denoting its importance was unveiled February 27, 2007, on a knoll adjacent to the Grand Bay–St. Elmo Community Center. One of those present for the unveiling ceremony was the school's oldest living graduate, ninety-six-year-old Clinton M. Hayes.

Monroeville: The Community of Atticus Finch
—JENNIFER LINDSAY

The Site

Monroeville, the hometown of novelist Harper Lee, celebrates her masterpiece, *To Kill a Mockingbird*, whose central character Atticus Finch embodies the values of racial tolerance and justice. Outside the courthouse, a marker, erected by the Alabama Bar Association, pays tribute to the book and to the principles upheld by Atticus Finch. The courthouse was

THE EASTERN SHORE

The village of Daphne, where Regina Benjamin was raised and where she learned many of the lessons of community that she brought to her work in Bayou La Batre, has long been rich in black history. Little Bethel Baptist Church on the town's main street traces its roots to 1867 when Major Lewis Starke, a Confederate veteran, deeded two acres to four of his former slaves. These four men, Nimrod Lovett, Stamford Starlin, Narcis Elwa, and Benjamin Franklin became trustees for the small wooden church, which became both a treasured place of worship and a symbol of newfound freedom.

One of the members of the church was Russell Dick, whose mother, Lucy, came to Mobile on the slave ship *Clotilda* (see chapter 8). Dick, who soon emerged as one of Daphne's most industrious citizens, once owned all of what is now its downtown. He is buried in the cemetery behind the church.

Less than two blocks away on Main Street, at what is now Daphne Middle School, another historical marker records the story of African American education in Baldwin County. In 1874, one-teacher schools sprang up in Daphne, Montrose, and Jonesboro. In 1889 the Reverend S. B. Bracy and the Eastern Shore Missionary Baptist Association purchased a ten-acre plot, currently the site of the Daphne Middle School, and established the Eastern Shore Baptist Academy for Negroes.

In 1894, as African Americans were building churches and schools, a group of white people settled on Mobile Bay just a few miles south of Daphne and established a community they called Fairhope. They held land in common and spoke of justice and "universal equality" for all people. Throughout the early years of the twentieth century, Fairhope's leaders spoke out strongly against lynchings, the Ku Klux Klan, and the disenfranchisement of African Americans. But the new community made one significant concession to the racial reality of the times. Fairhope, still one of the most beautiful villages on Mobile Bay, was a community established for white people only. Fortunately, in more recent times, that rigid segregation has broken down.

replicated for the movie version of *To Kill a Mockingbird*—which starred Academy Award–winner Gregory Peck, who became a close friend of Harper Lee's—and is now the scene of an annual play, where members of the audience are picked to serve on the jury of Tom Robinson, a black man falsely accused of rape. (In recognition of the times depicted in the play, only white men are selected as jury members.) There is something about the legacy of Harper Lee and her characters that is palpable in this Alabama town, even to a casual observer.

The Story

When my father was eleven, he and his brother took their new air rifles out into the woods, to make mischief if none could be found. Undoubtedly distracted by his newfound sense of power, my father accidentally shot and killed a mockingbird. His father did not chastise him; there was no need. My father's remorse and sorrow sufficed. He never hunted again.

For a young boy growing up in a small southern town in the 1950s, the beauty and intrinsic value of mockingbirds were cherished. The mockingbird, and the respect it engendered, spoke of small-town values and southern kindness. History tells us, however, that Alabama in the 1950s fell far short of valuing or showing kindness to its black citizens. The struggle of Alabama's black population to achieve some measure of equality and respect was waged in towns and cities across the state. In Monroeville, the motif of the mockingbird collided with the civil rights movement in a fictional tale that helped transform a southern town and touched the nation's conscience as well.

"They're certainly entitled to think that, and they're entitled to full respect for their opinions, but before I can live with other folks, I've got to live with myself. The one thing that doesn't abide by majority rule is a person's conscience." So says Atticus Finch, the central protagonist of

Harper Lee's 1961 novel, and somewhat surprisingly, since he is a fictional character, one of the cherished sons of Monroeville.

Despite a moment of glamour in 1961 when the town was inundated by Hollywood legends and national press during the filming of *To Kill a Mockingbird,* Monroeville is a quiet community in Monroe County in southeastern Alabama. What pulls it out of its small-town obscurity is its refusal to be stereotyped as either small or southern, along with any of the negative connotations either description might convey. Monroeville prides itself on being the Literary Capital of Alabama, a moniker conferred upon it by the Alabama State Legislature in 1997. As the hometown of Harper Lee and the childhood summer residence of Truman Capote, the town's designation is not without merit. However, Monroeville's true uniqueness stems from its ability to keep intact the best traditions of its small-town heritage, while shedding the burdens of its small-minded legacy.

Prejudice runs deep in Alabama. *To Kill a Mockingbird,* set in the state in the 1930s, portrays all too realistically what can happen to questions of guilt and innocence when they are placed in a context of social mores and conventions. In a Depression-era town in which black and white were segregated not only according to law but according to the traditions of both races, bias was rife. Although great legal and political strides were made toward civil rights in the 1960s, in many parts of the South residues of old prejudice remained. Monroeville was no exception. Even in the 1970s and 1980s, color lines were visible. But by the 1990s, residents of the town began interacting with one another in a way that blurred color lines, even within church services, one of the last bastions of segregation. *To Kill a Mockingbird* and the legacy of Atticus Finch were successful in helping Monroeville's citizens progress while many other small towns remained trapped in the past.

Each spring, the people of Monroeville honor Harper Lee and civil rights with an amateur production of *To Kill a Mockingbird*. Incorporating both local citizens and visiting audience members, this tradition serves as a yearly reminder of both the town's past and its growth. Having grown up in a small Alabama town myself, I know how insulated they can be. Often the traditions that give them their identity don't allow room for outside influences. Coming into these towns, some never quite escape the feeling that they just don't belong.

Monroeville avoids this tendency toward alienation. Sitting in bleachers erected on Courthouse Square, waiting for the play to begin, I was surrounded by local citizens, but I felt completely at ease. Welcomed, I guess, in the true southern fashion. I was struck not only by the ease with which Monroeville's citizens welcomed outsiders from all over the world but also by their kindness and their pride in their town and their performance. The play is not just an annual tradition for the town, it is a part of life for the citizens. Local girls who portray Scout, the young daughter of Atticus, grow up to play Mayella Ewell, the character who accuses a black man of rape.

Monroeville's citizens have continued to embrace this novel because the message is so powerful in their lives, and they take their responsibility to that message seriously. The cast travels the world, from England to Israel, a visible contradiction to the perception of small-town Alabama as ignorant and backward, racist and uneducated.

Since the publication of *To Kill a Mockingbird*, Monroeville's citizens have kept the novel from being just another classic read in high schools. They keep the message current by their dedication to it. Not just in honor of one of their own, but in honor of the message itself. The spirit of Atticus Finch lives on in the citizens of Monroeville. Black and white side by side performing and side by side observing. For this small town, in a state that is still fighting to shed the burdens of its past, this cooperation is an enduring testament to the power of *To Kill a Mockingbird*.

Old Monroe County Courthouse, Monroeville. Photograph courtesy of Tom Mason/ Monroe County Heritage Museum.

What to See

The Old Courthouse in Courthouse Square is preserved exactly as it was portrayed in the movie. In addition to the marker in Courthouse Square commemorating Atticus Finch, there are markers noting the location of Harper Lee's and Truman Capote's former residences. The annual production of *To Kill a Mockingbird* begins in April and runs through May. Tickets sell out very quickly, so reservations should be made early. Information about the play can be found at the Monroe County Heritage Museums website, www.tokillamockingbird.com/index.htm. Reservations may only be made in person or by phone (251-575-7433).

Joe Louis and Jesse Owens: Alabama Heroes

The Site

Alabama was the birthplace of two of the greatest sports heroes of all time, Joe Louis and Jesse Owens, whose historic victories in the 1930s offered a powerful refutation of white supremacy theories. Louis was born and spent his early years in Chambers County, just outside the community of LaFayette. Owens was born in Lawrence County near the community of Oakville. Today, both LaFayette and Oakville offer prominent tributes to their famous native sons.

Statue of Jesse Owens at the Jesse Owens Memorial Park and Museum, Danville.
Photograph courtesy of Susan Finch.

The Story

Joe Louis Barrow spent his boyhood in the Alabama hills, just a few miles west of the Georgia line. The town of LaFayette was a stone's throw away, but the black community in which the Barrows lived was known as Buckalew Mountain. Then as now, it was a rustic landscape of cotton fields and brambled forests and red clay gullies slashing through the trees.

Joe, the son of sharecroppers Munroe and Lillie Barrow, lived in the area until he was ten, at which point the family moved to Detroit. In 1935, at the age of twenty-one, Joe began to earn international fame as a boxer. Fighting under the name Joe Louis, he entered the ring thirteen times that year, defeating former champions Primo Carnera and Max Baer before facing off in 1936 with the German heavyweight Max Schmeling.

Schmeling stunned the boxing world by knocking out Louis in the twelfth round. But Louis rebounded quickly, winning a title fight with heavyweight champion James J. Braddock, and in 1938 Louis and Schmeling met in a rematch. By that time, the German fighter was a national hero. Adolf Hitler and the Nazi party had hailed Schmeling's earlier victory over Louis as one more proof of "Aryan superiority," and a Nazi publicist issued a statement before the second fight. The publicist declared that a black man could never defeat Max Schmeling, and that when the German fighter won, his prize money would be used to build Hitler's tanks.

On the night of June 22, 1938, more than seventy thousand fans gathered at Yankee Stadium for a bout that lasted two minutes and four seconds. Feeling that "the whole damn country" was counting on him, Louis knocked Schmeling to the canvass three times before the German's manager threw in the towel. The party line from Adolf Hitler was that Louis had won with an illegal punch to the kidney. But in the United States and other parts of the world the Brown Bomber's victory was viewed as yet another blow to German theories of racial superiority.

Portrait of Joe Louis.
Photograph by Carl Van
Vechten, courtesy of the
Library of Congress, Prints
and Photographs Division
[LC-USZ62-42521].

Two years earlier, another African American athlete had put his own dent in Hitler's worldview. At the 1936 Olympic Games, which were held in Berlin, American runner Jesse Owens won four gold medals. Born in the farmlands of northern Alabama, Owens was the tenth child of Henry and Emma Owens, sharecroppers living close to the land. They named their youngest son James Cleveland Owens, but when they moved to Cleveland, Ohio, in 1922 one of his teachers, who didn't understand his Alabama accent, called him Jesse instead of J. C.

The name stuck, and from the age of nine that is how he was known. By the time he entered junior high school, he decided despite his awkward stride that he would go out for track. "I always loved running," he explained. "I wasn't very good at it, but I loved it, because it was something you could do all by yourself, and under your own power. You could go in any direction, as fast as you wanted, fighting the wind if you felt like it, seeking out new sights just on the strength of your feet and the courage of your lungs."

At Fairview Junior High, track coach Charles Riley helped young Jesse refine his running style, and by the time Owens entered Cleveland's East Technical High School he was well on his way to becoming a star. In June 1933, he tied a world record by running the 100-yard dash in 9.4 seconds. But according to most of the people who knew him, he never let such achievements go to his head, and his high school peers, impressed in part by his quiet humility, elected him president of the student council.

In 1936, he went to the Olympics and won gold medals in the 100-meter dash, the 200-meter, the long jump, and the 400-meter relay. An angry Adolf Hitler stalked out of the Olympic stadium without congratulating the American champion. "As politics and sports became more intertwined," wrote Owens biographer Tom Gentry, "the black sprinter's showdown with the twisted theories of Hitler stands out as an eloquent statement against bigotry."

In the coming decades, as the struggle for equality shifted back to the United States, other black athletes, understanding their debt to Owens and Louis, would carry the same torch with dignity and pride (see chapter 8).

What to See

The Jesse Owens Memorial Park and Museum is located near the site of Owens's birth outside Oakville, Alabama. To get there, take Exit 310 off I-65 and travel northwest on Alabama Highway 157. After 24.8 miles, take a right onto County Road 187 and follow the dirt road until you come to the Owens Museum. Inside are photographs, memorabilia, and videos recording the Jesse Owens story. A three-room cabin replicating Owens's birthplace is also located on the site, and a recording from Jesse's brother, Sylvester Owens, describes the early life of the family.

Jesse Owens Museum, 7019 County Road 203, Danville. Photograph courtesy of Ginger Ann Brook.

The Joe Louis story is told in part at the Chambers County Museum, which is located in the historic and refurbished train station in LaFayette, Alabama. There are various pieces of memorabilia, including furniture that Louis purchased for his mother just before the second Schmeling fight. There are newspaper clippings, including a profile in the *Detroit Free Press,* noting that Louis was the grandson of slaves. In the same room of the museum is a display about the life of U.S. Senator Thomas "Cotton Tom" Heflin, another famous resident of LaFayette, who was, as his obituary noted on April 23, 1951, "one of the fiercest champions of white supremacy." Among other things, Heflin was known for shooting a black man in 1908 while serving as a member of the U.S. House of Representatives and for telling racist jokes on the Senate floor during a twelve-year stint that ended in 1932.

Helpful volunteers at the Chambers County Museum can also provide directions to the house where Joe Louis was born. A historical marker stands in front of the white, shingle-sided dwelling, which is still occupied, on a small dirt road off Alabama Highway 50, about six miles from downtown LaFayette.

The Legacy of Alabama Music

The Site

The north Alabama towns of Florence and Muscle Shoals have long been a hotbed of music, a place where performers and producers, black and white, have crossed racial barriers in pursuit of greater creativity. Florence was the birthplace of W. C. Handy, "the father of the blues," and of Elvis Presley's first producer, Sam Phillips, who set out to blend the white and black musical traditions of the South. Along with other artists with similar roots, they helped to change the culture of the nation.

W. C. Handy, 1941.

Photograph by Carl Van Vechten, courtesy of the Library of Congress, Prints and Photographs Division [LC-USZ62-42531].

The Story

In the 1950s, when the Alabama White Citizens Councils began to rail against rock 'n' roll, calling it the "mongrelization" of music, there was a kernel of truth at the heart of their attack. As the musicians themselves understood very well, they were breaking down walls, producing a cultural form of integration. One of the people at the heart of this movement was Florence native Sam Phillips, who began his career as a DJ in the neighboring town of Muscle Shoals.

In the 1940s, Phillips, who was white, was drawn to the format of station WLAY because it played both black and white music—those great and parallel traditions in the South that, in Phillips's mind, had more in common than many people realized. On January 3, 1950, Phillips opened a recording studio at 706 Union Avenue in Memphis, and for the first several years he recorded the great black performers in the region—Howlin' Wolf, B. B. King, Rufus Thomas, and Bobby Blue Bland.

Then in 1954, a young white singer named Elvis Presley came to Phillips's Sun Records studio. In an early recording session, Presley recorded two cuts for a record that became a double-sided hit. The first of the songs was "That's All Right, Mama," written by the Mississippi blues singer Arthur "Big Boy" Crudup, and the second was "Blue Moon of Kentucky," a bluegrass waltz by Bill Monroe. From the beginning, Phillips understood that it was a powerful moment—a white singer born in rural Mississippi who brought the same kind of energy and passion to songs from either side of the racial divide.

The result of that fusion would soon become known as rock 'n' roll, and for the next several years a stream of innovative performers poured into Phillips's studio—Carl Perkins, Jerry Lee Lewis, Roy Orbison, and Johnny Cash, among many others. Throughout that time Phillips saw clearly the link between what he was doing in Memphis and the music he had grown up with in Florence. There had long been a musical tie between the cities, certainly since early in the twentieth century when Florence native W. C. Handy came to Memphis and created the heart of its Beale Street legacy.

Handy, more than Phillips, had a deep understanding of the theories of music. Indeed, in 1900 the legendary educator William Hooper Councill, president of Alabama A&M (see chapter 7), invited Handy to come to the college and chair its growing department of music. Councill believed the arts were an important part of black advancement, and he thought that in choosing a professor of music he couldn't do better than W. C. Handy.

But the two men disagreed about music. Councill was a devotee of the classics, the work of European composers whose sophistication was admired worldwide. Handy, meanwhile, was deeply influenced by his life in the South. The grandson of a runaway slave, he was born in Florence in 1873 in a two-room cabin, where he grew up as the son of a Methodist minister. He loved the music of the church, but as he wrote in his autobiography, *Father of the Blues,* he was also moved by the sounds all around him—"the music of every songbird and all the symphonies of their unpremeditated art." And most importantly, there was the music of ordinary people, particularly the African Americans of the South, who played and sang in styles that were filled with subtlety and passion.

"The primitive southern Negro, as he sang," wrote Handy, "was sure to bear down on the third and seventh tone of the scale, slurring between major and minor. Whether in the cotton field of the Delta or on the Levee up St. Louis way, it was always the same. . . . I tried to convey this effect . . . by introducing flat thirds and sevenths (now called blue notes) into my song, although its prevailing key was major . . . , and I carried this device into my melody as well. . . . This was a distinct departure, but as it turned out, it touched the spot."

After moving to Memphis in 1909, Handy established a publishing company that helped legitimize the blues, and at the same time he began to publish the work of white artists. Music, he thought, provided a reprieve from the racism he saw all around.

As the years went by, that understanding of music became an article of faith, particularly in Florence. In 1959, three local white producer-musicians, Rick Hall, Billy Sherrill, and Tom Stafford, opened a studio; soon afterward Hall went out on his own. In 1961, he produced a song called "You Better Move On," written and sung by Arthur Alexander, a black musician in nearby Sheffield. Part soul, part country, the record became a hit, reaching number 24 on the national pop charts.

Hall took the money he made with Alexander and built a new studio in Muscle Shoals, and other black artists began to stream through the town. Montgomery soul singer Clarence Carter recorded such hits as "Slip Away" and the country-flavored "Patches" in Muscle Shoals; Prattville's Wilson Pickett cut "Mustang Sally" and "Funky Broadway"; and Percy Sledge, who was living in Sheffield, recorded his legendary hit "When a Man Loves a Woman."

These black singers, among the greatest and most respected of their era, were backed in every session by white musicians, and at the peak of the nation's civil rights turmoil, they developed a rapport that crossed racial lines. "We were like brothers," said Percy Sledge, "like family. We were just as one."

The white musicians—Roger Hawkins, Jim Johnson, and many others—emphatically agreed, explaining that they grew up on the music of R&B stars. As Rick Hall later put it, praising the great soul singers of the South, "That was us. That was what we wanted to be."

What to See

Four small cities in northern Alabama—Muscle Shoals, Sheffield, Tuscumbia, and Florence—are so close together they are almost adjacent. Each offers an important reminder of Alabama's black and white musical legacy. Rick Hall's FAME (Florence Alabama Music Enterprise) Recording Studios are still in operation at 603 Avalon Avenue in Muscle Shoals. The building that housed another legendary facility, the Muscle Shoals Sound Studio, is located at 3614 Jackson Highway in Sheffield and is listed on the National Register of Historic Places. In Tuscumbia, the Alabama Music Hall of Fame at 617 Highway 72 West pays tribute to Alabama's rich musical history, including the interracial harmonies from around Muscle Shoals.

Alabama Music Hall of Fame, 617 Highway 72 West, Tuscumbia.
Courtesy of Alison Stanfield.

W. C. Handy Home and Museum, 620 West College Street, Florence.
Courtesy of Ginger Ann Brook.

And finally, in Florence, the two-room log cabin where W. C. Handy was born anchors the W. C. Handy Home, Museum, and Library at 620 West College Street. For more information on the Handy Museum call 205-760-6434. To learn more about the Alabama Music Hall of Fame visit its website at www.alamhof.org.

The Scottsboro Boys

The Site

Scottsboro was the scene in the 1930s of one of the South's most heated civil rights controversies, the infamous trial of the Scottsboro Boys. The trials of nine young black men falsely accused of raping two white women not only resulted in a national debate but raised an international outcry. For many, the Scottsboro Boys trials, which began in Scottsboro but later continued in nearby Decatur, were the first significant precursor to the civil rights movement.

The Story

In the Depression-era South, poverty and unemployment were rife. Victoria Price and Ruby Bates were caught in this web of hard times. But they were white. And women. And in the South, those qualities afforded them a special status, despite their questionable morality. Haywood Patterson, Charlie Weems, Clarence Norris, Andy Wright, Ozie Powell, Olen Montgomery, Eugene Williams, Willie Roberson, and Roy Wright were also caught in that web of poverty. But they were black. And men. And in the South, those qualities conferred upon them immediate guilt, despite their incontrovertible innocence. The worlds of these white women and these black men collided on March 25, 1931, and that collision would not only transform the lives of all involved but also serve as a catalyst in mobilizing a nation of blacks and whites in a quest for civil rights.

Hoboing on trains was common during the Depression. On the Southern Railroad train from Chattanooga to Memphis, there were a variety of young white and black "passengers," traveling from city to city in search of jobs. On the March 25 run, the black boys on the train got involved in a scuffle with the white boys, who, save one, were subsequently thrown off the train. Those whites immediately reported the fight to authorities who phoned ahead to the next stop, Paint Rock, Alabama. When the train stopped, a posse was waiting for the black boys. They were apprehended, bound, and taken to the jail in nearby Scottsboro. At that point, the two white girls on board, upon being questioned by authorities, claimed they had been raped at knife and gunpoint by the nine black boys. Word of the arrests spread quickly. A crowd of hundreds gathered outside of the Scottsboro jail that night, intent on harm. They were stopped by the National Guard, sent in by the governor of Alabama, B. M. Miller.

Twelve days later, the trials of the boys began in Scottsboro. Ineffective defense lawyers and a biased panel of all-white jurors overrode contradictory testimony by Price and Bates and a lack of physical evidence against the accused. After a series of four trials lasting three days, the sentences were handed down. For all but the youngest boy, Roy Wright, for whom a mistrial was declared, the verdict was guilty; the sentence, death. The date for execution was set ninety days later, the least amount of time allowed by law between a death sentence and the execution of that sentence.

Initially, the NAACP, in a bid for self-preservation in such a potentially explosive case, refused to get involved. The Communist Party, however, took up the cause and began lobbying for its legal arm, the International Labor Defense, to be able to represent the boys. It's efforts were ultimately successful. Although the NAACP eventually became involved and invited Clarence Darrow to represent the boys, the defendants had placed their faith in the ILD.

An appeal to the U.S. Supreme Court served as a temporary reprieve for the Scottsboro Boys, as the nine youths had come to be called. The new defense began preparing for the retrials that would be held in Decatur. The national media reported continuously on the case. But the media in 1931 did not regularly adopt a tone of impartiality toward the Scottsboro Boys. The newspapers described gatherings of Negroes to protest the sentences as "mobs" but gatherings of whites in support of the sentences as "posses," not so subtly linking the whites to law enforcement and the blacks to vigilantism. Meanwhile, across the country and around the world, what had begun, and ultimately could have ended, as a "simple" matter of yet another case of white injustice was significantly complicated by the involvement of the Communist Party. The connection between Communism and the Scottsboro Boys, because of the role of the International Labor Defense, was repeatedly stressed. Presumably, this link between the early struggle for civil rights and Communism, in an era in which such comparisons would be sure to enflame people, was a tactic to discredit the movement toward equality. And while that strategy may have been successful nationally, or at least in the South, internationally the response was very different. The governor of Alabama received protests over the sentences from England, Germany, France, Switzerland, Canada, Cuba. and several South American countries.

Ultimately, the question of the guilt or innocence of the Scottsboro Boys was drawn out over two decades. Ruby Bates, who had disappeared under an onslaught of bad publicity regarding her alleged prostitution, reappeared in Decatur as a witness for the defense, admitting that she and Price had fabricated the charges. In a startling reversal, Judge James Horton, who presided over defendant Haywood Patterson's retrial, granted the defense's request for a new trial by overturning the guilty verdict and death sentence handed down by the jury. For the Scottsboro Boys, the momentum that began with Judge Horton's decision would influence the fates of all nine. Four of the boys had all charges against them dropped, two because of their youth, one because of his near blindness, and the fourth because he was suffering from a severe case of syphilis at the time of the crime and could barely walk, much less rape two women. These four young men spent six years on death row without a trial before the charges were dropped.

Of the remaining five, four were either paroled or pardoned. These men spent their youth in prison, only gaining their freedom fifteen to twenty years after the ordeal began. Haywood Patterson, who had been the first to be tried in Decatur, was convicted and sentenced to seventy-five years in prison. Patterson escaped in 1948 from an Alabama prison farm in Atmore and fled to Michigan. When he was caught by the FBI a few years later, the governor of Michigan refused to extradite him to Alabama. He died in 1952.

Obviously, much more was at stake in the trials of the Scottsboro Boys than the verdicts. People mobilizing either in support of or in opposition to the defendants viewed the struggle through the lens of race relations and as an issue relevant to the very survival of democracy. And while it is true that the case had far-reaching and long-lasting implications, what is sometimes lost in magnifying the series of events are the boys themselves. While the media debated, posses gathered, gangs protested, letters were passionately penned, and politicians pontificated, the lives of young, innocent black men were slowly eroding in prison cells both literal and figurative. Their very identities were erased in both the contemporary consciousness and historical memory, as they became collectively the Scottsboro Boys, not Haywood, Charlie, Clarence, Andy, Ozie, Olen, Eugene, Willie, and Roy, individuals in their own right, with all of the hopes and dreams they dared conceive of in a segregated South.

Hollace Ransdall, a white northern woman representing the ACLU, came to Alabama in May 1931 to investigate the case. After interviewing people involved with the case and those in the communities of Scottsboro and Huntsville to determine the larger societal aspects of the trials, Miss Ransdall wrote a report detailing what she considered to be a miscarriage of justice. At the end of her report, she posed the question, not only of why the accused had been denied basic legal rights but also why nine young black men in America "have never been given a chance to be anything but the illiterate, jobless young itinerants they are." Ransdall's question spoke to the issue of civil rights in America in the 1930s. Poverty, unemployment, even youth could not be equalizers in an American South so divided by race. The Scottsboro Boys were victims of that division, but in losing their own freedom, even their very identities, they raised not only the national consciousness but the world's, and in doing so became heroes in the fight for equality.

What to See

A marker commemorating the trial stands outside of the old courthouse in the city center of Scottsboro. Although the initial trials occurred in Scottsboro, the later trials were moved to Decatur when the situation in Scottsboro became too dangerous. A plaque honoring Judge Horton's bold action in overturning the jury's verdict against Haywood Patterson—a decision that cost him his future career—hangs on the back wall of the courthouse in Decatur where he presided. In nearby Madison, Judge Horton's antebellum home still stands at 27524 Old Highway 20. The property surrounding it, known as Macedon Farms, is the home of an award-winning herd of Angus cattle, first established by the judge in the 1920s and maintained by his son, Ed Horton, who became an Alabama state senator in 1963. In that capacity, the younger Horton sometimes found himself at odds with Alabama's segregationist governor, George Wallace. Among other things, he helped lead the opposition in 1966 when Wallace wanted to amend the Alabama constitution in order to run for a second consecutive term as governor.

Ardmore: Terror in the Night

The Site
One of the little-known stories of heroism and fear in the civil rights years occurred in Ardmore, a village on the Alabama-Tennessee line. It is the story of Bull Connor, a group of freedom riders, and an elderly couple who gave the young people sanctuary.

The Story
On the night of May 18, 1961, a small group of freedom riders huddled together in a Birmingham jail cell. They had been arrested as they headed into town, offering themselves as replacements for another group of riders who, a few days earlier, had been beaten too badly to continue with the journey.

John Lewis, the leader of the replacements, recalled years later how they sang freedom songs to buoy their spirits—and, not incidentally, he freely admitted, to annoy their captors at the jail. The music succeeded on both fronts, and around midnight Birmingham's police commissioner, Eugene "Bull" Connor, appeared at their cell and told them abruptly that they were going home.

The group of seven riders were shoved into a fleet of unmarked cars that headed north toward Tennessee, with Birmingham policemen at the wheel. One car was driven by Connor himself, and Lewis remembered how the commissioner—a renowned and feared Alabama segregationist (see chapter 2)—chatted amiably with Katherine Burke, a freedom rider and a student at Fisk University in Nashville.

"You should eat with us," he remembered Burke saying. "You should get to know us better."

"Well, you know," Connor replied, "I just might do that."

But in the town of Ardmore on the Tennessee line, Connor stopped the car near a desolate stretch of railroad track that formed the border between the two states. "This is where you'll be gettin' out," he said.

Suddenly, the freedom riders were frightened. This was Klan country in 1961, and they began to wonder if an ambush was already planned. It was pitch dark and they talked only in whispers as they walked along the track. They knew they needed a safe place to wait out the night, which could only mean a black person's house.

Finally, they came to a three-room cabin, set off beyond the outskirts of town. They approached it quietly and Lewis knocked on the door, hoping that the occupants were not white. After a few minutes, an old man appeared—a black farmer in his seventies who knew that the people at his door meant danger.

"We're freedom riders," John Lewis said. "We're in trouble. Will you help?"

The old man hesitated. "I'm sorry," he said, but after a moment an elderly woman appeared at his side. "Honey," she said, "let them in."

For the next several hours, the freedom riders tried to get some sleep, some on the bed, others on the floor, while their hosts kept watch at the windows and the door. At daybreak, the old man went out in search of food, returning with bologna, eggs, and cheese that he had bought, he explained, at several different stores. He said he didn't want to arouse curiosity with an order that seemed to be too large.

Lewis and the others ate breakfast and waited for another activist from Nashville to drive down and smuggle them back to Birmingham. When they left they said their grateful goodbyes. Looking back on it later, Lewis and the others clearly understood that people like these, intentionally or not, were the movement's heroes.

But there was another thing Lewis knew, a regret that has haunted him since that time. Caught up completely in the moment of danger—and his activist's resolve to resume the freedom rides—he never even got the old people's name.

What to See

The railroad track that cuts through Ardmore still divides Alabama and Tennessee, and still appears as desolate as it did in the 1960s. Every now and then, there is still the occasional shotgun cabin nestled close to the track. But almost certainly the freedom riders' sanctuary—their shelter on that night in 1961—is long since gone.

Acknowledgments and Sources

All entries in this book are based in part on research and interviews for an earlier book by Frye Gaillard, *Cradle of Freedom: Alabama and the Movement That Changed America*. That work has been supplemented for this book with additional interviews and readings. Here, chapter by chapter, are the sources on which this book is based.

Chapter 1

Montgomery. In addition to *Cradle of Freedom*, Taylor Branch's *Parting the Waters: America in the King Years, 1954–63* and David J. Garrow's *Bearing the Cross: Martin Luther King, Jr., and the Southern Christian Leadership Conference* offer excellent accounts of the Montgomery bus boycott. Branch in particular provides a revealing profile of the Reverend Vernon Johns. The entry on Hank Williams and the musical debt he owed to black performer Rufus Payne is based on accounts in Frye Gaillard's *Watermelon Wine: Remembering the Golden Years of Country Music* and Paul Hemphill's *Lovesick Blues*. Robert Graetz's story is based on interviews by Frye Gaillard and on Graetz's book *A White Preacher's Memoir*. The entry on the Montgomery attack on the freedom riders is based in part on John Lewis's memoir *Walking with the Wind* and on *The Children* by David Halberstam. John T. Edge, a brilliant writer at the Southern Foodways Alliance at the University of Mississippi, wrote a profile of Georgia Gilmore titled "The Welcome Table," originally published in the *Oxford American*. In addition, Mrs. Gilmore's story and that of Martha Hawkins were told in a film also titled *The Welcome Table* and produced by Joe York in 2004 for the Southern Foodways Alliance. The Southern Poverty Law Center's website offers detailed information about the work of that important organization.

Chapter 2

Birmingham. *Cradle of Freedom, Parting the Waters,* and *Bearing the Cross* form the basis for this chapter, along with Diane McWhorter's Pulitzer Prize–winning work, *Carry Me Home: Birmingham, Alabama: The Climactic Battle of the Civil Rights Revolution.* The stories of the drama at Boutwell Auditorium are taken primarily from two sources: John Egerton's *Speak Now Against the Day: The Generation Before the Civil Rights Movement in the South* and *Nat King Cole: A Personal and Professional Biography* by James Haskins with Kathleen Benson. Joan Baez's website offers details of her iconic recording of "We Shall Overcome" at Miles College. The story of Fred Shuttlesworth is based in part on the excellent biography *A Fire You Can't Put Out: The Civil Rights Life of Birmingham's Reverend Fred Shuttlesworth.* The story of Armstrong's barber shop is based on interviews by Frye Gaillard, as is Gaillard's personal reflection on the Birmingham church bombing. Another excellent source on the bombing is Frank Sikora's *Until Justice Rolls Down: The Birmingham Church Bombing Case.* The history of the Birmingham Civil Rights Institute is based on the institute's own 1997 video production *Inspired by the Past, A Vision for the Future.*

Chapter 3

Selma. This chapter is based primarily on accounts in *Cradle of Freedom,* John Lewis's *Walking with the Wind,* and on the book *Selma, Lord, Selma: Girlhood Memories of the Civil Rights Days* by Sheyann Webb and Rachel West Nelson, as told to Frank Sikora. In addition, Selma's excellent museums, especially the National Voting Rights Museum, the Slavery and Civil War Museum, and the Old Depot Museum provide substantial accounts of Selma's racial history. The story of Benjamin Turner, the former slave who became Alabama's first African American congressman, is told in those museums.

Chapter 4

The Black Belt. The history of the civil rights movement in the Black Belt is extraordinarily well preserved on the numerous historical markers scattered throughout those central Alabama counties and in museums such as those in Selma and the Safe House Museum in the Hale County town of Greensboro. The U.S. National Park Service operates an interpretive center on U.S. Highway 80 in Lowndes County, precisely at the spot where tenant farmers evicted from their homes for registering to vote built a tent city and spent a cold winter in 1965–66. The stories of Lowndes County are based primarily on accounts in *Cradle of Freedom;* so, in part, is the story of Jimmie Lee Jackson in Perry County. *Walking with the Wind* also offers an excellent account of the martyrdom of Jackson. The stories of Gee's Bend, Marengo County, and the prolific African American author James Haskins are based on interviews by Jane DeNeefe. Her principal sources in Marengo County were Julia Mae Haskins Foster, Bobbie Mitchell, and Mary Jones-Fitts, as well as the book *If White Kids Die: Memories of a Civil Rights Movement Volunteer* by Dick J. Reavis. In addition, John Fleming's article "Their Mother's House" in the Spring 2008 issue of *Longleaf Style* provided valuable information about the Faunsdale reunion.

In Gee's Bend, DeNeefe interviewed longtime residents Mary Lee Bendolph, Raymond Mosely, and Nettie Young, and she quoted from an interview with the Reverend Francis Walter in the *Encyclopedia of Alabama.* DeNeefe also relied on the books *Down Home, Camden, Alabama* by Bob Adelman and *Gee's Bend: The Women and Their Quilts* by William Arnett, Jane Livingston, John Beardsley, and Alvia J. Wardlaw. Also important in telling the story were the documentaries *The Quilts of Gee's Bend,* produced and directed by Matt Arnett and Vanessa Vadim, and *The Quiltmakers of Gee's Bend,* produced and directed by Celia Carey. And finally, we relied on the article "Dark Rivers of the Heart: A History of Gee's Bend" by Brett Buckner, appearing in the Spring 2008 issue of *Longleaf Style*.

The story of Greene County is based on Frye Gaillard's interviews with Thomas Gilmore, a former civil rights leader in that county.

Chapter 5

Tuscaloosa. The desegregation of the University of Alabama—both George Wallace's futile stand in the schoolhouse door and the earlier, heroic enrollment of Autherine Lucy—are told definitely in *The Schoolhouse Door: Segregation's Last Stand at the University of Alabama* by E. Culpepper Clark. In addition, we relied on the papers of Harry Shaffer, a University of Alabama economics professor who supported desegregation in the 1950s, and on accounts in the *Tuscaloosa News*. Shaffer's papers are preserved at the W. S. Hoole Special Collections Library at the university. The story of the belated desegregation of University of Alabama football is told in the monograph *The Black Athlete: 1970* by Bernard E. Garnett and Frye Gaillard, published by the Race Relations Information Center.

Chapter 6

Tuskegee. Perhaps the best single account of civil rights history in Tuskegee is Robert J. Norrell's *Reaping the Whirlwind: The Civil Rights Movement in Tuskegee*. Along with *Cradle of Freedom* and visits to Tuskegee and its two National Park Service sites, Norrell's work represents the principal source for this chapter. We also benefited from the excellent exhibits at Tuskegee Human and Civil Rights Multicultural Center. The story of the Tuskegee Airmen was based in part on the 2002 PBS documentary *The Tuskegee Airmen*. The story of the Tuskegee syphilis study and the Rosenwald schools in relation to the town of Notasulga was based on interviews with heirs of the study's survivors, especially Elizabeth Sims. Sims and many of her Notasulga neighbors are actively working to preserve their community's Rosenwald school at the Shiloh Baptist Church. Information on their efforts can be found at the website for the Shiloh Community Restoration Project (www.shilohcommfound.com/). And finally, Mab Segrest's *Memoir of a Race Traitor* provides a deeply personal reflection on race relations in Tuskegee, including an account of the tragic killing of Sammy Younge.

Chapter 7

Anniston, Gadsden, Talladega, and Huntsville. The story of the burning of the freedom riders' bus is based on accounts in *Walking with the Wind, Parting the Waters, Cradle of Freedom,* and Raymond Arsenault's *Freedom Riders: 1961 and the Struggle for Racial Justice.* We also interviewed Charles Doster, a key participant in the desegregation of Anniston's public library. Mr. Doster kindly shared with us a speech he has delivered on the subject, which records many of the specific details. The story of the *Amistad* murals at Talladega College is based on information available at the college's Savery Library and on the story "Living History" in *Vanderbilt Magazine,* which profiles Talladega graduate and Martin Luther King scholar Lewis Baldwin. We also relied on the book *Talladega College: The First Century* by Maxine D. Jones and Joe M. Richardson.

The account of the civil rights struggles in Gadsden is based on *Cradle of Freedom* and on Jane DeNeefe's interviews with Gadsden musician and activist Jerry "Boogie" McCain and civil rights leader Joseph Faulkner. The Gadsden entry begins with a quote from the essay "I'll Never Forget Alabama Law" by William Douthard published in the February–March 1965 issue of the *Liberal News.* We also quoted from "Gadsden Is Tough" by Maxwell S. Stewart, published in the *Nation,* July 17, 1937, and we relied on the excellent article "Southern Labor Relations in Transition: Gadsden, Alabama, 1930–1943" by Charles H. Martin in the *Journal of Southern History,* November 1981, and on the article "Call Her Miss," which appeared in *Time* magazine on April 10, 1964.

The best account of the civil rights movement in Huntsville and a principal source for this chapter is Sheryll Cashin's *Agitator's Daughter: A Memoir of Four Generations of One Extraordinary African-American Family.*

Chapter 8

Mobile. The stories of John LeFlore, Joseph Langan, and the more militant Neighborhood Organized Workers are based on accounts in *Mobile: The New History of Alabama's First City* edited by Michael V. R. Thomason. Keith Nicholls's essay in that book, "Politics and Civil Rights in Post–World War II Mobile," also tells the story of the *Bolden* case, which proved to be a landmark for the city. The inspiring but little-known story of the desegregation of Spring Hill College was documented in Charles S. Padgett's article "Albert Foley's Campaign against the Ku Klux Klan," published in the Winter 2004–5 issue of *Spring Hill Alumni Magazine.* Our entry on Africatown is based primarily on Sylviane A. Diouf's *Dreams of Africa in Alabama: The Slave Ship* Clotilda *and the Story of the Last Africans Brought to America.* The intriguing story of runaway slave Wallace Turnage is based on the accounts in David W. Blight's *A Slave No More: Two Men Who Escaped to Freedom.* That book contains in full Turnage's own narrative of his escape. For some of the details in the story of Hank Aaron, we relied on Tom Stanton's *Hank Aaron and the Home Run That Changed America.* The horrifying story of the lynching of Michael Donald is told on the website of the Southern Poverty Law Center. But our most important source was reporter Michael Wilson's excellent series of articles in the *Mobile Register,* running from June 1 through June 10, 1997.

Chapter 9

Other Places of Interest. The entry on the coastal village of Bayou La Batre is taken primarily from the books *In the Path of the Storms: Bayou La*

Batre, Coden, and the Alabama Coast by Frye Gaillard, Sheila Hagler, and Peggy Denniston, and *American Crisis, Southern Solutions* edited by Anthony Dunbar. The essay on Mobile Bay's Eastern Shore is based on the historian Paul Gaston's paper "My South—and Yours," which was delivered on the occasion of his retirement from the University of Virginia in 1997. The principal source for the section on Atticus Finch and Harper Lee's hometown of Monroeville was Charles J. Shields's *Mockingbird: A Portrait of Harper Lee.* The quotes about Olympic champion Jesse Owens are taken from an exhibit at the Jesse Owens Museum. For the section on the interracial legacy of Alabama music, we relied on W. C. Handy's autobiography *Father of the Blues,* and the quote from Handy about his songwriting comes from that book. The Alabama Music Hall of Fame offers extensive information on the Muscle Shoals sound, including quotes from many of the most famous producers and performers. For the entry on the Scottsboro Boys, we relied on Dan T. Carter's *Scottsboro: A Tragedy of the American South* and Douglas O. Linder's essay "The Scottsboro Boys Trials, 1931–1937," written for the University of Missouri Kansas City School of Law. And finally, the story of the freedom riders' ordeal in the town of Ardmore is based on the accounts in *Cradle of Freedom* and in John Lewis's *Walking with the Wind.*

Throughout our research, as we traveled around Alabama, we were aided by three travel books on the civil rights movement, all of them national in their scope. They are *A Traveler's Guide to the Civil Rights Movement* by Jim Carrier, *On the Road to Freedom: A Guided Tour of the Civil Rights Trail* by Charles E. Cobb, and *Weary Feet, Rested Souls: A Guided History of the Civil Rights Movement* by Townsend Davis.

For their ideas, time, and in some cases their encouragement and logistical support, we extend our special thanks to Susan Finch, Kate Lorenz, Sheila Flanagan, Dora Finley, William Gantt, Kent Rush, Paul Gaston, Wendy Watts, Ellen DeNeefe, Jessica Lacher-Feldman, Theresa

Burroughs, Elizabeth Sims, Juanita Syljuberget, Charles Doster, Bonnie Seymour, Odessa Woolfolk, Bishop Calvin Woods, David Carter, Dan Carter, Clyde Eller, Jay Lamar, Randall Williams, Robert Graetz, Jerry McCain, Kathryn Scheldt, Michelle Cagle, Bobby DeNeefe, and Nancy Gaillard.

Suggested Reading

Arsenault, Raymond. *Freedom Riders: 1961 and the Struggle for Racial Justice.* Oxford University Press, 2006.

Bass, S. Jonathan. *Blessed Are the Peacemakers: Martin Luther King Jr., Eight White Religious Leaders, and the "Letter from Birmingham Jail."* Louisiana State University Press, 2001.

Blight, David W. *A Slave No More: Two Men Who Escaped to Freedom.* Harcourt Brace, 2007.

Branch, Taylor. *Parting the Waters: America in the King Years 1954–63.* Simon and Schuster, 1988.

Carter, Dan T. *Scottsboro: A Tragedy of the American South.* Louisiana State University Press, 2007.

Chestnut, J. L., Jr., and Julia Cass. *Black in Selma: The Uncommon Life of J. L. Chestnut, Jr.* Farrar, Straus, and Giroux, 1990.

Clark, E. Culpepper. *The Schoolhouse Door: Segregation's Last Stand at the University of Alabama.* Oxford University Press, 1993.

Diouf, Sylviane A. *Dreams of Africa in Alabama: The Slave Ship* Clotilda *and the Story of the Last Africans Brought to America.* Oxford University Press, 2007.

Dryden, Charles. *A-Train: Memoirs of a Tuskegee Airman.* University of Alabama Press, 1997.

Eagles, Charles W. *Outside Agitator: Jon Daniels and the Civil Rights Movement in Alabama.* University of Alabama Press, 2000.

Egerton, John. *Speak Now Against the Day: The Generation before the Civil Rights Movement in the South.* Alfred A. Knopf, 1994.

Gaillard, Frye. *Cradle of Freedom: Alabama and the Movement That Changed America.* University of Alabama Press, 2004.

Garrow, David J. *Bearing the Cross: Martin Luther King, Jr., and the Southern Christian Leadership Conference.* HarperCollins, 1986.

Graetz, Robert. *A White Preacher's Memoir: The Montgomery Bus Boycott.* Black Belt Press, 1998.

Halberstam, David. *The Children.* Random House, 1998.

Howard, Ravi. *Like Trees, Walking: A Novel.* Amistad, 2007.

Lee, Harper. *To Kill a Mockingbird.* Lippincott, 1960.

Lewis, John, with Michael D'Orso. *Walking with the Wind: A Memoir of the Movement.* Harcourt Brace, 1998.

Manis, Andrew M. *A Fire You Can't Put Out: The Civil Rights Life of Birmingham's Reverend Fred Shuttlesworth.* University of Alabama Press, 1999.

McWhorter, Diane. *Carry Me Home: Birmingham, Alabama: The Climactic Battle of the Civil Rights Revolution.* Simon and Schuster, 2001.

Naslund, Sena Jeter. *Four Spirits: A Novel.* William Morrow, 2003.

Norrell, Robert J. *Reaping the Whirlwind: The Civil Rights Movement in Tuskegee.* Alfred A. Knopf, 1985.

Reavis, Dick J. *If White Kids Die: Memories of a Civil Rights Movement Volunteer.* University of North Texas Press, 2001.

Shields, Charles J. *Mockingbird: A Portrait of Harper Lee.* Henry Holt, 2006.

Sikora, Frank. *Until Justice Rolls Down: The Birmingham Church Bombing Case.* University of Alabama Press, 1991.

Webb, Sheyann, and Rachel West Nelson, as told to Frank Sikora. *Selma, Lord, Selma: Girlhood Memories of the Civil Rights Days.* University of Alabama Press, 1980.

Williams, Donnie, with Wayne Greenhaw. *The Thunder of Angels: The Montgomery Bus Boycott and the People Who Broke the Back of Jim Crow.* Lawrence Hill Books, 2006.

Index

Bloody Sunday, 102–109

Blow, Peter, 255

Bluff Hall, *159*; 160–161

Bodman, Jim, 286

Bolden, Wiley, 288–289

Bolling, Elmore, 132, 134

Bond, Julian, 158

Boone, Buford, 183, 185

Boston University, 69

Boston, Massachusetts, 148

Boswell Amendment, 261–262

Boutwell Auditorium, Birmingham, 59–62

Boynton, Amelia, 89–91, 93–96, 105

Boynton, Bruce, 94, 233

Boynton, Sam, 89–92, 94, 95

Bracy, S. B., 299

Braddock, James J., 305

Branch, Taylor, 24, 148

Branch, William McKinley, 110, 113, 168, 170

Brewton, John Anthony, 252

Brooks, Paul, *75*

Browder, Aurelia, 25, 28, 29, 30

Browder v. Gayle, 216

Brown Chapel AME Church, 100, 104, 109

Brown University, 110

Brown v. Board of Education, 66, 84, 268–269

Bryant, Paul "Bear," *196*; 173, 194–196

Buckalew Mountain, 305

Buddhist temples, Bayou La Batre, *297*; 294, 297–298

Buford, Kenneth, 217

Bunche, Ralph, 89

Burke, Katherine, 320

Burke, Richard, 200

Burroughs, Theresa, 141, 164–167

Butler Chapel AME Zion Church, *221*; 217, 220–221

Butler County, Alabama, 174

Butler, John, 201, 217

Byrd, Charlotte, 161

Byrne Hall, Spring Hill College, 270–271

California, state of, 193

Camden, Alabama, 150, 152–153

Cammeron, J. D., 241

Campbell, Justice John Archibald, 255, 290–291

Candlestick Park, 281

Capote, Truman, 301, 303

Carawan, Guy, 63

Carmichael, Oliver, 181, 183, 185

Carmichael, Stokely, *135*; 129, 135–136, 222, 224, 227

Carnegie, Andrew, 203

Carnegie Hall, 85

Carnera, Primo, 305

Carter, Clarence, 312

Carver, George Washington, *205, 206*; 89, 197, 199, 205–206

Carver High School, Gadsden, 240

Carver Performing Arts Theater, 85

Cash, Johnny, 310

Cashin, Joan, 251

Cashin, John, 251–252, 254

Cashin, Sheryll, 254

Jesus Christ, 13

Jet magazine, 163

Jim Crow laws, 201, 239, 295

John Archibald Campbell U.S. Courthouse, Mobile, 290

Johns, Vernon, *12*; 11–13, 18–19

Johnson, Colonel Stone, 235

Johnson, Ernie, 282

Johnson, Jim, 312

Johnson, Judge Frank M., *26*; 24–29, 288

Johnson, President Lyndon B., xviii, 40, 106, 111, 128, 136, 144, 158

Johnston, South Carolina, 218

Jones, Mayor Sam, 266, 290

Jonesboro, Alabama, 299

Jones–Fitts, Mary, 160–161

Jordan, Thomas E., 38–39

Juneteenth Celebration Week, 276

Kansas City Athletics, 283

Keck, Charles, 199

Kelly Ingram Park, *51, 57*; 50, 54, 56, 58, 65, 70, 83, 85

Kennedy, President John, 73, 177–178, 191, 240

Kennedy, Senator Edward, 215–216

Kennedy, Senator Robert, 40, 191–194

Kennedy Administration, 176–177

King, A. D., 58

King, B. B., 310

King, Coretta Scott, *145, 149*; 17, 100, 113, 145–149

King, Martin Luther, Jr.: xvii, xviii, 42, 70, 153, 155, 158, 240, 242, 246,

251, 253, 254, 280; and Coretta Scott King, *145*, 145, 148–149; assassination of, 168–170, 193; Birmingham demonstrations, *55*, 49–50, 52–58, 80–82; "I have a dream" speech, 45, 69; Montgomery years, *14*, 1, 8, 11–13, 15–20, 24–25, 27, 30, 33–35, 40–41; Safe House encounter, 164–167; Selma demonstrations, *95*, 89, 93, 95, 100, 105, 107–109, 111, 126

King, Martin Luther, Sr., 38

King, William Rufus deVane, 120–121

King, Yolanda, 17

Knowles, Tiger, 284–286

Korean War, 227

Ku Klux Klan, 13, 21, 31–33, 105, 140, 159, 177, 190, 200, 241, 299, 320; and freedom rides, 229, 231, 233, 235–237; and Southern Poverty Law Center, *44*, 44–46; in Birmingham, 57, 71, 74–76, 80; in Mobile, 259, 264, 267, 270–271, 283–287, 289; murder of Viola Liuzzo, 125, 127–128; targeting Martin Luther King, Jr., 164–167

LaFayette, Alabama, 304–305, 308–309

Lafayette, Bernard, 91

Lane, T. L., 67

Langan, Joseph, *262*; 257, 259, 261–262, 264, 270

Law, Moody, 271

Lawson, J. C., 136

Lee, Bernard, 30

Lee, Cager, 141–142, 144

Lee, Harper, 298, 300–301, 303

Lee, Peter, 160, 161, 164

Lee, Thomas, 149

LeFlore, John, *260*; 257, 259–265, 288

LeFlore, Teah, 264

Levern, Nathan, 149

Lewis, Cudjo, *274*; 274–275

Lewis, Jerry Lee, 310

Lewis, John, *33, 106*; 31–33, 103–104, 319–321

Lewis, Rufus, 30

Lin, Maya, *47*; 41, 45, 47

Lincoln, President Abraham, 177, 194

Lincoln School, *147*; 145, 147, 149

Lingo, Alabama, 238–239, 241

Little Bethel Baptist Church, Daphne, 299

Little Richard, 255–256

Little Saigon (Bayou La Batre), 297

Liuzzo, Viola, *131*; xviii, 42, 119, 123, 125–130, 136

Lockwood, Frank, Sr., 29

Logan, Bart, 61

Lottie's Restaurant, Marion, 144

Louis, Joe, *306*; 294, 304–306, 308–309

Lovett, Nimrod, 299

Lowery, Joseph, 251, 253, 257

Lowndes County, Alabama, xviii–xix, 89, 123–138

Lowndes County Courthouse, *137*; 137–138

Lowndes County Freedom Organization, *135*; 135–137

Lowndesboro, Alabama, *133*; 132–133

Lucy, Autherine, *181, 182*; 113, 156, 173, 180–185, 187

Lynne, Judge Seybourn, 25–27, 73

Macedon Farms, 319

Mack's Café, Marion, 144

Macon County, Alabama, 175

Macon County Courthouse, *225*; 224–226,

Madenica, Branko, 253

Madison, Alabama, 319

Malcom X, *101*; 100

Malone, Vivian, *176, 178*; 173, 176, 178–179, 266

Manis, Andrew, 85

Mann, Floyd, 31–33

Mantle, Mickey, 281

Mants, Bob, 129, 132, 222

March on Washington, 69, 251

Marengo County, Alabama, 123, 156–164, 252

Marengo County History and Archives Museum, 161

Marion, Alabama, *139*; 104, 138, 140–147, 149, 168

Marshall, Thurgood, 233

Martha's Place restaurant, *40*; 40–41

Massachusetts Institute of Technology (MIT), 201

Matthews, Frank, 112

Mays, Benjamin, 22

Mays, Josephine, 132

Mays, Willie, 281

McCain, Jerry "Boogie," 244

McCall, Nancy, 295

McClain, William B., 235–237

McCorvey, Gessner, 261

McCovey, Willie, 281–282

McDonald, Susie, 26, 28

McElroy, Tom, 119

McGlathery, Dave, 176, 252, 253

McLure Education Library, University of Alabama, 180, 183, 185

McNair, Denise, 79–80

McWane Science Center, Birmingham, 70

McWhorter, Diane, 85

Meaher, Timothy, 273

Memphis, Tennessee, 166, 169, 310–311, 315

Meredith, James, 177

Miles College, 54, 63

Miller, Dinah, 150–151

Miller, Governor B. M., 315

Milwaukee Braves, 281

Minge, Collier Harrison, 277–278

Mingo, Lucy Marie, *151*

Mississippi, state of, 2, 87, 270, 295

Mitchell, Bobbie, 159–160

Mitchell, Cecelia, 269

Mitchell, John, 196

Mobile, Alabama, *258*; xvii, 25, 59, 89, 173, 178, 257, 259–291

Mobile Bay, 272, 277–278, 296, 299

Mobile County, Alabama, 175

Mobile County Board of Registrars, 262

Mobile Hall, Spring Hill College, 272

Mobile Register, 269, 284–285

Mockbee, Samuel, 167

Monroe, Bill, 310

Monroe County, Alabama, 301

Monroe County Courthouse, *303*; 302–303

Monroe County Heritage Museum, 303

Monroeville, Alabama, 298, 300–303

Montgomery, Alabama, *xxii, 133*; xvii, xviii, 1–47, 59, 113, 132–133, 223, 227, 286, 288

Montgomery Advertiser, 8

Montgomery bus boycott, xvii–xviii, 2–9, 13, 15–19, 26–27, 66, 113

Montgomery, Olen, 315, 318

Montrose, Alabama, 299

Moore, William, 240

Moran, J. L., 256

Moran Hall, Oakwood University, 256

Morgan, Charles, 252

Morning Star Baptist Church, Demopolis, *162*; 158, 161, 163

Morrisroe, Richard, 130

Morton Hall, University of Alabama at Huntsville, 253

Most Pure Heart of Mary Catholic Church, Mobile, *265*; 263, 265

Motley, Fannie Ernestine, 267, 269–271

Moton, Leroy, 127

Moton Field, Tuskegee, *211*; 211

Mount Gillard Baptist Church, Lowndes County, Alabama, 134, 138

Mount Tabor A.M.E. Church, Perry County, Alabama, *146*; 146, 149

Murphy, Matt, 128

Murphy African American Museum, Tuscaloosa, 189

Murrell, Prince, 189

Muscle Shoals, Alabama, *292*; 310, 312–313

Muscle Shoals Sound Studio, 313

Myers, Pollie Anne, 180–181

NAACP, 6, 45, 72, 113, 136, 180, 208, 242, 257, 259, 261, 289, 316

Nashville, Tennessee, 31, 77, 320–321

Nation magazine, 239

National African-American Archives and Museum, Mobile, *266*; 265–266

National Democratic Party of Alabama (NDPA), 169, 252–253

National League (baseball), 281

National Park Service, 130, 204, 206, 222, 275

National Public Radio, 39

National Register of Historic Places, 9, 28, 111, 160, 179, 313

National Voting Rights Museum, *120*; 93, 108, 117–120

Nazi party, 305

Negro League (baseball), 280–281

Neighborhood Organized Workers (NOW), 259, 263–266

Nesbitt, R. D., 38

New Deal, 153–154

New England Conservatory of Music, 148

New Orleans, Louisiana, 269–270

New Republic magazine, 61

New York, New York, 154, 163

New York Times, 105, 141

Niagra Falls Conference, 203

Nixon, E. D., *5*; 2, 5–9

Noble, Phillips, 235–236

Non–Partisan Voters League, 259

Norrell, Robert J., 204, 225

Norris, Clarence, 315–318

Notasulga, Alabama, 199, 212–216

Oaks, the, *202*; 201, 203–204

Oakville, Alabama, 304, 307

Oakwood Cemetery, 37

Oakwood College. *See* Oakwood University

Oakwood University, *256*; 231, 251, 255–256

Oakwood University slave cemetery, *256*; 255–256

Obama, President Barack, 156, 253

Odetta, 42

Old Depot Museum, *122*; 108–109, 117, 120–121

Old Greene County Courthouse, *170*

Old Live Oak Cemetery, *118*; 114, 116–118

Old Monroe County Courthouse, *303*; 303

Old Slave Market, Mobile, 276

Olympic Games, 1936, 306–307

Orange, James, 66, 138, 140, 144, 158

Orbison, Roy, 310

Osman, David, 252

Owens, Emma, 306

Owens, Henry, 306

Owens, James Cleveland. *See* Owens, Jesse

Owens, Jesse, *304, 308*; 294, 304, 306–307

Owens, Sylvester, 307

Oxford American, 39

Padgett, Charles S., 271

Paige, Satchel, 282–283

Paint Rock, Alabama, 315

Panic of 1877, 116

Paris, Wendell, 204

Parks, Rosa *3, 4, 9, 28*; xvii, 1–10, 20–23, 26, 28

Patterson, Governor John, 30, 35, 175

Patterson, Haywood, 315, 317–319

Patton, Gwen, 223, 228

Paul W. Bryant Museum, *196*; 196. *See also* Bryant, Paul "Bear"

Payne, Rufus, 10

Pearson, Veronica, 252

Peck, Gregory, 300

Peck, Jim, 76

Penniman, Richard Wayne. *See* Little Richard

Perkins, Carl, 310

Perkins, Mayor James, 121, 145

Perry County, Alabama, 103–104, 123, 140–150

Person, Charles, 76

Peter, Paul, and Mary, 42

Pettus, General Edmund W., 115

Pettway, Arlonzia, *151*; 151, 154

Pettway, Georgianna, 152

Pettway, Loretta, 155

Pettway, Nancy, *151*; 151

Pharish, Ivey, 149

Phifer, J. S., 67

Phillips, Sam, 309–311

Phillips High School, Birmingham, 67–68, 70, 73

Pickett, Wilson, 312

Pierce, President Franklin, 121

Pippin, M. W., 79–80

Pittman, Judge Virgil, 287–290

Pitts, Lucius, 63

Pittsburgh Courier, 163

Plateau, Alabama, 272, 276

Pleasant Grove Baptist Church, Gee's Bend, 153, 155

Pollard, Charles, *217*; 215–216

Pollard, Mother, 16–17, 19

Ponquinette, Julia, 269

Poor People's March on Washington, 168, 170

Porter, John, 15, 81

Powell, Ozie, 315–318

President's Mansion, University of Alabama, *184*; 181, 185

Presley, Elvis, 309–310

Price, Victoria, 315, 317

Pritchett, Laurie, 53

Pruitt, G. E., 67

Ransdall, Hollace, 318

Rapier, James Thomas, 119

Rayfield, Wallace, 83

Reavis, Dick J., 159–160

Reconstruction, 90, 151, 200–201, 227

Redmont Hotel, 59

Redstone Arsenal, 251

Reeb, James, xviii, 105–106

Reese, F. D., 97

Republican Party, 201

Shaffer, Harry, 187

Sheffield, Alabama, *292*; 312–313

Shelton, Robert, 57–58

Sherrill, Billy, 312

Shiloh Cemetery, Notasulga, *217*; 216

Shiloh Community Restoration Foundation, 214

Shiloh Missionary Baptist Church, Notasulga, *212*; 212–216

Shores, Arthur, 86, 180, 247, 249

Shuttlesworth, Fred, *55, 65, 67, 68, 95*; 34, 37, 52, 54, 62, 65–70, 72–73, 76, 113, 235

Shuttlesworth, Pat, 67

Shuttlesworth, Ricky, 67

Shuttlesworth, Ruby, 67–68

Sikora, Frank, 85

Silver Moon café, 105

Sims, Elizabeth, 214–215

Sims, Frances, 251

Sims, Shepard, 160–161

Sixteenth Street Baptist Church, Birmingham, *78, 79*; 50, 56, 58, 71, 74–75, 78–83, 84, 236

Sixth Avenue Baptist Church, 51, 81

Slavery and Civil War Museum, *121*; 120–121

Sledge, Percy, 312

Smalls, Robert, 90

Smiley, Glenn, 27

Smith, Andrew, 268–269

Smith, Howard K., 76

Smith, J. H., 189

Smith, Mary Louise, 26, 28

Smith, N. H., 67

Smith, Ozzie, 282

Smith Hall, University of Alabama, *184*; 180, 182–185

Smitherman, Mayor Joe T., 121

Smoot, Fanny, 160

Smyer, Sidney, 57

South Africa, 148

South Carolina, state of, 90

Southern Christian Leadership Conference (SCLC), 52, 103–104, 111, 140, 142, 144, 158, 240, 253, 257

Southern Conference on Human Welfare, 61–62

Southern Poverty Law Center, *44, 47*; 41, 44–46, 286–287

Southern Railroad, 315

Spanish Fort, Alabama, 285

Speed, Thomas, 149

Spring Hill College, *268*; xvii, 267–272

Sproull, Miller, 236

St. James Hotel, 115, 117

St. Louis, Missouri, 255

Stafford, Tom, 312

Stanton, Tom, 281–282

Starke, Major Lewis, 299

Starlin, Stamford, 299

Steele, Rosa, 130

Stillman College, 189

Student Nonviolent Coordinating Committee (SNCC), *98, 106*; 77, 89, 91, 103, 111, 129, 132, 136–137, 222–224, 240

Sturdivant Hall, 120, 122

Summer Community Organizing and Political Education (SCOPE), 158

About the Authors

FRYE GAILLARD is writer-in-residence at the University of South Alabama. He has been a journalist for the Associated Press and the *Charlotte Observer*. He is the author of *The Dream Long Deferred: The Landmark Struggle for Desegregation in Charlotte, North Carolina*; *With Music and Justice for All*; *Some Southerners and Their Passions*; and *Cradle of Freedom: Alabama and the Movement That Changed America*, which won the Lillian Smith Award for best southern nonfiction.

JUAN WILLIAMS is a journalist and leading political analyst for National Public Radio and Fox News. He is the author of *Thurgood Marshall: American Revolutionary*; *My Soul Looks Back in Wonder: Voices of the Civil Rights Experience*; and *Eyes on the Prize: America's Civil Rights Years, 1954–1965*, the companion volume to PBS's landmark documentary of the same name.

JENNIFER LINDSAY is a resident of Fairhope and a history instructor at Faulkner State Community College. She has also taught at the University of South Alabama, where she received her master's in history.

JANE DENEEFE is a historian, journalist, and freelance writer in Huntsville. She is a former community columnist for the *Huntsville Times* and a frequent commentator on WLRH public radio in Huntsville.